U.S.-Japan Relations
and the Security of East Asia

Westview Special Studies in International Relations and Foreign Policy

*U.S.-Japan Relations and the Security
of East Asia: The Next Decade*
edited by Franklin B. Weinstein

Given the recent history of "shocks" to U.S.-Japan relations and the growing uncertainty about the future configuration of Japanese politics, there is ample reason to question whether the U.S.-Japan security relationship will survive the next decade in its present form. To ensure that Americans and Japanese have the clearest possible understanding of the assumptions and goals that motivate each other's policies, Stanford University's Project on United States–Japan Relations has established a continuing dialogue between American and Japanese specialists on security affairs. This book is a product of that dialogue.

The contributors look to the future with a sharp awareness that the Asian strategic context has changed since the end of the Vietnam war and that the basis of U.S.-Japan relations in the security field has also undergone important changes in recent years. Further changes of potentially great significance may be impending. The question of how to interpret and adapt to these changes represents a recurrent theme in this up-to-date book, although the authors differ sharply in their answers. Japanese and American experts offer contrasting perspectives on strategies for the defense of Japan, the role of nuclear weapons, the security of Korea, and conceptions of arms control. They give their recommendations for the kinds of policies that would best serve U.S. and Japanese security interests in the coming decade.

Franklin B. Weinstein is director of the Project on United States–Japan Relations at Stanford University, where he also teaches in the Department of Political Science. Professor Weinstein is the author of *Indonesian Foreign Policy and the Dilemma of Dependence*.

Prepared under the auspices of the

Project on United States–Japan Relations
Stanford University

U.S.-Japan Relations and the Security of East Asia: The Next Decade

edited by
Franklin B. Weinstein

Westview Press/Boulder, Colorado

Westview Special Studies in International Relations and U.S. Foreign Policy

Copyright © 1978 by Westview Press, Inc.

Published with the cooperation of the Sumitomo Fund for Policy Research Studies, administered by the Japan Society, Inc.

Published in 1978 in the United States of America by
  Westview Press, Inc.
  5500 Central Avenue
  Boulder, Colorado 80301
  Frederick A. Praeger, Publisher and Editorial Director

Library of Congress Cataloging in Publication Data
Main entry under title:
U.S.-Japan relations and the security of East Asia.
  (Westview special studies on China and East Asia)
  1. United States—Foreign relations—Japan—
Addresses, essays, lectures. 2. Japan—Foreign
relations—United States—Addresses, essays,
lectures. 3. United States—Foreign relations—
East Asia—Addresses, essays, lectures. 4. East
Asia—Foreign relations—United States—Addresses,
essays, lectures. 5. Japan—Defenses. I. Weinstein,
Franklin B.
E183.8.J3U74   327.73'052   77-13752
ISBN 0-89158-053-9

Printed and bound in the United States of America

Contents

Acknowledgments

This book, and the U.S.-Japanese dialogue of which it is a product, would not have been possible without the assistance of numerous institutions and individuals. Financial support came primarily from the Sumitomo Fund for Policy Research Studies, administered by the Japan Society in New York. Supplementary support was provided by the State Department's Office of External Research and by a Ford Foundation grant to the Stanford Arms Control and Disarmament Program, of which the Project on United States–Japan Relations is a component. Of course, the institutions that have funded this effort bear no responsibility for the book's contents.

The book owes much to all of those who took part in the dialogue, but special mention should be made of the leadership roles played by John K. Emmerson and Kiichi Saeki in helping to establish the dialogue and make it a meaningful one. John W. Lewis and Robert E. Ward provided important encouragement, support, and advice at every stage. The Japan Center for International Exchange gave essential assistance in both planning and logistics; we are indebted to Tadashi Yamamoto, the center's director, and to Yoji Yamamoto, the principal staff member assigned to work with our project. In the preparation of this book we were fortunate to have cheerful secretarial support from Barbara Johnson. Geraldine Bowman, Nancy Okimoto, and Patsy Tutsch helped with conference arrangements, and Gaye Passell with typing.

F. B. Weinstein

The Contributors

Ralph N. Clough is a guest scholar at the Brookings Institution, where he has also been a senior fellow. He has served as director of the State Department's Office of Chinese Affairs and as a member of its Policy Planning Council.

Morton H. Halperin is director of the Project on National Security and Civil Liberties, Washington, D.C. He has formerly served as a deputy assistant secretary of defense and as a member of the staff of the National Security Council.

Selig S. Harrison is senior associate at the Carnegie Endowment for International Peace. He spent many years in Asia as a correspondent of *The Washington Post* and has been senior fellow in charge of Asian Studies at the Brookings Institution.

Ryukichi Imai is general manager, engineering, of the Japan Atomic Power Company. He is also a special assistant to the minister of foreign affairs, dealing mainly with nuclear and arms control matters.

Fuji Kamiya is professor of international relations at Keio University and also research director of the Japan Institute of International Affairs.

Takuya Kubo is secretary-general of the National Defense Council of Japan. He served previously as vice minister of defense.

John W. Lewis is director of the Arms Control and Disarmament Program at Stanford University, where he is also William Haas Professor of Chinese Politics.

Makoto Momoi is director of international security studies and professor of international relations at the National Defense College of Japan.

James William Morley is chairman of the Department of Political Science at Columbia University.

Daniel I. Okimoto is assistant professor of political science at Stanford University.

Henry S. Rowen is professor of public management in the Graduate School of Business at Stanford University. He has served as president of the Rand Corporation, assistant director of the Bureau of the Budget, and deputy assistant secretary of defense.

Franklin B. Weinstein is director of the Project on United States–Japan Relations at Stanford University, where he also teaches in the Department of Political Science.

Toru Yano is professor of international relations at the Center for Southeast Asian Studies, Kyoto University.

U.S.-Japan Relations and the Security of East Asia

Introduction

Franklin B. Weinstein

Few would deny that U.S.-Japan relations have in most respects been remarkably close over the quarter century since the end of the American occupation. Nor would many deny that the ties between the two countries in the security field have been a central component of that relationship. Japan, perhaps more than any other major power in history, has depended for its security on the power and wisdom of another nation—the United States; on the other hand, the military facilities maintained in Japan by the United States have been, and remain, of major importance to the maintenance of America's strategic posture in Asia.

For all its closeness, however, the U.S.-Japanese relationship has long been characterized by paradoxes and misunderstandings. Nowhere is this more obvious than in the security field. It was, of course, under American auspices that Japan adopted the so-called peace constitution, wherein the nation forever renounced war as a sovereign right and undertook never to maintain an army, navy, or air force. Yet from the days when John Foster Dulles negotiated the mutual security treaty in 1951 right down to the present, Americans have pressed the Japanese to develop their "self-defense" capabilities at a rate faster than most Japanese have been prepared to accept. The same U.S. president who proposed that Japan assume security responsibilities and become America's partner in maintaining Asian security

1

chose to seek a rapprochement with the People's Republic of China—an initiative dramatically affecting Japanese interests—without even consulting Tokyo.

Furthermore, the U.S.-Japanese security relationship, despite its intimacy, has long been underlain by diametrically opposed conceptions of how its benefits and costs are distributed between the two nations. Americans, observing Japan's resurgence as an economic power and freedom from the burden of maintaining a costly defense establishment, have accused the Japanese of taking a "free ride" at the expense of the U.S. taxpayer. Many Japanese, on the other hand, have emphasized that the U.S. bases in Japan are maintained not merely to defend the Japanese islands but to serve American strategic purposes elsewhere in Asia. Japanese public opinion has traditionally been much more skeptical than the Japanese government about the desirability of the security relationship with the United States. In the view of many Japanese, the bases are a "service" to the United States for which Japan receives little in return.

The importance of cordial U.S.-Japan relations to the peace and security of Asia is scarcely a matter of great debate. Even the communist powers seem now to have accepted this. But U.S.-Japan relations have been far from untroubled during the 1970s. The alliance has been shaken by recurrent "shocks," from the surprise announcement in 1971 of President Nixon's plan to visit Peking to the Lockheed scandal of 1976. Although U.S.-Japan relations seemed smoother in 1977 than in 1971, the Carter administration's policies on nuclear energy and troop withdrawals from Korea did create some significant new strains. If the Japanese people have grown more tolerant of the mutual security treaty and the U.S. military presence, they wonder what further changes will occur in U.S. policies and how these changes will affect Japan. Nor can anyone predict how Japan will respond should the oil-exporting Arab states bring heightened pressure on Tokyo to adopt a more hostile attitude toward Israel; if Japan were to yield to such pressures, the impact on U.S.-Japan relations could be significant.

Adding to the uncertainty surrounding the future of U.S.-Japan relations is the changing configuration of Japanese politics; the diminution of Liberal-Democratic party control could have far-reaching implications for U.S.-Japan relations. This trend comes at a time when many Americans have concluded that Japan should carry a larger share of the burden of its own defense and perhaps that of the rest of East Asia as well. There is, in short, a growing awareness that the premises and assumptions that have underlain the alliance for so many years are changing significantly. There is ample reason to question whether the U.S.-Japan security relationship will survive the next decade in its present form.

Given the importance of the relationship and the uncertainty about its future, the need for better communication between the United States and Japan is manifest. As the United States and Japan lay the conceptual groundwork for security and arms control policies that will carry them through the 1970s and into the 1980s, it is essential that Americans make every effort to acquire a deeper understanding of the way Japanese view their own security and that of the rest of Asia, and that Japanese come to have a clearer understanding of American purposes and expectations. Future changes in the policies of the communist powers and, perhaps more important, in Japanese domestic politics may lead Japan toward a looser association with the United States than in the past. This is not necessarily undesirable. But whatever course the future of U.S.-Japan relations may take, it is important that each country maintain the clearest possible understanding of the assumptions and goals that motivate the security policies of the other. This process can best be facilitated if communication between the two countries takes place not only through government channels, but through unofficial discussions and research involving nongovernmental specialists, who might feel freer to raise questions about basic assumptions in the relationship and to speculate about the long-run implications of new approaches.

In 1974, in recognition of the need for discussions of this kind, the Stanford University Project on United States–

Japan Relations undertook to initiate a continuing dialogue between U.S. and Japanese specialists on security affairs and arms control. Distinguished groups of Americans and Japanese, including academics, government officials, and journalists, were assembled. The various meetings held over the years since 1974 have focused mainly on three topics: (1) strategies for the defense of Japan, with special attention to the role of the United States; (2) adaptation to the post-Vietnam strategic context in order to maintain peace in Asia, especially in Korea; (3) possibilities for arms control and the prevention of nuclear proliferation in Asia. The present volume is one product of these discussions.

The contributors to this book look to the future with a sharp awareness that the basis of U.S.-Japan relations in the security field has undergone important changes in recent years and that further changes of potentially great significance may be impending. Although varying interpretations are presented as to the implications of these developments, the question of how to adapt to a changing situation is a recurrent theme in the book.

Daniel I. Okimoto sketches the background of U.S.-Japanese security relations, highlighting a number of underlying asymmetries and differences in modes of communication and conceptualization that have made it hard for Japanese and Americans to understand one another's views on national security affairs. Okimoto observes that changes in Japan's domestic and international environments may well add to the existing sources of tension. Ryukichi Imai picks up the theme of change, showing how the nature of arms control has been transformed and how, as attention has shifted to questions of direct relevance to Japan, the Japanese have begun to demonstrate more interest in, and more realism about, arms control. He notes that there is considerable potential for conflict stemming from the differences between Japanese and U.S. conceptions of arms control, as Tokyo's response to the Carter administration's nonproliferation policies has made clear.

Japanese and American roles in the defense of Japan are considered by James William Morley and Makoto Momoi.

Given the increased willingness of the Japanese to tolerate the Self-Defense Forces and the U.S.-Japan Security Treaty, what, if any, changes in Japan's defense role may now be appropriate? Morley, in arguing that the time has come for greater "realism," suggests that the viability of the U.S. commitment may depend at least in part on Japan's determination to play a more meaningful role in its own military defense, as demonstrated by a readiness to make a more significant contribution to joint defense efforts. Momoi analyzes the factors that influence Japanese defense planning. He notes a growing awareness of the limitations on the U.S. capacity to deter conflict, and he indicates the instruments, both military and nonmilitary, that Japan may bring to bear on its own behalf.

Morton H. Halperin and Takuya Kubo examine one aspect of the defense question—the meaning of the U.S. nuclear umbrella for Japan's security. Both find the U.S. nuclear guarantee sufficiently credible. Halperin clarifies this often muddled subject by reducing the question of credibility to a series of subquestions intended to specify what the umbrella is, and is not, intended to do. Kubo is concerned not only with the question of credibility but also with the Japanese political context and ways in which questions relating to the deployment of U.S. nuclear weapons have stimulated political controversy in Japan.

The discussion then shifts to the broader Asian context. John W. Lewis and I offer an analysis of the new strategic situation in Asia, concluding that there is need for a more conditional view of U.S. security commitments. We suggest that the United States and its Asian allies might place greater reliance on economic and diplomatic relationships with potential adversary nations as a means of providing the latter with incentives to avoid resolving conflicts by military means. The Asian area of sharpest concern in the post-Vietnam era is Korea. Fuji Kamiya analyzes the prospects for peace on that peninsula, focusing mainly on the factors that make a North Korean attack unlikely and on the desirability of building a basis for longer-term stability through "cross-recognition" of the two Korean states by the major powers.

Selig S. Harrison views the strength of Korean nationalism, analyzes U.S. and Japanese interests and options in Korea, and concludes that Washington and Tokyo should move toward relationships with Pyongyang even in the absence of reciprocal actions by the communist powers vis-à-vis Seoul. In parallel commentaries, Ralph N. Clough expresses his skepticism about the feasibility of the unilateral moves proposed by Harrison, and Toru Yano draws attention to some of the differences between U.S. and Japanese approaches to the Korean question.

Addressing both the Japanese and broader Asian dimensions of the security issue, Henry S. Rowen sets forth his analysis of the options for Japan. He believes that expanded Japanese defense efforts may be required sooner or later, and he sees latent support in Japan for such efforts. Rowen suggests ways of helping to ensure that Japan's military role is developed within a framework of close U.S.-Japanese cooperation. In the concluding chapter, I summarize the discussions we have had and offer my own observations, which are at odds with those of some of the other contributors, about the kinds of policies that would best serve U.S. and Japanese interests in the changing Asian situation.

There is an omission, the reasons for which may be of interest. In this collection on the security of East Asia there is no chapter on China; nor is there any explicit proposal concerning relations with China in the conclusions and recommendations presented at the end of the book. At our first meeting, we proposed to discuss ways of encouraging China to become an active participant in arms control discussions. This was something to which a number of the American participants attached a high priority, but it did not elicit much interest on the part of the Japanese, who felt there were many other more important issues to discuss. As a result, there was no session specifically devoted to China. How this experience relates to what we learned about Japanese conceptions of arms control is described in the final chapter of the book.

This is a time of growing uncertainty for the Japanese and for the future of the U.S.-Japanese security relationship.

That much remains unclear is indicated by the divergent views presented in this book. It is to be hoped, however, that this collection of essays, together with future products of our ongoing discussions with the Japanese, will cast light upon the problems we face and will contribute to mutual understanding between Japan and the United States.

F. B. Weinstein

1
Security Policies in the United States and Japan: Institutions, Experts, and Mutual Understanding

Daniel I. Okimoto

The U.S.-Japanese security alliance has survived for over a quarter century in the face of strong and sustained opposition, periodic outbursts of violent protest, and major changes in the domestic and international environment. The United States and Japan have managed to avoid many of the tensions that one might have expected, given the degree of asymmetry between the military forces of the two allies and the dissimilarities in the institutional and social context within which they formulate and implement their national security policies. The remarkable durability of the alliance is due mainly to two factors: a benign international security environment for Japan and the dominance of domestic political forces committed to limited Japanese defense capabilities within the framework of a close military relationship with the United States.

These conditions are now changing. The security picture in the region has become more complicated, and pressures, both internal and external, for a larger Japanese defense capability are mounting. This comes at a time when the dominance of the Liberal-Democratic party (LDP) has been steadily weakening. The end of LDP hegemony promises to introduce new strains into the U.S.-Japanese military alliance, since the progressive parties have tended to oppose long-term continuation of the security treaty. So long as the larger framework of U.S.-Japan relations remains firmly bound by economic interdependence and shared interests in other fields, the security treaty may not be in any immediate danger of being terminated, even if a coalition government comes to power. But the alliance may become considerably more difficult to manage if domestic and international conditions evolve in ways that bring out latent tensions stemming from the gap between the two nations' military forces, the differences between their infrastructures for making security policy, the roles in policy making played by national security experts, and their styles of conceptualization and communication. If potential misunderstandings are to be averted, the importance of these asymmetries and dissimilarities must be fully recognized.

Differences in Institutional Context

There are marked disparities in the scale and scope of institutions organized to deal with security issues. In the United States, a vast national security infrastructure has been erected both within and outside the government, attesting to the high priority attached to military preparedness. In Japan, there exists only a modest security infrastructure, reflecting the low emphasis on the development of military capabilities. Among the most telling indicators of the disparity are budget figures for military expenditures. In fiscal 1976 the United States allocated $102.7 billion for national defense, an amount that accounted for roughly 26 percent of the total national budget and 5.9 percent of the GNP. Defense allocations in Japan for the same year came to only $5.06 billion, or roughly 6.2 percent of the national budget and less than 1 percent of Japan's GNP. The statistics show that U.S. expenditures exceeded Japanese outlays by twenty times in absolute terms, ten times in per capita costs, and four times in percentage figures. Japan spends proportionately less on national defense than any other major nation.

Government Institutions

The authority of the Japanese prime minister over defense and security policies is much less sweeping than that of the U.S. president. This is an important difference between the two systems. If Americans assume that the Japanese prime minister can speak for his country on security affairs with as much authority as the U.S. president speaks for his, there is a basis for serious misunderstanding. There are a number of major constraints on the prime minister's role. The president can rely on the National Security Council (NSC) to coordinate interdepartmental views and present policy alternatives, but the prime minister has only a handful of staff assistants on loan from other agencies to help him carry out his national security responsibilities. Japan's counterpart to the NSC, the National Defense Council (NDC), has so far failed to perform its intended functions; instead, it has tended merely to approve what has already been decided. Moreover, the consensual style of politics and the important role of political parties in Japan make it extraordinarily difficult for a prime minister to carve out an independent base of action. He must be careful to consult widely with a broad cross section of people before coming to a decision. The norms of consensus often require what from an American perspective appears to be an inordinate amount of time, energy, and attention to form. Indeed, this is sometimes a source of frustration for Americans, but it is the mode of operation in Japan; failure to adhere to these norms can be politically costly. It would be almost inconceivable, therefore, for a Japanese prime minister to conduct foreign and defense policies with the secrecy and concentration of power that characterized Nixon-Kissinger diplomacy. Power is too widely diffused in Japan to permit such an approach.

The prime minister's ability to direct the framing and implementation of security policies is further hampered by the way Japanese cabinets have been selected under the LDP. The U.S. president has considerable leeway in forming a cabinet of members loyal to him and, at least to a reasonable degree, willing to work together toward the realization of common administration goals. Japanese prime ministers usually appoint senior LDP politicians to cabinet posts on the basis of factional considerations; cabinet posts are meted out as rewards for support in intraparty elections, or as a means of ensuring an equitable representation of the party's factional balance.[1] A prime minister often has been obliged to appoint leaders of strong rival factions to key posts in his cabinet. Some of these have used their posts to expand their own power at the expense of the incumbent prime minister. It has not been uncommon for prime ministers to be ousted from office because of the maneuverings of their own cabinet members.

Nor can the Japanese prime minister expect to draw upon bureaucratic agencies with a breadth of expertise in the security field comparable to that available to the U.S. president. Although the competence of the Japanese bureaucracy is high, especially where economic issues are concerned, security problems have not commanded the sustained attention needed to develop extensive analytic skills. The Japan Defense Agency (JDA) does not even have the status of a full-fledged ministry. Its scale of operations is dwarfed by that of its counterpart, the U.S. Department of Defense. The Defense Department, which has been described as the "primary employer, contractor, purchaser, owner, and spender in the nation,"[2] employs more than a million people, but the JDA staff numbers only around 28,000. The JDA has tended to take a low profile on most policy questions, except on such narrowly military matters as weapons procurement and deployment of military forces. On most issues of foreign and security policies, the JDA has deferred to the Foreign Ministry, even though the latter's analytic capabilities in the politico-military sphere are also far from extensive. There is no bureau within the Foreign Ministry that specializes in problems of military security.

These limitations are perhaps most graphically captured in the paucity of resources devoted to arms control and disarmament policies. Unlike the United States, which has an Arms Control and Disarmament Agency with a staff of 214 and a budget of $10 billion, Japan has only a small Office of Disarmament, housed within the United Nations Bureau of the Foreign Ministry. This office is normally staffed by nine junior-ranking bureaucrats, few of whom have had special training for this assignment; the practice of regular rotation every two years or so makes it hard to acquire expertise on the job. Efforts to keep informed of current developments in the field are hampered by the absence of basic materials from abroad, such as daily editions of the *New York Times* and *Washington Post* or more specialized journals like *Aviation Week* and the *Bulletin of the Atomic Scientists*. Everyone reads English and several can handle Chinese, but almost no one in the office has the language competence to utilize materials in Russian. The Disarmament Office, understaffed and inadequately funded, commands little prestige or influence within the Foreign Ministry.

Equally striking is the absence of specialized agencies for the gathering and processing of intelligence, particularly with respect to matters of military security. The Japanese government must rely on the modest in-house capabilities of the Foreign Ministry, the Office of the Prime Minister, and other agencies. The United States has provided classified information from time to time, but the laxness of Japanese laws governing the protection of classified information has forced U.S. leaders to be concerned about possible leaks. In contrast, the network of intelligence agencies available to the president is one of the most extensive in the world.

Important differences between the United States and Japan are evident in the legislative branch as well. Deliberations on national security operations in the National Diet are much more sharply partisan than in the U.S. Congress. Indeed, the policy-making role of the Diet is less important than that of its American counterpart, largely because of the long dominance of the LDP and weaknesses in the Diet's own structure of operations. There are no Japanese counterparts to the Senate and House committees on armed services. Such discussions of national security issues as do take place in the Diet occur within the Budget and Foreign Affairs committees. The lack of analytic capabilities renders the Diet more dependent on information supplied by the executive branch than is the U.S. Congress. Although the Diet has the legal authority to affect the shape of national

security policies through its jurisdiction over military
budgets and other defense-related legislation, its ability to
exercise that authority has been severely restricted by the
strength of the bureaucracy and the LDP's control over the
two houses. Opposition parties have generally lacked the
numerical weight to block proposed appropriations for
weapons procurement and other legislation relating to
defense, although this situation seems to be changing as the
LDP's dominance erodes.

The opposition parties, of course, have always been able to
exert some impact on the formulation of defense policies by
using the Diet as a forum to subject cabinet members and
other government officials to intensive grilling. By raising
hard questions, delivering partisan soliloquies, and occa-
sionally making dramatic revelations, they have often put
the government on the defensive. Preparation for Diet
interpellations has been a time-consuming burden for LDP
leaders and government officials fearful of embarrassment at
the hands of opposition party spokesmen seeking to use
military issues to score political points. Thus, even when its
ability to dominate the Diet has been virtually unchallenged,
the LDP-led government has not felt free to move rapidly
toward major military expansion programs.

Private Institutions

Japan has few nongovernmental institutions that are
involved in the study of military security problems. In the
United States, an extensive network of private "think tanks,"
research institutes, and study centers, employing thousands
of highly trained scientists and strategists, has developed
since World War II. The best known are the Rand Corporation, the Hudson Institute, and the Brookings Institution.
All three have committed substantial human and financial
resources over the years to studies in the field of arms control,
deterrence, and defense; some of their studies have had a
major impact on the thinking of government officials on
such matters as force deployments, targeting doctrine, and
the conceptual implications of new weapons technologies.
In addition, private foundations and government agencies

have enlisted the services of some of America's academic talent by funding the establishment of research centers at major universities across the country. Many prominent academics have gained membership in the Council on Foreign Relations, probably the most influential of the private groups organized to study and discuss security policies. Specialized professional organizations such as the Arms Control Association and the Federation of American Scientists maintain lobbies in Washington to act on a range of arms control and security issues.

The closest approximation to a Japanese "think tank" in the field of national security is the International Problems Research Institute. Funded primarily by the Foreign Ministry, the institute draws upon a small pool of specialists who write on political-diplomatic affairs. Nor are the resources of Japanese universities extensively utilized to bring academic expertise to bear on policy problems. Japanese campuses have been centers of strong antimilitary sentiments, and the pervasiveness of powerful normative sanctions against military-related research has inhibited the study of national security on college campuses. This atmosphere has also prevented the kinds of linkages between universities and the government that are common in the United States. Under present circumstances it is very hard to imagine that a weapons laboratory such as the Lawrence Radiation Laboratory could be created as an affiliate of a major Japanese university. Although the antipathy toward studies of national security may be diminishing, it will be some time before universities are willing to participate directly in studies in this field.

Another major difference in the institutional context within which security policies are made in the United States and Japan relates to the fact that in Japan the most active private organizations with an interest in the security field have strongly opposed programs aimed at greater military preparedness. Japan has far fewer industrial interests that are dependent on expenditures for weapons procurement and that therefore lobby for increased military spending. There are also fewer research-and-development facilities engaged in work on military hardware, in part because many Japanese scientists are averse to military-related research. Moreover, the largest and most visible citizen groups in Japan have tended to criticize government policies on national defense. *Gensuikin* and *Gensuikyo*, two well-known "ban-the-bomb" organizations affiliated with the Japanese Socialist party (JSP) and the Japan Communist party (JCP), respectively, have staged regular rallies and demonstrations calling for termination of the security treaty and the immediate and complete abolition of all nuclear weapons. Japan's mammoth national dailies, which have generally opposed large-scale increases in armaments and an expanded military role in the region, have had a significant impact on public opinion. Although opposition may be softening, the constant threat of criticism from the press, students and intellectuals, labor unions, and citizen groups continues to limit the range of options open to policymakers in the national security field.

The national security infrastructures in the United States and Japan could hardly pose a sharper contrast. Discrepancies in the scope and level of institutional development reflect basic differences in the salience of military issues, the security environment of both countries, the hierarchy of national priorities, and the legacy of the war. Because of the absence of worrisome threats and because of the credibility of the U.S.-Japan defense alliance, few demands have been made on Japan's security capabilities. As a consequence, Japan has managed to get through the past quarter century with only a very modest security infrastructure. But the contrasting institutional contexts for the making of security policies in the two countries reflect, and reinforce, important differences in the way Japanese and Americans think.

National Security Experts: Contrasting Characteristics

The Intellectual Context in the United States

World War II brought American scientists and scholars into the field of military affairs on an unprecedented scale. They were mobilized to bring their knowledge and skills to bear on a variety of tasks, including weapons development, analysis of intelligence data, selection of target sites, and development of propaganda. With the advent of nuclear weapons, civilian strategists emerged to deal with the complex array of problems these new weapons introduced: how to avoid the use of nuclear warheads, how to regulate their production and proliferation, where to deploy and how to deliver these weapons, and what implications changes in military technology might have for international relations.

Physical scientists gravitated to the field of strategy not only because their technical expertise was increasingly in demand, but also because many felt a moral obligation to find ways of preventing the awesome power of nuclear energy from ever again being unleashed against mankind. Political scientists took an interest in the field because it was becoming an important feature of international relations. Economists, attracted to study problems of managing the substantial resources being allocated for military purposes, found that their skills in such areas as operations research, systems analysis, and game theory could be put to effective use in the selection of weapons systems, deployment of military hardware, and development of scenarios for strategic planning.

The majority of experts engaged in the study of military strategy subscribe to the view that deterrence is the only feasible means of maintaining the balance of power, the sine qua non for world peace. Any reduction of arms, they believe, has to be implemented without upsetting the balance of power. There are those, however, who reject the concept of deterrence. These analysts, who belong to the disarmament school, believe deterrence actually creates circumstances that guarantee instability. The concept of deterrence legitimizes not only the existence but also the constant expansion of nuclear and other arsenals; the irony is that ever-rising levels of armament fail to guarantee any greater sense of security, since there is always the danger that the balance will tip in favor of the adversary. The only sure way to disengage from this vicious cycle, according to the critics of deterrence, is to take bold steps toward disarmament.

What are the background characteristics of these experts on national security? What are their educational backgrounds, occupational patterns, and links with government? To gather background data on American and Japanese experts, national samples were drawn of specialists who have published on national security affairs.[3] Perhaps the most striking characteristic of American experts as a group is the continued dominance of the same core of specialists who pioneered the field in the 1950s. This continuity is partly attributable to the youthfulness of these individuals at the time of their rise to prominence. During the 1950s, Henry Kissinger, Albert Wohlstetter, and Thomas Schelling were in their thirties, and even "senior" analysts such as Bernard Brodie were only in their forties.

Advocates of disarmament represent only 15 percent of the American experts in the sample, which probably reflects the general lack of broad support for the disarmament movement in the country. There was much sympathy for the banning of all nuclear weapons in the immediate postwar years, but such sentiments began to fade with the onset of the Cold War. By the late 1950s, advocates of unilateral disarmament had moved to the periphery of the nuclear debate, and it became difficult for them to gain a hearing.

The overwhelming majority of U.S. experts (85 percent) belong to the deterrence school. This category, however, covers a broad spectrum of views. Some, like Herbert Scoville and Paul Warnke, advocate arms control agreements and even bold measures for arms reduction so long as the balance of power is maintained. Others, like Edward Teller and Robert Strausz-Hupé, regard arms limitation as dangerous and destabilizing; these advocates of military preparedness believe that maintenance of a credible deterrent requires almost unquestioning support of ever higher levels of armament. Although they sometimes voice token support for arms control efforts, they consistently oppose specific efforts at arms limitation and urge the production and deployment of new weapons systems in order to "negotiate from strength." These "hawks" represent only a minority of the deterrence group, but they express sentiments that have significant support among top-ranking officers of the armed services, key leaders of Congressional committees, spokesmen for certain industrial interests, elements of the media, conservative associations, and the public at large. Underlying these hawkish views are an intense anticommunism and a deep suspicion of the Soviet Union.

The Japanese Intellectual Context

Unlike their American counterparts, Japanese scientists and scholars reacted to the war with a profound aversion to military power. The nightmare of Japan's wartime experience generated powerful undercurrents of pacifism, neutralism, and Marxism from 1945 to roughly the early 1960s. During the years when the fever of anticommunism was running high in the United States, Marxist thought sunk deep roots at college campuses and within intellectual circles in Japan. Most Marxists and "progressive" intellectuals opposed both the peace and security treaties, the stationing of U.S. troops on Japanese territory, and the establishment and expansion of Japan's Self-Defense Forces. Left-leaning magazines such as *Sekai*, then at the height of their prestige, carried articles that advocated global disarmament, unarmed neutrality for Japan, and the amelioration of relations with both the Soviet Union and the People's Republic of China. The dominance of left-wing scholars put the intellectual community sharply at odds with the government, and there was significant public support for the idea of unarmed neutrality and the abrogation of the security treaty. This support began to fade after the convulsive demonstrations in Tokyo opposing President Eisenhower's planned visit to Japan in 1960.

During the late 1950s and early 1960s, the strength of left-wing thought began to wane. A group of young international relations specialists known as "neo-realists" appeared on the scene, including such scholars as Shinkichi Eto, Fuji Kamiya, Masataka Kosaka, Kei Wakaizumi, and Yonosuke Nagai. Born in the 1920s and 1930s, conversant in English, and experienced in research and study abroad, these scholars challenged the prevailing orthodoxy of left-wing thought. They assumed that coercive power was an unavoidable reality of international relations; they criticized "unarmed neutrality" and "complete and immediate disarmament" as dangerous and irresponsible policies that no country could afford to implement. They argued that Japan's national interests, as well as stability in the region, required the continuation of the U.S.-Japan security alliance. The alliance, in their eyes, did not preclude amelioration of relations with the Soviet Union and China; it meant that normalization with the communist bloc would have to be pursued within the enduring framework of the American-Japanese alliance.

The rise of the neo-realists coincided, not accidentally, with the development of international relations as a field of study and with Japan's own emergence as an economic power. The late development of international relations as a discipline at Japanese universities helped neo-realists gain a foothold in the field, since it was not dominated by a Marxist orthodoxy, as were history and economics. Japan's newly acquired status as a major economic power was said to require more "realistic" and "pragmatic" approaches to the study of Japan's changing role in the world order. Since 1960 the neo-realists have succeeded in establishing a firm foothold in Japan as the mood of the country has shifted gradually away from left-wing solutions to security problems. Indeed, at international conferences, the views of neo-realist analysts tend to be overrepresented, and American participants often fail to appreciate the continued importance of more "progressive" points of view in Japan.

Like their American counterparts, Japanese adherents of deterrence theory include advocates of a wide range of viewpoints—from strong opposition to Japan's assumption of a larger military role to support for a nuclear weapons program. The thinking of neo-realists, for the most part, comes closer to that of arms reductionists in the United States than to that of the more hawkish proponents of maximal military preparedness. Most neo-realists have tended to believe that a low military posture is Japan's only feasible course, though they are not inflexibly committed to that position. The small group of Japanese hawks who have gone on record in favor of large-scale rearmament and nuclear weapons consists mainly of former military officers such as Akio Doi and Hideo Sekino and literary figures such as Shintarō Ishihara. They represent only a small fraction (5 percent) of the Japanese sample, and their arguments have so far struck few responsive chords in either the government or the general public. They are seen as a tiny fringe element.

Although support for the disarmament perspective has eroded considerably since the early 1960s, this view still exerts a strong influence through the writings of "idealist" scholars. Nearly 40 percent of the Japanese sample can be identified as advocates of disarmament, compared to only 15 percent of the Americans. Nor should we underestimate the significance of continued support for the cause of disarmament among opposition party leaders, labor unions, student activists, peace organizations, and the mass media. In contrast to the United States, Japanese discussions of national security take place within an atmosphere of deep uneasiness concerning any expansion of the country's military capabilities. For many years the weight of these forces and public opinion led to a special hostility toward nuclear weapons, commonly referred to as Japan's "nuclear allergy." Judging from public opinion polls, the allergy seems to be on the wane, but Japanese leaders still do not feel completely free about discussing nuclear-related issues in public, because the subject remains extremely sensitive even today.

Educational Background, Occupational Patterns, and Government Experience

One of the most obvious differences between American and Japanese experts on military affairs is the substantially smaller number of physical scientists among the Japanese. Although specialists trained in political science represented the largest number in both samples, 32 percent of the Americans were physical scientists, as compared to only 12 percent of the Japanese.[4] As a result of this underrepresentation of scientists, much of the Japanese writing on security

issues lacks concreteness and technical specificity. There is
rarely any evidence of mastery over the nuts and bolts of
weapon systems.[5] Nor can much of the public discussion be
readily translated into clear policy alternatives. Most
writings on national security are very general and are
produced for popular consumption. Related to the paucity
of physical scientists is the lack of the interdisciplinary
collaboration that has yielded some of the most important
American studies in the field.

Another difference between American and Japanese experts lies in the length of their formal training, as measured
by the number of doctorates and other advanced degrees.
Only 15 percent of the Japanese specialists had earned
doctorates, as opposed to 74 percent of the Americans. This is
largely due to the fact that the Japanese educational system
places much less emphasis upon graduate training than does
the American system. But whatever the reason, there is no
denying the fact that American experts have had more
training than their Japanese counterparts. They are also
more specialized. A large number of the Americans who
work in the national security field consider this their
primary research interest and professional commitment.
Very few Japanese regard national security as their major
area of specialization.

Notwithstanding the disparities in years of formal educa-
tion, the two groups are similar in the prominence and
prestige they enjoy within their respective nations. A large
number of specialists on both sides are alumni of elite
universities. Nearly half the Americans received their degrees
from Ivy League institutions; many of the rest graduated
from other first-rate universities, such as Chicago, California (Berkeley), and the California Institute of Technology. More than half the Japanese graduated from either
the University of Tokyo or Kyoto University, the two most
distinguished institutions in the academic hierarchy. Eight
Americans and two Japanese in the sample have won Nobel
prizes. Clearly, both groups stand among the intellectual
elite of their countries.

Nearly all of the analysts are employed at one of three

types of institutions: universities, research institutes, or government. Yet the occupational patterns of American and Japanese experts are quite different. Japanese tend to work solely within a single sector, but Americans move freely from one to another. The majority of American experts are based at universities; 75 percent have worked on college campuses at some point in their careers. Forty-two percent have held full-time positions in the government, and 34 percent have worked full time for research institutes. Members of the American sample have served in the following agencies of government: Defense Department (23), State Department (17), the President's Scientific Advisory Committee (10), Atomic Energy Commission (10), Arms Control and Disarmament Agency (9), National Security Council (6), and Central Intelligence Agency (3). If consultantships are included, the percentage with government experience increases from forty-two to seventy-two.[6] Although most of the positions held have been at the middle ranks, a handful— including Henry Kissinger, James Schlesinger, Fred Iklé, Harold Brown, and Zbigniew Brzezinski—have served in top-level posts.

In Japan there is very little movement between government and academic circles. Only 23 percent of the sample have worked full time for the government, and the vast majority of these were employed by the National Defense College, an appendage of the Defense Agency, which is not an important center of policy making. Japan's higher civil service is a tightly enclosed, elitist structure into which lateral entry from the outside is rare. It is staffed by career civil servants whose mode of operations would be disrupted by the American system of "in-and-outers."[7] The self-sufficiency of Japan's bureaucracies extends even to the level of outside consultants; not many Japanese have been asked to serve as part-time consultants to the government. Some government agencies maintain "deliberative councils" comprised of leading outside experts, but neither the Foreign Ministry nor the Defense Agency draws heavily upon such advisory bodies.[8]

Even if the Japanese government did make more extensive

use of consultants, or if the bureaucracy actively sought to recruit outside talent into its ranks, there would probably still be barriers to the free flow of scholars into government service as a consequence of strongly held norms against such mobility. Japanese intellectuals, reacting to their wartime cooptation by the military government, tend to feel that the intellectual's role in society is to serve as "pure critic," free from entanglements with the government. Intellectuals who fail to maintain such detachment—especially academics seduced by the allure of operating close to the centers of power—are likely to be scorned by colleagues as "kept scholars," "scholars on the make," or "intellectual flunkies" of the establishment. Derision of intellectual opportunism is much stronger in Japan than in academic circles in the United States. The existence of such norms, together with the exclusivity of the bureaucracies, have thus tended to keep the worlds of academia and public service distinctly divided.

Even though outsiders encounter obstacles to participation in government, many deterrence-oriented experts feel it is the responsibility of intellectuals to see that their beliefs are translated into better government policies. They have therefore been less hesitant to accept government positions or to consult unofficially with politicians and bureaucrats. These contacts, however, do not necessarily signify influence, even though the policies advocated by these scholars may be very close to those adopted by the government.[9] It may be that members of the deterrence group who have developed ties with the government have played a more important role in lending intellectual legitimacy to government policies than in actually molding those policies.

In summary, the contrasts between American and Japanese experts on security affairs are striking. The Americans have had more years of advanced training, represent greater diversity of fields, and include more physical scientists; they move much more freely in and out of government. The intellectual context in the United States has supported participation by scholars in the making of government security policies; in Japan, prevailing norms and the closed structure of the higher civil service have strongly discouraged such participation. As a result of these differences, American experts have had many more opportunities than their Japanese counterparts to become involved, directly and indirectly, in the policy-making process. It is therefore not surprising that American specialists, with their greater technical expertise and government experience, have played a much more important role in the framing of national security policies than have their Japanese counterparts.

Potential Obstacles to Mutual Understanding

It is easy to see how the differences discussed so far can lead to misunderstandings between Americans and Japanese. Americans who urge that Japan play a larger military role may fail to realize that such a change would involve far more than a decision by the prime minister and a few other leaders close to the top. As we have seen, the prime minister's freedom to direct national security policies is sharply limited by the peculiarities of the policy-making process in Japan. Americans may not fully appreciate the extent to which the underdevelopment of Japan's institutional infrastructure inhibits any rapid expansion of the country's military role. Nor do American national security experts always understand the constraints imposed on their Japanese counterparts by the intellectual context in Japan and by the relative isolation of Japanese academics from the policy-making process. But problems such as these are by no means the only obstacles to mutual understanding. It is necessary also to consider some basic differences in American and Japanese conceptions of national security.

American Globalism and Japanese Insularity

America's perspective on security is a global one, reflecting the magnitude of U.S. military power and the global reach of U.S. military commitments. The United States, viewing itself as the chief barrier to the expansion of communism across national boundaries, has, at least until quite recently, rarely questioned its right, even obligation, to bring its awesome powers of coercion to bear on behalf of allied nations. Similarly, Americans see their country's

role in arms control negotiations as being of great consequence for all nations. The United States acts within what it
perceives to be a global framework.

The Japanese, in contrast, have had no pretensions to such
sweeping global designs. Rather, their perspective has been
relatively narrow. Their security conceptions have focused
much more explicitly on their own national needs and, to a
limited extent, on regional concerns. A central component of
the Japanese security perspective has been the absence of any
serious military threat to their country. The Japanese
propensity to view their military security in insular terms is
reinforced by a belief that in any case Japan can do little to
influence the larger military balance. Moreover, Japan's lack
of natural resources and consequent dependence on world
trade make the Japanese keenly aware of their own vulnerabilities and inclined to maintain their low military posture.
Indeed, most Japanese believe that their security hinges
more on economic relationships than on military ones.
Their conception of security explicitly emphasizes economic
interests, and Japanese experts on security affairs often
criticize the United States for taking an excessively military
view of security. Whether the Soviet naval buildup, the U.S.
withdrawal of its ground forces from Korea, or other
international developments will significantly alter Japanese
perceptions of their national security is as yet unclear.

Differences between Japanese and American approaches
to security are apparent in the arms control field as well.
Japan has acted with much less vigor in this area than
Japan's commitment to a low military posture would lead
one to expect. It is sometimes hard for Americans to
understand how a major industrial state and ally such as
Japan can fail to appreciate the significance of such negotiations as the SALT rounds. Japan's dependence on the U.S.
nuclear umbrella should, theoretically, suggest a high level
of interest in SALT. But SALT has been of relatively low
salience in Japan—even among intellectuals and political
leaders. The Japanese show much less interest in SALT than
do their European counterparts. The reason is not that the
Japanese are unaware of SALT's potential significance;

rather, they feel that there is little they can do to affect the course of events. What strikes Americans as indifference may merely be a reflection of the belief that what goes on between the superpowers at SALT is far beyond the scope of Japan's influence.

Even outside the SALT arena, the Japanese have been reluctant to undertake arms control initiatives. In part, this is a product of a long-standing psychological dependence on the United States and a tendency to follow Washington's lead. Tokyo's reluctance to push for a nuclear no-first-use pledge, a measure that would seem to serve Japan's interests, may be attributed to the dependence of the Japanese on the U.S. nuclear umbrella and their desire to respect Washington's concern about the European implications of such a pledge. Moreover, the Japanese have felt that any arms control proposals they might make would lack weight because Japan, not being a heavily armed nation, would not be required to make its own sacrifices as part of a quid pro quo. Japan has, however, gradually begun to show more signs of independence from the United States in the arms control field, as indicated by some of its recent stands on peaceful nuclear explosions, a comprehensive test ban, and nuclear proliferation. The Japanese have come to realize that because they clearly possess the capability to develop nuclear weapons, they do possess more potential weight than many other nations on such matters as nuclear proliferation.

Some American arms control advocates have assumed that Japan should at least be able to take a leading role in working toward arms control arrangements for the Northeast Asian region. The failure of the Japanese to do so is partly attributable to their pessimistic estimate of the feasibility of such measures and their reluctance to risk antagonizing any of the major powers with interests in the region. Japan's passivity in the arms control field also reflects Tokyo's awareness of the deep suspicion with which Japan is viewed by its neighbors. Nothing in Europe compares in intensity to the residue of resentment and suspicion coloring Japan's relations with Korea. Americans tend to think of Korea's security in terms of global strategic calculations; the Japanese, on the other hand, are more inclined to view the problems of the peninsula within the context of the deep animosity between Korea and Japan. Americans who urge that Japan take "initiatives for peace" by acting as a bridge to Korea often fail to appreciate the constraints imposed by these "parochial" concerns.

Contrasting Modes of Communication

The tendency of the Japanese to view their security in isolation from that of other nations is reinforced by the linguistic and cultural insularity of the country. Because so few foreigners know the Japanese language, security discussions in Japan are not exposed to as much critical feedback from audiences outside the country as similar discussions in Western Europe or the United States. On security and arms control issues, Japan's internal debate has been largely cut off from the ferment of international give-and-take; this isolation has contributed to the sterility and stridency of the exchange. Although a fair number of English books on national security have been translated into Japanese, few Japanese works have found their way into the English language. This situation has given rise to yet another asymmetry: the Japanese know a great deal more about American views on security (as well as most other issues) than Americans know about Japanese perspectives. The appalling American ignorance about Japanese ways of thinking, and about even the fundamentals of Japanese politics and policy making, is in itself a major source of potential misunderstanding between the two countries.

The language problem is not merely a matter of inadequate translations. It reflects important differences in the way words are used and in modes of communication within the two societies. American culture is highly verbal, but the intricacies of human interactions in Japan's homogeneous and ritualized society are conveyed by both verbal and nonverbal means with an extraordinary degree of subtlety. The social context, the choice of appropriate levels of politeness in addressing another person, a variety of hidden cues, and the leaving of certain things unsaid, often obviate the need to spell out explicitly that which is being communicated. Even skillful translation cannot always capture the real message of Japanese statements. It should be remembered that the Japanese language has evolved within patterns of social relationships quite unlike those found in the United States.

One indication of the role of indirect communication in Japanese political discourse is the importance attached to the distinction between explicit statements *(tatemae)* and private intentions or beliefs *(honne)*. It is not unusual for Americans to draw this distinction in certain situations, such as election campaigns, but statements that do not mean what they appear to mean are much more common at all levels of interaction in Japan. Most Japanese are aware of the real messages being transmitted by such statements, but Americans are apt to take these pronouncements literally as accurate expressions of the speaker's beliefs. Foreigners are usually not sensitive to the cues that enable Japanese to distinguish between *tatemae* and *honne*.

A policy statement may be meant to convey a message to other political parties, to project a distinctive public image, to strengthen party morale, or, on occasion, merely to test the political air. To interpret a statement, one must know a great deal about the context within which it is made. Certain Japanese political parties sometimes issue statements critical of the security treaty, even though their leaders are known privately to favor its continuation. The JSP's rhetoric on unarmed neutrality has been intended, in part, to bolster the party's image as a distinct alternative to the LDP. Unarmed neutrality may be viewed by the JSP as a desirable long-term goal, but most party leaders are realistic enough to know that, if the party came to power, it could not immediately attain that goal. Similarly, some observers believe that there are *tatemae* elements in the LDP's "three non-nuclear principles." The three principles have been characterized as a formulation originally devised to forestall criticism of the terms by which Okinawa was returned to Japan; the principles have subsequently been used to enable the government to pursue a close military relationship with a nuclear-armed United States without arousing the public's strong antinuclear sentiments. When a number of LDP members called for disavowal of the third non-nuclear principle during the 1975 Diet debate on NPT ratification, this was taken by some critics as conclusive evidence that earlier statements of support for the principles had been mere *tatemae*. The criticism is probably exaggerated, but the point is that Americans can easily be misled if they take Japanese statements on security and arms control, or any other subject, at face value without attempting to discern the hidden messages being transmitted.

Further evidence of the importance of indirect communication in Japan emerges from a comparison of Japanese and American styles of persuasion. American bureaucracies serve as clearinghouses for a voluminous traffic of memoranda. Indeed, these memorandums may be said to represent the bureaucracy's lifeblood—information pumped through a maze of communication arteries to every part of the organism. Ideally, policy proposals are set down succinctly, rigorously, and impersonally; the memorandum's impact depends on the persuasive force and logic of its argumentation. American experts on national security affairs are especially prone to rely on this style of persuasion.

In Japan, persuasion and decision making are more loosely structured to accommodate personal factors. In lieu of endless reams of memorandums, there are endless rounds of formal and informal meetings full of meandering discussions that would drive most efficiency-minded Americans to distraction. The final result of these discussions is decision by consensus. In the process of reaching a consensus, the human interaction is central. It is not unusual to see rigorously logical arguments go unheeded because of their advocate's brashness or some other idiosyncratic factor. The Japanese usually do not reach a decision solely on the routinized basis of a detailed elaboration of all policy options, careful speculation on the implications of each, and a detached weighing of costs and benefits.

The American disposition to communicate through logical, explicit argumentation usually dictates the format of U.S.-Japanese discussions. It is the Japanese who normally are called on to make the adjustments, for Americans probably would find it hard to adapt to the more elliptical Japanese patterns. As a result, the Japanese often find themselves pinned down unnaturally and forced to provide Western-style explanations of Japanese views or events that are not readily rendered in those terms. By expecting Japanese to argue, discuss, explain, and persuade in the Western mode, Americans leave themselves open to disappointment and misunderstanding. Few Americans are aware of the invisible pressure of human relationships at work among the Japanese, inhibiting the expression of views that might be asserted in other settings. Although these differences in modes of argumentation and persuasion should not be exaggerated, they can on occasion lead to considerable frustration on both sides.

An excellent example of the kind of misunderstanding that may arise from the differences between Japanese and Americans in their use of language and patterns of persuasion relates to Prime Minister Satō's reply to President Nixon's request for voluntary curbs on textile exports to the United States. Satō is reported to have responded with a very ambiguous statement, which most Japanese would interpret as a deliberate evasion and an indication that nothing should be expected, but it was taken by Nixon as a firm promise to resolve the textile problem.

Discussion of national security issues is further complicated by confusion about the meaning of key terms. The language of nuclear strategy is full of ambiguities. Does "credibility" require demonstration of a willingness to use nuclear weapons, or does it mean the creation of circumstances in which the use of nuclear weapons would be so costly as to be inconceivable? Is the distinction between "strategic" and "tactical" nuclear weapons based on the distance they travel, their throw weight, the type of target selected, or the degree of collateral damage?

The imprecision of this vocabulary is compounded by the translation of these terms into Japanese. Until the mid-

1960s, even such a central concept as "deterrence" lacked a standard Japanese equivalent. The term finally accepted as standard, *yokushiryoku*, does not fully capture the nuances of the English word. *Yokushiryoku* conveys rather passive and mechanistic connotations of checkmating; the subtle but vital ideas of psychological gamesmanship associated with the concept of "nuclear deterrence" or the French term, *dissuasion*, are not at all suggested by the Japanese translation. Similar problems arise in the translation of other important terms, such as "credibility" *(shinraisei, shimpyō-sei*, and *kashinsei*), "first-strike" *(daiichigeki)*, and even the term "arms control" *(gunbi kanri)*. Unless one is familiar with the original terms, the Japanese words can be quite misleading. The failure, even today, to establish a set of standardized terms that adequately convey the nuances of the English originals has not only restricted the circle of those who genuinely understand the strategic vocabulary; it has also opened the way to argumentation based on distorted ideas of what these concepts really mean. Indeed, many Japanese idealists have rejected the idea that any effort should be made to understand those concepts on the ground that doing so requires an acceptance of the conceptual framework of nuclear strategy and, with it, the legitimacy of power politics and coercive diplomacy.

Cleavages in conceptual vocabulary and related differences in modes of argumentation suggest the magnitude of the gap between idealists and realists in Japan. To begin with, they have different conceptions of the purpose of argumentation. Realists tend to use instrumental words and phrases in order to facilitate dispassionate analysis leading toward some "practical" solution. Argumentation aimed at promoting lofty ideals is seen as extraneous unless "feasible policy options" emerge. These experts regard the language of the idealists as rife with emotionalism and empty abstractions. The realist vocabulary, which is full of concepts drawn from American strategic writings, emphasizes the role of rational calculation even in areas where profound moral and ethical questions impinge.

Idealists, on the other hand, believe it is necessary to

address security issues on a high moral plane, even if this is denounced by their critics as irrelevant philosophical rambling. Idealists feel it important to consider "what ought to be," not merely "what is." The idealists do not feel that their aspirations are impossible to attain. In their view, there is every reason to gear their arguments to appeal to healthy human reactions against weapons of mass destruction. Thus, they stress such themes and words as "balance of terror," "ashes of death," "lessons of Hiroshima-Nagasaki," and "complete and immediate elimination of nuclear weapons." The idealists refuse to accept the criticism that they are unrealistic; they believe that history will show them to have been more realistic than those myopic defense intellectuals who are now ironically referred to as realists. Indeed, they believe that realists who accept the assumptions and linguistic terms of reference of strategic thought have allowed themselves to be swept into the framework of an American strategy which aims at the perpetuation of U.S. military and political hegemony.

The growing influence of the realists in Japan reflects an increasing reliance on American concepts, terminology, and modes of communication. The nature of Japanese discussions of security has changed. But Americans should be cautious about assuming that this necessarily bodes well for the future of the U.S.-Japan security alliance. Even realists immersed in American strategic doctrines operate within a Japanese context in which indirect communication remains important. Idealist intellectuals may be less influential than before, but their ideas remain a powerful force. Moreover, the LDP's loss of its majority in the Diet would create new uncertainties about the future of the security relationship with the United States. It is quite conceivable that the external environment could develop in ways that lead to mounting pressures on Japan to revise its national security policies and institutions to make them fit more closely with those of the United States. No one can predict what sort of balance may ultimately be created among these conflicting trends and pressures. But considering the fundamental differences between the United States and Japan in each of the areas we have surveyed, it is hard to escape the conclusion that there are many potential obstacles to mutual understanding as the U.S.-Japan security relationship moves into its second quarter century.

Notes

1. The process of selecting cabinets has been changing as the LDP's control over the Diet has weakened. Stronger pressures are being felt to appoint younger Diet members on the basis of ability rather than of factional balance or of seniority. If the operative power of factions continues to wane, and if the LDP is forced to enter coalitions with one or more of the reformist parties, the old way of forming cabinets may undergo further changes.

2. James Clotfelter, *The Military in American Politics* (New York: Harper and Row, 1973), p. 54.

3. The procedure by which the two samples were selected is as follows. Two journals of comparable prestige and visibility, *Foreign Affairs* and *Chuo Koron*, were surveyed over a twenty-five-year period to identify analysts who had written at least one article on national security, especially related to the problem of nuclear weapons. The core lists were then expanded to include other analysts who had written major books or articles for magazines of diverse political leanings, including *Sekai, Kokubo, Bulletin of the Atomic Scientists,* and *Orbis.* The final lists contained 110 American and 60 Japanese experts; they represent a fairly broad cross section of participants in the national security debate in both countries.

4. The variance is statistically significant at the .01 level of probability, using standard chi-square measures of association.

5. All the physical scientists in the Japanese sample belong to the disarmament school. Thus, even those with the technical competence to discuss the details of military hardware have generally refrained from doing so.

6. Since information regarding employment as consultants is not always listed in standard biographical reference works, it can be assumed that the figures underestimate the actual number of those who have had experience as consultants.

7. Cases of outsiders gaining lateral entry without passing the entrance examination are rare but not unknown; in fact, their numbers may be on the rise in some agencies such as the Foreign Ministry, where there is some recognition of the need to tap the wealth of expertise existing outside the government.

8. The Foreign Ministry and Defense Agency do draw upon the services of some outside specialists as consultants. But the numbers are small.

9. Interviews with bureaucrats and LDP leaders indicate that outside scholars exercise very limited influence over the policy-making process. Politicians feel that intellectuals are too narrow and are not attuned to domestic political factors that must be taken into account in formulating policies; bureaucrats tend to believe that as career civil servants they have more administrative experience and access to better information. Over forty were interviewed; they included bureaucrats from the Foreign Ministry and Defense Agency and LDP leaders involved in national security affairs. Of these individuals, only one thought intellectuals made a significant contribution to the making of national security policies in Japan.

2
Commentary: Changing Conceptions of Arms Control

Ryukichi Imai

It is much more difficult to explain and compare U.S. and Japanese conceptions of arms control than to evaluate the merits of specific arms control proposals. Mr. Okimoto has done an excellent job in preparing a background paper. I agree with most of what he says, but disagree on some points. Rather than go into those details, however, I would like to take up the problem from a somewhat different angle. I shall first address the question of why there is a seeming lack of interest in Japan regarding arms control matters and then focus briefly on a recent example of how differing conceptions of arms control can lead to strains in U.S.-Japan relations.

In the past, arms control was never an issue involving Japan's direct interests. This is changing, however, as arms control discussions shift to weapons systems that are within the practical reach of Japan. The character of arms control is being transformed. It is becoming less superpower-dominated, strategic nuclear weapons–oriented, and NATO-centered; increasing attention is being paid to tactical/conventional issues directly involving the defense, industrial, and trade concerns of many nations. People have not officially changed the name of the game; as a result, many are discussing the subject without realizing that they are talking about the central focus of today's arms control.

The current confusion about the meaning of arms control is to a great extent the result of the superpowers' traditional use of arms control primarily to serve their own political purposes. Arms control has often seemed to mask efforts to attain relative strategic supremacy. Although SALT is very significant as a manifestation of shared U.S.-Soviet strategic nuclear interests contributing to the creation of an atmosphere of détente, it certainly is not aimed at arms reduction. In fact, it is often regarded as merely a means of legitimizing a qualitative, rather than quantitative, nuclear arms race between the two superpowers. In reality, arms control is much more than SALT and MBFR (mutual balanced force reductions); it should be broadly conceived of as a hardware-oriented exercise involving reduction of arms in order to strike a stabilizing balance between competing military forces.

For many nations, including Japan, the Nonproliferation Treaty (NPT) provided the link between the "old" arms control, which looked like superpower political gamesmanship, and the "new" one involving many more nations. Nuclear arms control began in the United Nations after World War II as an attempt to control the international spread of military nuclear power, and then narrowed its focus to the vertical proliferation of strategic nuclear weapons. With the rising concern about direct control to prevent "military diversion from peaceful nuclear industry," nuclear arms control has once again come to involve directly more than just two nations. This new version of arms control is not limited to concern over proliferation of the capability to produce and deploy nuclear weapons; it extends as well to modern conventional arms and especially to their sale across national boundaries.

Japanese Indifference toward the "Old" Arms Control

The absence for many years of any active public interest in arms control among the Japanese is partly attributable to the lateness of Japan's entry into postwar arms control forums. During the long period in which most Japanese were concerned about nuclear weapons only from a moralistic point of view, the realpolitik of bipolar arms control negotiations seemed remote. In addition, knowledge of the hardwares that make up a nuclear arsenal was very limited. It is only fairly recently that descriptions of these hardwares, formerly closely guarded secrets, have become available in public documents. As a consequence, although there was some intellectual interest in the strategic doctrines expounded by the major powers, this was confined to a very limited circle. Strategic doctrines were undoubtedly of vital concern to the United States and to the NATO planning group, but they lacked relevance, not to mention urgency, to the Japanese, whose national security scenario differed greatly from that of Western Europe, even during the height of the Cold War.

With Japan's economic resurgence and the growing sense that the country would have an important role to play in international politics, Japanese interest in arms control slowly began to develop. In 1969 Japan was admitted to the Geneva Eighteen Nation Disarmament Committee (ENDC), subsequently renamed the Conference of the Committee on Disarmament (CCD). Although membership in the CCD gave Japan an increased sense of participation in the "old" strategic nuclear-centered arms control process, this was limited by the fact that the focus of that process had already moved away from the CCD forum. The game had become so delicate and complicated, and the hardwares under consideration so sophisticated and expensive, that the subject was now beyond the reach of any but the two superpowers. Only between them could really serious negotiations take place. In a sense, the Nonproliferation Treaty was the last great act of the ENDC/CCD. As the focus in the development of arms control issues moved from the CCD into the hands of the superpowers and the arena of SALT, this kind of arms control classed itself out of immediate Japanese interests. Although the European nations also were left behind, they felt a closer relationship to the SALT proceedings because scenarios for U.S. nuclear involvement in central Europe are more sharply defined than in Northeast Asia.

Of course, even though SALT seemed more or less remote for the nonsuperpowers, they were extremely interested in the outcome of those negotiations because of the obvious

global implications. But they largely gave up any hope of
influencing that outcome. Even where the superpowers had
undertaken formal obligations within a multilateral arms
control regime, such as the NPT, it was very difficult to
counter the argument that the treaty represented a mechanism to perpetuate nuclear domination by the great powers,
while they themselves violated the spirit of the NPT's article
VI, which pledged them to negotiate faithfully toward
effective reduction of nuclear arms.

Nevertheless, a minority of Japan's foreign policy leadership took a more than passing interest in strategic nuclear
arms control. They even argued that Japan, because of its
unique constitutional renunciation of war and the constitution's imposition of arms control requirements, was in an
ideal moral and political position to exert an influence on
arms control negotiations between the superpowers. It could
try to bring the superpowers back to a truly meaningful
effort at nuclear arms reduction, rather than letting their
narrow national interests dominate, leading to arbitrary
compromise positions. One way to internationalize the
SALT process, it was argued, was for Japan to propose
international satellite surveillance of strategic arms. Those
who took such a position, however, remained a very small
minority among the Japanese political leadership. The
majority either failed to take any interest or gave up in
frustration at the conduct of the superpowers in their
bilateral negotiations. This frustration was heightened by
the realization that Japan had gained membership in the
CCD only when that body had already become virtually
irrelevant.

Japan's Rising Interest in the "New" Arms Control

Against this background of frustrated Japanese efforts to
play a meaningful role in superpower-dominated strategic
nuclear arms control, we now see the rising importance of a
new dimension of arms control not so clearly dominated by
the superpowers. This reflects the transition from a bipolar
world to one with many more centers of military power, both

nuclear and conventional. As evidence of the new focus, one need only point to the current international concern about proliferation of nuclear capabilities and about the rapidly increasing transfer of advanced conventional weaponry. Of especially intense concern in Asia is the proliferation of these advanced military technologies to Korea; a related question is the possible use of U.S. tactical nuclear weapons deployed in South Korea.

In connection with this new dimension of arms control, several points should be noted. First, developments in the technology of tactical nuclear weapons (such as mini-nukes) and ambiguities in the doctrines relating to their use are blurring the line of demarcation between nuclear and conventional warfare. Moreover, advances in precision-guided munitions technology (PGMs) have brought into question the usefulness of tactical nuclear weapons, except in the case of antisubmarine warfare. At the same time, the widespread deployment of U.S. tactical nuclear weapons in Europe and Northeast Asia increases the likelihood of nuclear war, as well as the danger that nuclear weapons will be seized by terrorists or other "unauthorized people."

Second, growing concern about the supply of fossil fuels to meet the world's energy needs has greatly heightened interest in nuclear technology as an alternative source of energy. Meanwhile, changes in the global economic climate, especially the difficulties encountered by industrialized economies and the strengthened bargaining position of resource-rich Third World countries, raise the possibility that advanced conventional arms and nuclear technology may become leading export items for industrialized states hard-pressed for petroleum or for foreign exchange. Examples of this trend may be found in the proposed export of nuclear technology from West Germany to Brazil, from France to South Korea and Pakistan, from the United States to Iran, and from Canada to South Korea and Argentina. The sale of advanced conventional weapons has become one of the most salient features of the relationship between the industrialized countries and certain OPEC nations.

In contrast to the expensive and sophisticated systems

represented by ICBMs, SLBMs, MIRVs, and supersonic long-range bombers, a small-scale arsenal of nuclear weapons or PGMs lies well within the reach of Japan and many other countries. The importance of this fact was evident in the 1975 debate in Japan over ratification of the NPT. This debate marked a notable turn in the country's handling of security-related issues. Although positions were stated cautiously, reflecting the psychological restraints of the past, the national security issue was discussed much more openly and concretely, in terms of weapon hardware, than before. There were even some serious exchanges about the advantages and disadvantages of acquiring a nuclear weapons capability. Discussion of this question focused on an assessment of Japan's technical capabilities to produce nuclear and other sophisticated weapons, and on how its peaceful nuclear industry would be affected if the country embarked on a nuclear weapons program. Some people asked whether Japan's Self-Defense Forces might not be made more effective by the acquisition of PGMs, rather than nuclear weapons. As an active particpant in these debates and a strong opponent of the nuclear option, I can testify to the growing tendency among Japanese on both sides to consider these questions in much more concrete and realistic terms than before. Moving away from the simple, moralistic arguments of the past for worldwide and complete disarmament, more Japanese discussed the issue in terms of a serious assessment of the hardware and a realistic analysis of benefits and risks.

This change clearly was a result of the fact that, unlike previous arms control discussions, the subject matter related directly to Japan's immediate interests and to decisions that were to be taken by neighboring countries and by Japan itself. Some opinion leaders warned of the dangers for Japan if its neighbors were to acquire nuclear weapons. India's successful test of a nuclear device was cited as a case in point; the Indian detonation had a lot to do with Japan's insistence on stronger restrictions regarding peaceful nuclear explosives (PNEs). Defense Secretary Schlesinger's statement in the summer of 1975 about the possible use of nuclear weapons in Korea helped to set off a new round in the debate over the extent of Japan's involvement in Korea's defense

and about the role of U.S. nuclear weapons in Korea. This
weapons in Korea. This stimulated arguments for the
creation of a nuclear weapons–free zone on the Korean
peninsula.

It would be quite wrong to conclude that most Japanese
have suddenly awakened to the need for arms control. It is
still only among a limited number of experts that these
subjects are explicitly considered. But the nationwide debate
over NPT ratification, reported almost daily in the mass
circulation newspapers, has created an atmosphere very
different from that of the past. To an unprecedented degree
the public has been exposed to debate on the problems of
nuclear weapons in Korea, post-Vietnam U.S. defense commitments in Asia, and the vulnerability of the Japanese
economy if its sea-lanes should be attacked. For the first time,
questions have been asked about what Japan itself should
do, rather than whether to urge the superpowers to "exercise
restraint" in their conduct.

The Japanese public has not clearly identified the subject
of this ongoing debate as arms control. There is as yet no
sharply defined conceptual framework within which the
questions being debated can be related to a consistent
strategy of seeking to guarantee national security through
arms reduction or through nonacquisition of arms. Of
course, there is a similar inconsistency and ambiguity about
the relationship of various national policies to arms control
in Korea, India, the Middle East, and other areas of the
world. It is certainly true of the United States. Washington is
very eager to press for nuclear nonproliferation but wants
simultaneously to protect the competitive position of the
United States in the world nuclear power market. The
United States also exports a tremendous volume of the most
advanced conventional weapons to various nations around
the world; these weapons are also capable of serving as the
most effective delivery vehicles for nuclear warheads. Outside of SALT and MBFR, Washington's arms control policy
is far from consistent or clearly established. The same
criticism can be made of several Western European countries.

There is one additional point worth noting in the case of

Japan. This concerns the lack of any central coordinating body within the bureaucracy to reconcile the conflicting interests of various agencies with respect to arms control. The Foreign Ministry is in charge of foreign policy and thus is the principal agency in matters relating to arms control, but it cannot dictate to the Ministry of International Trade and Industry, which is more interested in ensuring that arms control does not jeopardize Japan's energy supply, industrial development, and trading position. The position of the Science and Technology Agency tends to be quite uncertain. There is a definite need for better coordination among these three ministries. Of course, the failure to establish effective coordination when issues traditionally viewed as domestic take on international ramifications is certainly not an exclusively Japanese problem.

This discussion has dealt mainly with changing conceptions of arms control, as emphasis has shifted from a superpower-dominated, strategic nuclear weapons–oriented, and thus, for nations like Japan, only peripherally relevant set of issues to broader concerns with direct relevance to the security and economic interests of many countries. To summarize, the central issues of the new arms control include: (1) efforts to stem the proliferation of nuclear weapons through such instruments as tightened international safeguards and restrictions on the transfer of technology; (2) the future of tactical nuclear weapons spread around the world as the military utility of those weapons comes increasingly into doubt; and (3) placing limits on the international trade of conventional weapons, the rapid expansion of which has been stimulated by the natural resource and foreign exchange needs of the industrialized states. At the same time, the old arms control continues, and so do efforts to influence the superpowers in their bilateral negotiations so that more meaningful strategic nuclear arms control may be realized. Of course, it is difficult to enumerate in a short space all the factors involved in arms control today. But it does seem useful and important to take note of the changing situation, and to point out that Japan's interest in this new arms control, though not yet nationwide, is a significant departure from the indifference of the past.

Japanese and American Conceptions of Arms Control

A rising Japanese interest in the new arms control does not, of course, mean that Japan and the United States will necessarily agree on how to approach these problems. Indeed, major differences in the way the two countries view the nuclear proliferation problem became manifest in early 1977. A central component of the Carter administration's nonproliferation policy has been the de-emphasis of plutonium in the generation of nuclear power, because of its suitability for use in the manufacture of bombs. Specifically, President Carter made clear in April 1977 his desire to postpone indefinitely the commercialization of "reprocessing" (the separation of plutonium from spent fuel rods) and to retard the development of plutonium-burning "fast breeder reactors" (which produce more plutonium than they consume).

Although Mr. Carter has formally requested all of the industrialized nations to take similar steps to restrict the role of plutonium in their nuclear industries, the new policy would have an exceptionally severe impact on Japan. The agreement governing cooperation between the United States and Japan in the nuclear energy field requires U.S. approval of any Japanese reprocessing of fuel containing enriched uranium provided by the United States. Since Japan relies on U.S. enrichment services in fueling all of its light-water reactors, the United States could effectively prohibit Japanese reprocessing. The Japanese find this situation particularly irksome for three reasons: (1) Japan has just completed construction of a demonstration-scale reprocessing plant at Tokai-mura; (2) in the past, the United States has consistently urged Japan and other countries to make use of plutonium as a fuel both for light-water reactors and for fast breeders; and (3) the U.S.-EURATOM agreement, governing nuclear cooperation between the Americans and the West European nations, does not contain provisions similar to those found in the U.S.-Japan agreement.

The negotiations between the United States and Japan in

the first half of 1977 made clear the inability of Americans and Japanese to understand each other's concepts of arms control. The Americans could not appreciate the impact of their plutonium policy on a resource-poor country such as Japan. Given its much more secure supply of energy, the United States did not hesitate to put the nonproliferation issue ahead of energy considerations. For Japan, however, the possibility of finding itself with inadequate energy supplies in the coming decades is a matter of the gravest national concern. The U.S. policy thus has given rise to a strongly nationalistic response on the part of Japan.

The Japanese, on the other hand, could not really appreciate the American inclination to view the nonproliferation problem in global terms. There is little understanding among Japanese of the role of nuclear weapons in the current phase of international politics. Thus, the early Japanese reaction to the Carter administration's new policy emphasized Japan's lack of interest in nuclear weapons and the importance of nuclear power in the country's strategy for meeting its future energy needs. The Japanese have tended to deal with the issue only as it affects Japan, not as a broader problem affecting global security.

The gap between American and Japanese conceptions of arms control is further illustrated by the way they have discussed the possibility that South Korea might develop an independent nuclear weapons capability. Neither side has been entirely consistent. The U.S. government reminded the Japanese of its earlier successful intervention to prevent the export of French reprocessing technology to South Korea and asked whether Tokyo would have favored the Koreans' acquisition of plutonium extraction capabilities. The Japanese replied that it was meaningless to talk in such abstract terms—as if an abstract nuclear weapon were to emerge in an abstract international situation. The principal goal, from the standpoint of nonproliferation, had to be the creation of a political atmosphere in East Asia in which the countries concerned would not have strong incentives to go nuclear. In this connection, the Carter administration's policy of military withdrawal from South Korea does not help the cause of nonproliferation.

Without speculating as to the ultimate outcome of Mr. Carter's nonproliferation policy, either in its global context or with respect to the confrontation it has generated between Washington and Tokyo, we can conclude that as Japan's interest in the new arms control develops, both Japanese and Americans will need to make greater efforts to understand each other's conceptions of arms control.

3

A Time for Realism in the Military Defense of Japan

James William Morley

From the Japanese standpoint, the arrangements for Japan's defense over the past twenty-five years—a minimal commitment to its own defense in the form of the Self-Defense Force (SDF) and a maximal reliance on America's protection under the U.S.-Japan Security Treaty—have been remarkably effective. Perhaps no other country in the world has enjoyed such military insurance at such low cost. The United States, too, has benefited enormously, securing a peaceful and valuable ally and, in addition, bases from which to protect its other interests in the region. Under these circumstances, one may well ask why Japan's defense arrangements should be reconsidered now. The answer is that the attitudes and elite structures on which these arrangements have rested are now shifting.

Shifting Attitudes and Elite Structures

In the United States the present arrangements are the product of Cold War attitudes shared originally on a bipartisan basis by the overwhelming majority of the American people. It will be remembered that when the security treaty was ratified in 1952, fighting raged in Korea; everywhere the line was drawn between the United States and its allies, and the Soviet Union, the People's Republic of China, and their allies. Japan was seen by the United States as too vital to the Korean war effort and too essential to the world balance to be left a hostage of fortune.

Now, more than two decades later, most Americans see the world as a different place. The Soviet Union is far stronger, having attained rough nuclear parity with the United States. The PRC has demonstrated not only its independence of the Soviet Union, but its mortal fear of it and its readiness to look on the American presence in Asia, even its military presence, as welcome. And since the U.S. failure in Indochina, the danger posed by communist-led insurrection in Asian states has seemed less threatening. In the last stages of. the Vietnam war and in its immediate aftermath, the American people plunged into a wide-ranging foreign policy debate. There could be no doubt that the human and material costs of the Vietnam war had been hard to bear. Most Americans longed for a reduction in the confrontation with the Soviet Union and the People's Republic of China, a cutting of the military budget, withdrawal of American forces from exposed positions in the world, and a respite from involvement in other people's quarrels. To many, a drastic reorientation seemed possible and required.

But as the debate wore on and as the efforts of the government for détente seemed to yield such modest results, a strong sense of the dangers of the world returned. By the end of the presidential campaign in the fall of 1976, it was apparent that a broad consensus had once again been formed: the United States would now take a more restrained, more accommodating stance than in the past several decades, but it would not drop its allies or lower its own military guard. Concerning relations with East Asia, most Americans seemed agreed:

- that relations with the industrialized democracies, particularly Japan, must be strengthened;
- that although every effort must be made to reduce tensions with the Soviet Union, the United States must maintain an adequate deterrent force;
- that normalization of relations with the People's Republic of China should be sought, but not at the expense of Taiwan's autonomy; and

•that a demilitarization of the Korean conflict is desirable, but not at the one-sided expense of the Republic of Korea.

The U.S.-Japan Security Treaty has been strongly reaffirmed. Attitudes toward it are perhaps more favorable today than they have ever been.

On the other hand, one must recognize that most Americans perceive very little likelihood of Japan's being attacked. Thus, their support for the treaty may be more accurately understood as a symbol of gratitude for Japan's peaceful posture and an expression of goodwill than as an indicator of the depth of the U.S. commitment. The treaty, after all, only obligates the United States, should there be "an armed attack against either party in the territories under the administration of Japan," to consider this a threat to "its own peace and safety" and to "act to meet the common danger in accordance with its constitutional provisions and processes." Consequently, it is only prudent to recognize that the specific action that can be expected depends not only on the preservation of the treaty, but more fundamentally on the strength of the underlying relationship and its place in America's new, more reserved posture toward the world.

In Japan a very different process is bringing these defense arrangements into question. They were not born in a Cold War consensus as in the United States. When the National Police Reserve (the forerunner of the present-day Self-Defense Force) was first set up in 1950, it was bitterly attacked. The great debate that followed over the advisability of signing the San Francisco Peace Treaty and entering into a military alliance with the United States in the face of Soviet and Communist Chinese objections was abortive. No agreement on Japan's postwar security policy emerged. So polar in fact were the positions assumed—the conservatives calling for minimal self-defense in alignment with the United States and the socialists denouncing both and calling for unarmed neutrality—that ever since, there has been little, if any, reasoned public debate on Japan's defense requirements. Hardly a month has gone by when some question

about the behavior of the SDF or the American use of
Japanese bases has not agitated the public. The constitutional legitimacy of both the SDF and the security treaty
has itself been attacked. Indeed, in 1959-1960, the question of
revision of the security treaty brought Japan to the brink of
civil war.

But over the years, beneath the surface of this partisan
vituperation, the deeper currents of Japanese opinion have
gradually shifted to the side of the SDF. In recent years,
public opinion polls have shown that more than three-
quarters of the Japanese people look on it with favor.
Hostility to the U.S.-Japan Security Treaty has been slower
to change, but it now appears that the treaty too is gaining
supporters.

The collapse of the Thieu regime in Vietnam following
the U.S. withdrawal from Indochina brought home to many
Japanese the fragility of survival in a world without U.S.
military support. A fear of isolation began to mount. Tokyo
commentators queried: What if the United States were now
to withdraw from Northeast Asia? Would South Korea be the
"big domino" next to go? And if it did, how secure would
Japan then be? The "oil shock" administered when the
OPEC countries threatened in 1973 to turn off Japan's oil
supply had raised similarly disturbing fears. For both
military and economic reasons, the tie with America seemed
more important than ever, and the treaty symbolized that tie.

At the same time, support for the treaty has become less
costly. For many years, Japanese feared that their treaty
obligation to provide bases for U.S. forces carried the serious
danger of dragging Japan into a war it did not want. The use
of these bases for the war in Indochina, for example,
although not questioned by the government of Japan,
nevertheless fanned an emotional, if abortive, drive to
denounce the treaty in 1970. But what most disturbed the
Japanese was the long American hostility toward the PRC
and the possibility, through Japan's commitment to the
United States and the U.S. commitment to the Republic of
China on Taiwan, that Japan might be dragged into a U.S.-
China war. Even though that war was avoided, so long as

Peking denounced the U.S.-Japan Security Treaty as an obstacle to good relations with Japan, the Japanese people felt a deep uneasiness. But in the last few years, the situation has changed. The end of the war in Indochina ended the danger of Japan's hostile involvement there; the deepening of the Sino-Soviet split and the establishment of a U.S.-PRC détente have converted Peking's attitude toward the treaty from opposition to support.

These changes in Japanese attitudes are particularly influential because they are bubbling up at a time when a restructuring of party power in Japan appears imminent. Since the landslide election of 1949, the conservatives have ruled Japan without interruption. In fact, this control of the Diet enabled them to proceed formally with the defense arrangements they favored—even though vehement opposition prevented them from taking these arrangements up realistically. For a variety of reasons, however, their power has steadily eroded: now, they are accorded only minority support by the voters and are enabled to retain office only by the peculiarities of the electoral system. What was so long unthinkable now seems quite possible, that within the foreseeable future the conservatives may in fact be unable to form a government alone and will have to look for partners from among their erstwhile opponents. Each of the parties, therefore, conservative and opposition alike, is now showing a strong interest in trying to work out a new position on defense, a position that will have greater public appeal or perhaps make coalition possible.

Each country must resolve these problems for itself, of course; however, the U.S. role in Japan's defense has been so vital in the past and the continued interdependence of our two countries would appear to be so mutually beneficial, indeed, essential, that it behooves each of us, Japanese and Americans alike, to take serious account of the attitudes and requirements of the other as we seek to clarify our own attitudes and requirements. It is to be hoped that out of this period of reconsideration will emerge not only a higher level of agreement on defense policy within each of our countries, but also a greater consensus between us on mutual defense.

Defense Issues Needing Clarification

In such a binational discussion, what are the issues we need to clarify? I believe three are of primary importance.

The Relationship of Military Defense to National Security

There has been confusion in the public discussion of military matters on both sides of the Pacific. We in the United States have often talked, budgeted, and acted as though our own national security—and Japan's as well—depended almost exclusively on a military readiness for war. The Japanese, on the other hand, have sometimes sounded as though military defense played little or no part in their own thinking, the keys to their security being found primarily in the skills of their diplomacy, the vigor of their economy, the strength of their political system, and the health of their public morale. Each has been responding essentially to its situation, the United States to its confrontation with the Soviet Union and Japan to the urgency of national reconstruction. Neither view is comprehensive enough to serve as a guide for future policy.

First of all, the U.S. view must be enlarged. Surely the conception of national security as the capacity of the people to maintain the ultimate values and institutions that bind them together as a community is fundamental. In highly industrialized, democratic, cosmopolitan societies such as those of Japan and the United States, this involves physical safety, to be sure; but it involves far more than that. It includes also the ability of the industrial system, for example, to secure the markets, materials, technology, and capital required for production. It involves the ability of the distribution system to allocate fairly the goods and services produced. It involves the ability of the political system to hold the people's confidence and win their participation; and of the cultural institutions to educate and enrich the lives of all citizens. It follows that the fundamental security question to be determined at any one time is: from what quarter do the most pressing threats to these vital community-support systems come and what are the most realistic instruments for coping with them?

In the late 1940s and early 1950s, for example, when Japan was threatened more by internal division and international isolation than by external attack, the emphasis on domestic reconstruction and the drive for international acceptance were obviously more appropriate security policies than the rapid rebuilding of the armed forces. Had rearmament then been given higher priority, it would most likely have disrupted the orderly political process, delayed economic recovery, and frozen Japan out of the Asian community, thereby weakening the very security it would have been designed to ensure.

But what about today? Is Japan today in greater danger of external attack than it was more than twenty-five years ago? It would be difficult to argue so. Its mammoth Soviet and Chinese neighbors have fallen into such deep hostility to each other that each is courting rather than threatening Japan. The situation of the two Koreas is similar. Elsewhere in Asia, now that the Chinese have shelved the Taiwan problem and fighting has ceased in Indochina, the possibility that Japan might, however unwillingly, be drawn into hostilities in these regions is much more remote. No, the most salient threats to Japanese security today would seem to lie still in the political and economic areas—incomplete normalization of relations with the Soviets and the Chinese, political instability in the Third and Fourth Worlds, recession in the market economies, uncertainty in the international monetary system, and interruption of the supply of food, energy, and other raw materials.

It is precisely the acceptance of this holistic conception of national security that lies behind the economic and political pledges that Japan and the United States gave to each other in Article II of the revised Treaty of Mutual Cooperation and Security in 1960. It reads:

The Parties will contribute toward the further development of peaceful and friendly international relations by strengthening their free institutions, by bringing about a better understanding of the principles upon which these institutions are founded, and by promoting conditions of stability and well-being. They will seek to eliminate conflict in their international economic policies and will encourage economic collaboration between them.

The conception therefore is not new. It has simply not been given high enough priority in U.S. policy—or there would have been no Nixon "shocks" in 1971 and 1972. Fortunately, the jolts these gave to Japan's sense of security are now widely recognized here. The time would seem to be ripe, therefore, for rearticulating what appears to be a growing consensus in both countries that national security is a broader concern than military defense. We have mutually pledged ourselves to that broader concern, and because of it, we now give priority attention to our economic, political, and cultural needs.

On the other hand, the Japanese view also must be enlarged to recognize that at some time in the future their physical safety may well be threatened. History gives no support to the view that the peaceful circumstances Japan now enjoys will never change. A realistic security policy must therefore include secondary attention to an effective military insurance policy as well.

The Political Requirements

A reconsideration of the defense arrangements cannot proceed in a political vacuum. It must go forward along the consensual lines that are evolving in our two societies. One cannot be sure where these lines will ultimately lead, but for purposes of discussion it may be useful to try to set forth a preliminary list of some propositions that seem to have gained significant support.[1]

In the case of Japan, the growing acceptance of the SDF and of the security treaty does not presage the accelerated rearmament of Japan or the acceptance of joint peace-keeping missions with the United States in distant regions. Rather, it is the result of more than two decades of partisan confrontation, in the course of which the limits of public toleration were gradually felt out. It is the tacit or explicit acceptance of these limits by most of Japan's political leaders that is the ground of the current consensus. Any acceptable reformulation of Japan's defense arrangements will, therefore, need to take those limits into account.

How much should Japan spend for national defense? Only so much as would not seriously detract from Japan's economic growth or welfare objectives. Expenditures have risen as high as 2.93 percent of the GNP (in 1952), but for the past decade they have been held to less than 1 percent. Unless there is a significant change in the international environment, it seems unlikely that in the foreseeable future expenditures greater than 1 percent or so will be acceptable.

How large a force should be raised? Since conscription is unthinkable, only the number a volunteer system can produce.

What weapons should be deployed? Nuclear weapons are clearly excluded. To allay public fears on that score, the government has even gone so far as to proclaim "three nonnuclear principles": that Japan will not manufacture nuclear weapons, will not possess nuclear weapons, and will not allow them into the country. In addition, long-range weapons such as bombers, carriers, and ICBMs are ruled out. In fact, only such weapons as can be said to have a limited, defensive purpose are acceptable.

Everything about the SDF, in fact, must have an exclusively defensive character. This requirement springs, of course, from the prohibition in article IX of the Japanese constitution against the maintenance of "land, sea, and air forces, as well as other war potential" and against the recognition of even "the right of belligerency" of the Japanese state. Former Premier Yoshida's argument that these provisions did not preclude "the inherent right of self-defense" sets the criterion of legitimacy. It is reflected also in the SDF's official aim, which limits it to "defending the country against both direct and indirect aggression." And it applies to the SDF's area of operations. Almost no one in Japan could tolerate having ground forces capable of going overseas, or air and naval forces capable of operating beyond the air and sea space immediately adjacent to the country.

Political conditions also attach to the growing public acceptance of the security treaty. Some are limitational, like those relating to the SDF. The presence of U.S. forces in Japan, for example, must be minimal, as the decades-long mass movement against U.S. bases has demonstrated. Nuclear weapons must not be deployed in the country, although there is ambiguity about the tolerability of their passage. Under article VI of the treaty, the United States is legally permitted to use its Japanese bases—not only for the defense of Japan but also for "the maintenance of international peace and security in the Far East"—but it is difficult to imagine the circumstances under which they would be available for purposes other than Japan's defense. They could not be used for the defense of the Republic of China, which Japan no longer recognizes; nor can one feel certain about their availability for the defense of the Republic of Korea, even though Japan's concern for that country's security is often stressed. In short, the "cost" to Japan in peacetime must not be too high. On the other hand, it is also apparent that there is another requirement of a different character—namely, that the will and capability of the United States to defend Japan in time of emergency must remain convincing.

These are Japanese political realities that Americans need to consider seriously. At the same time, there are American political realities that the Japanese people on their side would do well to ponder. Up until now, the Japanese have felt able to take the U.S. military commitment to the defense of Japan pretty much as given. The United States has never wavered in its support for the treaty, and it has kept sizable forces in the Japanese area. But given America's disillusionment in Indochina and the depth of the present debate in the United States about the deployment of U.S. forces overseas, it would be unwise, I believe, for this commitment to be taken for granted. Clearly the concern is growing in Japan that it cannot be. Therefore, it is important to try to spell out, if we can, some of the political considerations that can be expected to affect the vitality of America's interest in Japan's defense in the future.

One consideration is the Japanese determination in an emergency to defend themselves. Unfortunately, Japanese public opinion polls are not reassuring on this point. Nor are the statements of leading defense planners. Osamu Kaihara, former chief of the Secretariat of the National Defense Council, for example, has said that the SDF could hold out for no more than a matter of days against the Soviet Union.[2] Makoto Momoi, staff member of the Defense College, seems to accept this estimate and proposes that the SDF conceive of its wartime role as simply "buying time" until the United States steps in to mediate Japan's surrender.[3] The model for this doctrine of "strategic accommodation" is said to be the mediation of Theodore Roosevelt that extricated Japan from the Russo-Japanese War in 1905. But the conditions of 1905 are unlikely to be duplicated in any foreseeable future engagement between Japan and an opponent. Under present arrangements the United States is likely to be a belligerent from the start. Moreover, its capacity to compel a negotiated end to the war favorable to Japan will depend basically on its capacity and will either to defeat the attacker or fight him to a draw.

If the Japanese forces were to indicate a readiness to give in after a very short period, it is difficult to imagine that the Americans would want to go on alone. In these circumstances, the Americans could only bring pressure to bear on the enemy to ameliorate his surrender terms by threatening to escalate the fighting to the strategic level. But is it credible that the United States would indeed be prepared to bring on the holocaust of a nuclear war in order to defend another country that wished to end the fighting? The conclusion seems inescapable: in any foreseeable military engagement between Japan and an opponent, although the United States will in all likelihood be a belligerent from the beginning, the duration and strength of the U.S. response—and therefore the effectiveness of Japan's defense—will depend as much on Japan's own will and capacity to resist as on those of the United States. Or, put another way, the U.S.-Japan Security Treaty cannot substitute for Japan's own self-defense effort; it can only supplement it. The value of the U.S. commitment to Japan's defense must be seen therefore to depend on the reliability of Japan's own determination to defend itself.

Many in Japan are beginning to recognize this fact, as seen in the recent contention of the Japan Defense Agency that an effective collective security system requires that "every member nation . . . must have a strong will and capability to defend itself by itself."[4]

A second requirement is the existence in Japan of a stable, democratic government, capable of mobilizing the human and material resources necessary for a serious defense effort in time of emergency. The war in Indochina testifies to the difficulty of securing the support of the American people for the sustained defense of any other country that does not meet these minimal political conditions.

A third requirement is the existence of a deep bilateral interchange, perceived as essential to the way of life we value: a trade and investment flow, for example, vital to our economy, and a cultural sharing that is integral to the health of our own technology, arts, and sciences.

And a fourth is the convergence of Japanese and American foreign policy objectives on the building and maintenance of a peaceful world order of independent states by balancing power, reducing tensions, and promoting cultural and economic interchange.

Put in a more summary way, the United States can be counted on to come to the defense of Japan to the extent that a sense of trust and interdependence has become so strong that neither can imagine communal survival without the other. It is the liveliness of that sense and the strength of that interdependence that is the basic guarantee of any joint defense community.

Strategic Relevance

A third issue that needs clarification is the strategic relevance of existing defense arrangements. In the early days, when Japan's military expenditures were too small to have real military meaning, its willingness to rely on the United States was total. There was little need for either a purely Japanese strategy or a strategy coordinated with that of the United States. But today, small though the ratio of Japan's defense expenditures may be to its GNP, the absolute size of these expenditures is not inconsiderable. Budgeted at $4.95 billion for the fiscal year beginning April 1, 1976, they are believed to be the seventh largest in the world. As already noted, the Japanese people are now prepared to accept sums of this character: they believe that the SDF is useful and are inclining more and more to the view that Japan should do what it can in its own defense. The question therefore is now being raised pragmatically for the first time: given the political requirements we have outlined, what can and should the SDF do in Japan's defense? And how can and should this autonomous effort be related effectively to the U.S. commitment?

The answer must be sought in the ultimate purpose to which these forces might be put. We might begin by recognizing two important characteristics of Japan. Its economy is heavily dependent on external resources; and its population and industrial and administrative centers are concentrated in a small geographic area. The most likely potential military threat to Japan and its life-support systems would therefore seem to be the cutting off of supplies by the interdiction of its air and sea lanes. Less likely, because it would probably be unnecessary, is a bombing attack or an invasion by ground assault forces, either alone or in cooperation with some kind of local uprising.

What defensive strategies might be most effective against such attacks? Let us begin with the interdiction threat. Japanese maritime supply lines stretch all over the globe and are therefore vulnerable to inderdiction by almost any country. On the other hand, those most vital would seem to be two: the southern route, extending down to Indonesia, the other ASEAN states and Australia, and branching westward to Iran and the Persian Gulf; and the eastern route extending across the Pacific to the Americas. Interdiction of these lanes would require a substantial naval or air force capable of operating effectively in the Pacific or Indian Oceans. Today only the Soviet Union has that capability.

Accordingly, three defensive strategies might be considered. One would be to set up narrow shipping lanes and provide naval and air convoys. A second strategy would be to try to exclude the hostile ships from the entire region by setting up what might be called naval containment lines. The most realistic line might be at the Soya, Tsugaru and Tsushima Straits for the purpose of bottling up the Soviet Far Eastern Fleet in the Sea of Japan. Of course, it may be that in the remote future the Chinese, Koreans, or Vietnamese also will build a distant offensive capability; alternatively, were the Sino-Soviet coalition to be formed again, they might provide the Soviet fleet with bases somewhere on their coasts. In that event, another line of naval containment might be required to seal off the East and South China seas. Still another is conceivable at the western entrances to the Indian Ocean or off the USSR's European shores. But from Japan's standpoint, a naval containment line centering on the straits leading to the Sea of Japan would seem to make the most sense. A third defensive strategy would be a counter-base approach, aimed at catching the marauding planes, ships, or missiles before they leave their home bases or launching pads. In any event, stockpiles would be needed. Defense against a bombing or a ground attack on the home islands would also require a range of defensive and counter-attack capabilities.

The point here is not to try to outline each of the contingencies and how it might be met. It is rather to suggest that, given the obvious size and complexity of the strategic problem, two conclusions are inevitable:

- that in a crisis the SDF alone could not possibly defend Japan;
- that close coordination with American forces would be essential.

But the question may well be raised, given the low level of the actual threat to Japan's military security today, as to why either Japanese or Americans should worry about the strategic relevance of Japanese defense planning now? After all, the primary purpose of Japan's armed forces and the U.S. security treaty as well is to deter war, not to fight it.

True, but deterrence, we must remember, is a state of mind

in which a potential adversary is persuaded not to aggress by the estimate that the operation would be too costly. Unless it is demonstrably clear that, in the foreseeable contingencies, Japan, combined with the United States, can indeed exact that cost, deterrence is an imaginary shield.

Of course, a rule of reason needs to operate. Contingencies may be viewed as ultimately possible without appearing to be immediately probable. Japan today is in so favorable a position that, as the Japan Defense Agency concludes, "it is almost unthinkable that a large-scale military aggression might be launched against Japan."[5] It therefore argues that Japan's "defense capability" should be conceived in terms of "defense power in peacetime."

Clearly, larger budget shares for defense or immensely more powerful forces are not needed in either Japan or the United States today. Expense and force size, the Defense Agency argues, should be "minimal." On the other hand, one would hardly want them to be strategically irrelevant. Rather, three standards of relevance might be suggested. One is that the SDF be adequate to meet and, therefore, deter such small-scale threats as might be thought possible even in this peacetime. Another is that it be so planned that, should the international environment change, it could be expanded smoothly to meet the changing threat. Finally, at both its present and its potential strength, the SDF should be so designed and trained as to be able to coordinate effectively its operations with those of U.S. armed forces should the necessity arise.

What Should Be Done?

The Treaty

In the decade preceding the withdrawal of the United States from Indochina and the rise of the current debate on overall American defense policy, there appeared to be a growing current of opinion in Japan inclining toward the revision of the security treaty and the attenuation of military relations with the United States.[6] If, however, the impression is accurate that this view is now being overtaken by a greater concern to revitalize the U.S. military tie, it would seem best for treaty revision talk to be put aside. The treaty is after all a remarkably broad and permissive document. In its 1960 form it sets forth reasonably clearly a mutual concern for the overall security of both countries. It does so in terms that are flexible enough to facilitate, in the emerging era, a strengthening of combined emphasis on the political, economic, and cultural underpinnings of the relationship. At the same time there is sufficient latitude to permit alteration of actual defense arrangements as required by changing circumstances. It is to these arrangements and not to the treaty that rethinking should be directed.

Contingency Planning

Within the framework of the treaty, it would seem desirable for experts on both sides of the Pacific to get together to try to work out the requirements for meeting various potential military emergencies. A central question to be considered concerns the missions to be assigned to the units of each force.

A few years ago it was suggested that the SDF should prepare itself to take on the duty of relatively exclusive defense against a close-in conventional attack, carrying out surveillance and response in a ground zone limited to Japanese territory and an aerial and maritime safety zone extending perhaps 300 to 1,000 miles from the main islands. To the United States was given full responsibility for strategic and distant defense, as well as supply.[7] But for that period the Japanese government found this to be an excessive expectation. Unless conditions drastically change, it seems likely that Japan will be unable to mount the intelligence apparatus, force structure, and strength required for such a capability, certainly before 1980 and probably before 1985.[8]

Now the Defense Agency speaks less about autonomous defense. It states as its goal the acquisition of capabilities "sufficient to take minimum, necessary steps in dealing with possible aggression staged by any of the conventional means." At the same time, it indicates an appreciation of the importance of the U.S. role.[9] Greater defense autonomy would seem to be a reasonable long-term goal; but for the next five to ten years, contingency planning which does not provide for an American role in Japan's close-in conventional defense, as well as its distant and strategic defense, would seem to be unrealistic.

A close coordination of Japanese and U.S. efforts in Japan's defense poses many questions. What force structures, for example, will each need to fulfill such responsibilities as may be agreed on, in the near- and mid-term, and in the long-term? If the level of joint readiness for actual war is to be kept relatively low, it would seem prudent to maintain forces on a cadre basis in order to permit their expansion in time of need, should intelligence reports suggest an imminent danger. Each government is responsible to its own people in these matters, but it is important to establish some degree of overt mutual understanding so that each side will be reassured about the reliability of the other and so that potential opponents will take these defense arrangements seriously.

With these objectives in mind, particular attention needs to be directed at arrangements for the use of bases in Japan by American forces. Clearly, a U.S. presence is needed as an earnest of American intent; but, in addition, certain cadre facilities would seem to be required in order to maintain intelligence operations and enable air and naval units to respond quickly if the need arises. But which facilities? Has not the time come for the two governments to sit down together and determine in conference which bases the Americans should have, with each side announcing the mutual decision publicly and the Americans evacuating all other facilities promptly?

A greater sharing of intelligence information seems called for. Although the political and strategic situations seem to justify a relatively low state of readiness, the two countries must be ever on the alert for changes—in weapons technology, the size and disposition of potentially hostile forces, and the attitude of the governments raising and deploying those forces. Since the United States and Japan have mutually pledged themselves to each other, it would seem essential that they share fully the results of surveillance and intelligence-gathering activities. Procedures to facilitate this need to be worked out.

Finally, it is difficult to imagine an effective joint defense of Japan unless the two forces are thoroughly informed about each other and accustomed to working together. It is not easy to coordinate one country's forces. It is far more difficult to coordinate an allied force when language, social relations, and military experiences are so different. Training in joint maneuvers is essential. How can it best be done?

Presumably, it is questions like these which will be taken up by the United States–Japan Defense Cooperation Committee, which met for the first time in the fall of 1976. Bringing together uniformed officers of the two countries, as well as civilian officials, the new committee has been instituted to consider practical problems of operational coordination.

Korea

There is one other issue about which greater realism is needed: Korea's security and its relation to that of Japan. Throughout modern times there have been those who have argued that the defense of Japan is inextricably dependent on the defense of Korea. Before 1945 it was the entire Korean peninsula that the Japanese government considered vital— so vital that it annexed and ruled it for thirty-five years. In the postwar period this theme has been taken up by the Americans with a slight difference. The American doctrine since 1950 has been that the safety of Japan requires keeping at least the southern half of the peninsula from falling into hostile—that is, communist—hands. The Japanese government has acceded to this conception. It has approved a provision in the security treaty and accompanying understandings concerning the U.S. right to request permission to use its bases in Japan for the defense of the Republic of Korea.

But there are ambiguities surrounding this conception. There can be little doubt that turmoil in Korea would be politically disturbing in Japan. The Korean minority in

Japan is divided into highly partisan groups; moreover, the Japanese people have felt so close to Korea over the past century that emotional as well as practical strains would be high. On the other hand, it is not clear strategically why, if it is militarily tolerable to Japan for the communists to control the northern half of the peninsula, it would be so intolerable for them to extend their power over the southern half as well. If the Japanese people and government do indeed believe that their fate is bound up with that of South Korea, it is hard to understand why they have allowed their political relations with Seoul to deteriorate so badly in recent years. Nor is it apparent why, in the event of hostilities on the peninsula, they are unwilling to contemplate doing more than facilitating a response by the United States. If contingency planning for the defense of Japan is to become more realistic, it would help if these ambiguities were cleared up.

On the other hand, in view of the long time over which these uncertainties have persisted, the Japanese government may well find it impossible now, as in the past, to clarify just what it will do in a Korean emergency. The United States thus may have to plan to act alone if need be, without the use of Japanese facilities. Even so, it is important for Americans to recognize that the Japanese would be deeply affected by any instability in Korea. In the interest of preserving the solidarity of the U.S.-Japan alliance, it behooves the United States to pursue a security policy toward Korea which takes Japan's interests into account and has Japan's continuing understanding.

Underlying each of these proposals is a basic theme: that the only realistic defense for Japan is a joint defense. If that is true, while it is essential that the responsible and concerned communities in Japan and the United States should each be thinking and planning nationally, binational planning must be given greater priority than in the past. Until recently the Japanese people have been so divided on defense matters and the capability of the SDF has been so limited that the practical defense of Japan was assumed to be almost exclusively the responsibility of the United States. Now it would appear that the Japanese people wish to play a somewhat more important role in their own defense; the SDF is now sufficiently large to justify a serious consideration of what that role should be. It is no longer enough for American leaders to compound doctrines of "massive retaliation" or "flexible response" and the like, leaving it to the Japanese to ponder the implications for them and determine what they must do to adapt. Nor is it enough for Japanese leaders to devise new concepts of "essential," "autonomous," or "basic" defense, leaving it to the Americans to contemplate the implications of these ideas for the U.S. defense role. There is need for a more practical coordination of mutual efforts in Japan's defense. It is time to set up such structures and initiate such discussions as may be needed to achieve that coordination.

Notes

1. It is within these limits that the government's search for a new defense policy to carry the country into the 1980s seems to be progressing. See the informative report on the Committee to Think About Defense (*Bōei o kangaeru kai*), a group of scholars and opinion leaders appointed in April 1975 to advise the director-general of the Defense Agency, in *Asahi Shimbun*, November 1, 2 and 3, 1975. See also *Defense of Japan: Defense White Paper* (Summary) (Tokyo: Japan Defense Agency, June 1976).

2. Interview of Kaihara in *Mainichi Shimbun*, January 31, 1973. This article was one of seven installments in *Mainichi Shimbun* from January 30 to February 5, 1973.

3. Makoto Momoi, "Pax Russo-American and Its Theoretical Impact on Japan's Defense Concept," in *Contrasting Approaches to Strategic Arms Control*, ed. Robert L. Pfaltzgraff, Jr. (Lexington, Mass.: Lexington Books, 1974), pp. 193-210.

4. *Defense of Japan*, p. 5.

5. Ibid., p. 11.

6. One of the most thoughtful arguments for this point of view is that of Katsumi Kobayashi, "Nixon Doctrine to Nichibei anzen hoshōtaisei" [The Nixon Doctrine and the U.S.-Japan security structure], *Shinbōei ronshū* 2, no. 4 (March 1975): 16-35.

7. See, for example, the statement along these lines by Yasuhiro Nakasone, former director-general of the Defense Agency, on the

rationale of the (abortive) draft fourth defense buildup plan, reported in *Nihon Keizai*, October 22, 1970, as related in John Emmerson, *Arms, Yen & Power: The Japanese Dilemma* (New York: Dunellen, 1971), p. 146.

8. See the brief discussion in Fred Greene, *Stresses in U.S.-Japanese Security Relations* (Washington: Brookings, 1975), pp.83-86.

9. *Defense of Japan*, p. 12.

4

Are There Any Alternative Strategies for the Defense of Japan?

Makoto Momoi

For more than a quarter century, Japan has had no choice but to stake its security on the strategic concepts of its ally, the United States. American strategic doctrines, however, were designed for a nation with a reasonable damage-absorbing capability and a relatively invulnerable retaliatory strike force; these two strategic factors are prerequisites to any concept of deterrence based on the threat of retaliation. Unlike the United States, Japan has neither of these prerequisites. The first is ruled out by the country's geopolitical and demographic characteristics and the second by the prevailing sociopolitical and psychological climate in Japan. Thus, it is hard to conceive of any defense posture that is feasible for Japan, unless it is based on some concept other than the conventional theory of deterrence, which requires a demonstration of retaliatory punitive potential.

Deterrence for Japan: Past and Present

Japan has, however, relied on several kinds of deterrents: (1) the invulnerable deterrent represented by the U.S. nuclear umbrella; (2) prevailing international inhibitions on the actual use of nuclear weapons either for psychological purposes (nuclear blackmail) or in combat; and (3) Japan's industrial establishment, a potential "war trophy" that an aggressor might be reluctant to destroy by using nuclear weapons.

The central concept on which the defense of Japan has been based is reliance on the United States. The U.S. commitment has continued and is likely to remain unchanged, unless there is a major breakdown of U.S.-Japan relations, which seems a remote possibility. But the nature of the commitment itself has undergone a series of changes, even though the security treaty has not been altered.

In the 1950s, Japan's security was totally dependent on the U.S. commitment. At a time when the United States enjoyed safety from an attack on its homeland and overall nuclear supremacy, the commitment was simple: although Japan itself could not strike back, the United States almost certainly would retaliate against any country that had launched an attack on Japan. This commitment was one in which the Japanese could have confidence. Moreover, in the early years after the end of the occupation, the security relationship with the United States and, in particular, the American military presence in Japan, were accepted as things over which the Japanese public had no say.

In the 1960s, when the Soviets began to catch up with the Americans in the nuclear field and particularly in the development of delivery systems, the United States for the first time faced the possibility that its continent might be the first to be hit. Hence, the Americans developed a second-strike capability, invulnerable and technologically superior. The nuclear umbrella over Japan thus remained credible. In consultation with the Japanese government, the United States began to reduce its military presence in Japan during the 1960s. But the U.S. commitment to Japan remained firm, partly due to the Americans' urgent need for bases in Japan as staging areas and logistical support centers for their operations in Vietnam. This clear U.S. interest in and commitment to Japan functioned as a credible deterrent to conventional aggression by the Soviet Union.

With the advent of the 1970s, doubts were raised about the value of the U.S. commitment as a deterrent to both nuclear and conventional aggression against Japan. The United States made a subtle about-face in its use of the threat of nuclear retaliation as an element in its structure of deterrence. Washington appeared to move away from its earlier reliance on a strategy of nuclear brinkmanship and toward a commitment to avoidance of central nuclear wars. How this new emphasis on the avoidance of war affected U.S. nuclear guarantees to its allies was not made clear. The problem became evident to America's allies when the U.S. and Soviet leaders, meeting at the Washington summit in June 1973, agreed to "refrain from the threat or use of force against . . . the allies [of the parties] . . . and other countries" [article II] and to "immediately enter into urgent consultations" in order to avoid a nuclear confrontation [article IV]. Gone were the days when allies could comfortably (and perhaps naively) count on instant, near-automatic, and massive U.S. nuclear retaliation against any country that launched a nuclear attack on them. Of course, whether the nuclear umbrella had actually been furled depended on the extent to which the behavior of the two superpowers would actually be governed by their 1973 agreement.

With respect to conventional forces, the U.S. strategic posture evidently shifted from a universal to a selective commitment. This was probably an inevitable reaction to America's Vietnam experience, and one may expect the "no-more-Asian-ground-wars" sentiment to prevail among Americans for some time. Public antipathy toward U.S. involvement in Asian land wars contrasts sharply with a continued willingness to commit U.S. ground forces to the defense of Western Europe, as reflected in the attitudes of both the legislative and executive branches. Hence, Washington could propose a phased withdrawal of U.S. ground forces from Korea while promising a continued presence of such forces in Europe.

Indeed, the enunciation of the Nixon Doctrine persuaded many Japanese that the United States would not come to Japan's defense in the event of a conventional attack.[1] This statement may seem an exaggeration, but it reflects the view that prevailed in Japan during the early 1970s. The reliability of the U.S. commitment appeared to be further jeopardized by a series of developments that irritated Japan and strained the alliance. These developments included: the surprise Sino-U.S. rapprochement, the rise of trade and monetary frictions between the United States and Japan, American criticism of Japan's "free ride" in defense at the expense of the U.S. taxpayer, and the 1973 oil crisis.

Furthermore, Japanese defense analysts grew increasingly suspicious about the credibility of U.S. policy pronouncements. For example, a U.S. leader (reportedly Henry Kissinger) was quoted in 1970 as having made the following comments about Japan in a background briefing:

> If Japan should draw the conclusion that the United States, for whatever reason, is no longer a factor to be reckoned with in Asia, then Japan has two choices: it can either try to carry the load that we did, in which case we might see a resurgence of Japanese militarism, or it might try to join forces with these other Communist countries, in which case we might also see a growth of Japanese military power, but more overtly directed against us.
>
> So from many points of view, from the point of Japan alone, it is quite important for us to remain a Pacific power, or to remain interested in Asia so that Japan pursues compatible policies with ours, and still feels sheltered to some extent by the American military presence, so they don't decide to go it alone.[2]

In Japanese eyes, this was an extremely rational statement of the U.S.-Japanese relationship, although it exaggerated the options open to Japan. What the Japanese found confusing, and somewhat upsetting, was the fact that this statement was made *before* the United States began to apply the pressure tactics that led to a sharp, if short-lived, strain in U.S.-Japan relations. If even a U.S. leader who demonstrated such a deep understanding of U.S.-Japan relations had to go along with President Nixon's high-handed treatment of Japan, what were the Japanese to make of future policy statements by U.S. officials?[3]

If the early 1970s saw a significant change in U.S. attitudes concerning both nuclear brinkmanship and the commitment of ground forces, as well as a series of other developments that strained Japanese confidence in the U.S. commitment, there was another important change in the international environment. As fears that ideological expansionism would lead to a nuclear showdown between the superpowers subsided, there was a new recognition of the need for interdependence in solving a variety of nonmilitary problems, such as natural resource allocation, the development of revised laws of the sea, and the adoption of measures to deal with international terrorism. Although the Nixon-Brezhnev agreement of June 1973 may have weakened the credibility of the nuclear umbrella as a contract between the United States and its allies, it was welcomed in Tokyo as a means of fostering an atmosphere of détente, without which international efforts to deal with such nonmilitary problems would be very difficult. The agreement provided a political framework supportive of efforts to assure that economic activities vital to Japan were not catastrophically disrupted as a result of a global confrontation between the superpowers.[4]

This new situation was not without potential danger for Japan, however. As the credibility of the U.S. nuclear umbrella declined, Japan might find the expectation of enduring peace generated by the U.S.-Soviet détente to be illusory. To be sure, the Soviet Union's ideological expansionism seemed to have lost momentum because of the continuing Sino-Soviet dispute, weakening ties between Moscow and the East European capitals, and growing difficulties experienced by the Soviets in dealing with economic problems and political dissidence in their own country. But the continued expansion of Soviet military capabilities, especially their growing naval presence in certain critical regions, raised serious questions among the Japanese concerning the viability of the present peaceful order.

Indeed, Japanese defense planners were coming to feel their country to be under increasing pressure from the Soviet Pacific Fleet. In the mid-1970s, for the first time since 1945, defense planners were prepared to single out the Soviet Union as a potential threat. Moreover, there was concern not only about the credibility of the U.S. nuclear umbrella, as already noted, but also about the increased possibility that

U.S. naval and air support might come too late or prove to be insufficient. This concern related to two potential scenarios. First, armed conflict between Japan and the Soviet Union might arise not as an isolated contingency but as part of a chain of international crises in various regions of the world, crises that could leave the United States overburdened and unable to respond adequately to the situation in Northeast Asia. The second scenario was one that seemed very unlikely, but not inconceivable. It assumed that if conflict in Northeast Asia were to develop in isolation from any hostilities elsewhere in the world, the Soviets might believe that they could avoid provoking a U.S. response either by staging a blitzkrieg that would be over before the Americans could intervene or by undertaking a series of piecemeal operations, perhaps coupled with the use of proxies to fight the war.

The calculus of deterrence was affected not only by changes in the international environment but also by a clearer sense of Japan's own national potential—including both its strengths and vulnerabilities. Until the 1973 oil crisis, the Japanese economy had expanded in a linear fashion; then, suddenly, Japan was forced to confront the profound vulnerability of its economy. As one official reportedly put it, "With or without a nuclear deterrent, there is no national security without oil." The Japanese reaction to the oil crisis was first complacent, then pessimistic, and finally fatalistic.[5] Civilian oil consumption was curtailed, and some military exercises were halted. On November 22, some thirty-five days after the embargo was announced, Japan made manifest its deep sense of vulnerability by abandoning its neutralism for a pro-Arab stance, even at the risk of antagonizing the pro-Israeli United States.

Japan's inherent economic weaknesses thus became apparent, but the Japanese also discovered that their country was one of the few industrialized nations to make a quick recovery from the initial "shock." Japan's industrial potential was now taken as a given. As already indicated, barring a complete loss of rationality on the part of a potential aggressor, the productivity and technological prowess of Japan's economy would probably play an important role in deterring an attack, either by providing resources that might be offered as a "bonus" in exchange for cooperative relations or by serving as a "trophy" that a potential aggressor would be reluctant to destroy lest a military victory prove empty.

By the middle 1970s, then, reliance on the United States, which had been the conceptual basis of Japan's defense since the 1950s, was being questioned on a number of grounds. But the Japanese were by no means disposed to abandon the security relationship with the Americans. The basic vulnerability inherent in Japan's dependence on foreign sources of energy had become manifest, as had Tokyo's lack of political leverage. The Americans, for their part, had begun to refrain from referring to the Japanese as "free-riders." Some form of cooperative security relationship with the United States still seemed essential. President Ford's Pacific Doctrine, set forth in Honolulu in December 1975, appeared to provide a sound framework within which to coordinate Japanese and U.S. policies in the next decade.

Such cooperation, however, still must overcome some basic differences between the two nations in defense concepts. These differences, which derive from the dissimilar strategic and domestic environments of the two countries, do not necessarily pose a threat to cooperative U.S.-Japan relations. But unless those differences are fully appreciated, it will be impossible for Americans to understand the way Japanese defense planners perceive the alternatives available to their country.

The key conceptual difference between Japanese and Americans concerns public attitudes toward national security, and, in particular, toward the role of the military in assuring security. The longstanding political constraints on the development of Japanese defense capabilities are well known. Although some opposition parties have been subtly changing their attitudes, they have generally continued to feel uneasy about the concept of maintaining U.S. forces in Japan as a "hostage" to ensure that the Americans will come to Japan's assistance in the event of an attack. The differences go beyond attitudes toward the expansion of the Self-Defense Forces (SDF) or the maintenance of a U.S. military presence. At a more basic level, the Japanese public is broadly skeptical about the utility of military power as a means of assuring national security. Most Japanese believe that military power in itself does not symbolize either national prestige or glory. Nor do they see it as effectively serving political or economic purposes, as was assumed to be the case prior to World War II. Even a former defense minister dismissed the concept of using military power to protect overseas assets as "not only anachronistic but useless."[6]

The problem is that the Japanese public tends to dismiss military power altogether as a means of helping to maintain national security. Ruling out even a limited military role is risky, for it could leave Japan with only two options— unconditional surrender or national suicide. Japanese policymakers need to have some choices apart from those two unacceptable extremes. The country needs at least some capacity to deter others from taking hostile actions, and this would seem to require a capability to deny a potential aggressor the possibility of an easy victory. But it is not only the Japanese public that fails to perceive accurately what military power can and cannot do for Japan. Many experts, both Japanese and foreign, argue for or worry about a full-scale military buildup without any real appreciation of Japan's inherent limitations and strategic vulnerabilities.

Given the changes that have occurred in the 1970s and the lack of realism in much of what has been said about Japan's defense alternatives, the need for a systematic reassessment of Japan's strategic context and, accordingly, the nation's basic defense posture has become manifest. Japanese defense planners have been endeavoring to carry out such an analysis. In so doing, they have been aware of the difficult dilemma they face: are there ways, within the limitations imposed by public attitudes toward military development, for Japan to prepare itself for the possibility that in certain situations the U.S. commitment may prove inadequate? Japanese defense planners have begun to talk not of defense strategies, but of *defense philosophies*, which suggests a broader approach then merely countering specific threats.[7]

To date, the major product of that ongoing reassessment has been a Defense White Paper published in 1976. What follows is a description of the considerations leading to that white paper and some further thoughts about Japan's alternatives in providing for its national security.

Japan's Inherent Vulnerabilities and Strategic Alternatives

Japan's geopolitical, historical, and socioeconomic characteristics impose a set of vulnerabilities which are unlikely to change significantly in the foreseeable future. To begin with the geopolitical situation, Japan lacks strategic depth. No place in Japan is farther than seventy-five miles from the coastline. Moreover, Japan's proximity to the Asian continent precludes an effective air defense. Hokkaido, the northernmost island, and the coast of northern Honshu bordering on the Sea of Japan lie within the operational range of Soviet MIG-21s or IL-28s; the entire archipelago falls within the range of the USSR's TU-16s, as well as its Backfire aircraft, should the latter be deployed in the Soviet Far East. And, of course, Japan is vulnerable to Soviet medium-range ballistic missiles (MRBMs) based on the continent. Japan's demographic distribution heightens the country's vulnerability to a massive attack or to disturbances centered in the urban areas. As of October 1975, Tokyo and its three neighboring prefectures had a population accounting for about 25 percent of the national total, and Osaka and its three neighboring prefectures had another 15 percent.[8]

From the standpoint of historical experience and psychological considerations, Japan is ill prepared to fight a war on its homeland. The Japanese have never fought a war on their own soil; nor have they ever had to confront urban guerrillas or external infiltrators. A country so lacking in strategic depth theoretically must rely on a forward defense, but in Japan there is no popular support, from either a legal or a psychological standpoint, for such a defense, much less for the development of a capability to launch a preemptive, retaliatory, or even a damage-limitation counterforce attack. Moreover, there is little public understanding and psychological preparedness for popular resistance against an invader. Strategists often forget that an invader might be able to take a large number of civilian hostages, thereby making it very difficult for Japanese forces to stage a counterattack against his beachhead.

As a corollary of the above, Japan has extremely limited emergency stockpiles of oil, food, medical supplies, and other strategic materials. No precrisis dispersal plans have been made, no public shelters designated, and no emergency laws established. Furthermore, in peacetime, legal restrictions inhibit the operational maneuverability of the SDF. There are limits on the use (and sometimes even the maintenance) of military bases, exercise grounds, overland transportation of arms and ammunition, and access to air space for military aircraft.

Japan's economic dependency on overseas markets and supplies is a well-established fact that needs no further elaboration, except to mention a near 90-percent dependency on oil from the Middle East. It is sometimes forgotten, however, that Japan cannot possibly defend militarily all of its merchant ships. They are simply too widely dispersed across the globe and too numerous (as of January 1972, there were 1,258 ships heavier than 3,000 tons) to be offered military escorts. In any case, their importance in resupplying Japan with raw materials and other vital imports would depend on the duration of any armed conflict involving Japan and, more important, on the extent to which other elements of the transportation system—such as harbor facilities, offshore safety, and overland transportation—had been disrupted.[9]

The implications of these inherent vulnerabilities for the defense of Japan are, of course, subject to varying interpretations. The four most commonly proposed alternatives are the following:

1. *Accept military impotence.* Japan should forego any effort to mount a military defense; it should rely on political maneuverability within the framework of a posture of unarmed neutrality and should spend its

money on the development of economic instruments with which to buy off potential aggressors by offering them a "bonus" for remaining at peace with Japan.

2. *Rely on the United States.* Japan should base its defense on the U.S. deterrent. In order to make that deterrent credible, a continued U.S. military presence is needed as a hostage to ensure timely U.S. retaliation against any country that attacks Japan.

3. *Seek an independent deterrent.* Without a military defense, Japan is at the mercy of predatory countries; the United States cannot be relied on to come to Japan's defense. Hence, it is argued, Japan has no choice but to develop adequate means of defending itself.

4. *Develop a "new military" concept.* This line, advanced by the Japan Communist party, calls for abolition of the security treaty with the United States and dissolution of the SDF. Then, after Japan has become "truly democratic," the constitution should be revised, and the nation should develop means of defending itself against possible threats from the United States "and other imperialists."[10]

The diversity of these views merely reveals how bewildered and worried the Japanese are about their defense. Given recent international and domestic developments, and the subtle revival of nationalism, the Japanese generally feel that their existing concepts of national security need to be overhauled. But there is far from a consensus as to the direction in which the country should move.

The first and fourth alternatives—military impotence and the "new military" concept—represent extreme views and have support from only small minorities. The third course—seeking an independent deterrent—is more seriously considered as a reasonable option for Japan. This line of argument, however, fails to consider in a realistic way the overwhelming obstacles Japan would face in any effort to develop an independent deterrent.

To be sure, the technology for making an unsophisticated

nuclear weapon (or an Indian-style peaceful nuclear device) is no longer secret, and Japan certainly possesses some peripheral technological background that could be applied to such an effort. But an independent deterrent requires more than a few simple bombs; it requires a meaningful strategic nuclear force with sophisticated weapons and delivery systems. It is simply beyond Japan's capabilities to develop such a force; it is not a matter of intentions or desires, but of unbearable costs and virtually insurmountable obstacles that would almost certainly keep Japan from becoming militarily self-sufficient.

To begin with, a nuclear-armed Japan would face a hostile international environment. The nuclear arming of Japan, like that of Germany, would have international repercussions entirely different from those associated with other countries that have developed a nuclear capability; both Japan and Germany remain designated as "ex-enemies" in the United Nations Charter, and the fear of "resurgent militarism" in those countries is far from dead among their neighbors. If Japan were to go nuclear, the hostility this would engender in the international environment would have the most serious implications for the economic relationships that are vital to Japan. Indeed, key economic activities could be brought almost to a standstill as a result of Japan's emergence as a nuclear power.

Domestically, the acquisition of nuclear weapons would almost certainly give rise to extreme instability, given the prevailing nuclear phobia. If, as seems most unlikely, the Japanese people were to indicate their support for an independent nuclear deterrent, there would be intense pressure to preempt a potential attack by striking first. Given the vulnerability inherent in a country with 40 percent of its population concentrated in two industrial complexes, the Japanese might not want to wait until an attack had been launched against them before retaliating.

From a technological standpoint, Japan lacks the required number of scientists and engineers who would be willing to work on a nuclear weapons project. It would be extremely difficult to find a suitable plant location in a country already short of industrial sites. Japanese delivery systems would have to be developed in a crash program, but Japan still lacks the capability to produce jet engines, nuclear-powered submarines, or sophisticated missile guidance systems. Japan's deposits of uranium, estimated at only 6,000 metric tons, are far from adequate for a significant nuclear weapons program. Moreover, Japan has come under strong pressure from the Carter administration to abandon the development of reprocessing facilities. Japan has not yet put into operation a uranium enrichment plant.

Even if Japan could produce a bomb and a delivery system, there would be no place on Japanese territory to test it. It is extremely doubtful that an arsenal of untested nuclear weapons could serve as a credible deterrent. Furthermore, a second-strike strategy requires an adequate early warning system, but there is no site in Japan distant enough to provide more than a twenty-minute warning. Japan has yet to develop any space warning system. To make matters worse, Japan would need to have a 360-degree ballistic missile early warning system (BMEWS) to guard against submarine-launched ballistic missiles (SLBMs); not even the United States is capable of installing such a system.

Finally, there would be few suitable targets for a Japanese nuclear force based on submarines located in the Sea of Japan, the only place where such a force could conceivably be protected. Soviet targets are too remote; Moscow, for example, is 6,000 miles from the Sea of Japan. Chinese targets, with 11 percent of the population located in 1,000 major cities, are simply too numerous to achieve any reasonable tradeoff with a Chinese nuclear attack. Most other Asian targets are too small for nuclear warheads. American targets, with about 25 percent of the population in 10 major cities, remain "too friendly" to serve as hostage targets. What, then, is the strategic purpose of a submarine-based, second-strike Japanese nuclear force?[11]

If an independent deterrent would be virtually meaningless, Japan would seem to have little choice but to base its security on some variation of the existing system, which involves a heavy degree of reliance on the United States.

Within the framework of continued dependence on the U.S. deterrent, however, there may be need for substantial change in Japan's strategic concepts. It may not be sufficient to indicate a desire for a continued U.S. naval and air presence. Consideration needs to be given to the role that Japan might play in its own defense.

The 1976 White Paper and the "Standard Defense Force"

The Defense White Paper published in June 1976 was the first attempt by the government to define a new Japanese defense role within a structure of continuing reliance on the U.S. deterrent. According to then Defense Minister Michita Sakata, this Defense White Paper, the first one published since October 1970, differed from its predecessor in that it sought to define "the role of military power in the context of rapidly changing international environments . . . and of peculiar Japanese environments, political and strategic."[12] In his press conference explaining the white paper, Sakata set forth some new concepts with a candor not found in the white paper itself. His explanation was based on the Defense Agency's own analysis of the international strategic context, in itself a departure from established practice—such analyses had previously been undertaken only by the Foreign Ministry.

Sakata outlined his interpretation of détente and, by implication, of the nuclear umbrella. He emphasized that the avoidance of war, whether a nuclear conflict or a conventional war that might escalate to nuclear strife, was the primary objective of détente. Even if war should break out, he added, the major powers would probably seek to limit the extent of hostilities and to avoid a nuclear exchange. Thus, it was quite possible that the military means actually employed would be significantly less than those that the parties to a conflict might have at their disposal.

How does the major powers' determination to avoid or, failing that, to limit armed conflict affect Japan? Sakata stressed that "to *avoid wars* of any kind, a chain of nations should have no feeble link which might provoke a military challenge; only an international system whose every link is strong and enduring can survive any test it faces." Thus, he concluded, Japan's defense would require, first of all, "a collective security system based on common will and mutual responsibility." Second, he argued, "every member nation of the [collective security] system must have a strong will and capability to defend itself by itself." This means, he explained, that each nation should be capable of *"denying others easy armed aggression."* (Emphasis added.)

The U.S.-Japan security system, Sakata noted, is designed to prevent aggression against Japan or, in the event of such aggression, to *limit* its scale. What Japan needs, he argued, is a "basic standing force," which was renamed a "standard defense force" in the published version of the white paper. This force would be intended to fill a gap in Japan's defense strategy by denying a potential aggressor the possibility of an easy victory through a limited action to which the United States might for some reason be unable or unwilling to respond. The concept of a standard defense force entails the maintenance of a limited military force in peacetime and the qualitative improvement of hardware and of capabilities for combat and logistic support.

The primary missions of the standard defense force would be as follows:

1. air-sea surveillance and intelligence collection;
2. quick response to indirect aggression and violation of Japan's territorial boundaries;
3. maintenance of manpower and hardware in a state of readiness to respond to a near-surprise attack;
4. maintenance of smooth operational coordination with U.S. forces;
5. readiness for "smooth expansion and reinforcement to a necessary level, if and when a political decision should be made . . . in response to changes in the international situation."[13]

This outline of a standard defense force remains, as of

1977, a basic "guideline," which may be modified as circumstances require. As presented in the Defense White Paper, the standard defense force concept is surrounded by a good deal of euphemistic rhetoric that reflects the prevailing antimilitary climate in Japan. Clearly, the inherent vulnerabilities and political factors that have constrained Japan's military development in the past are likely to persist for some time. Nevertheless, it may be appropriate here to speculate as to the kinds of contingencies in which the standard defense force outlined above might play a role and as to the specifics of such a role.

The Defense of Japan: Contingencies and Responses

In the first instance, Japan's defense strategy must provide for an all-out effort to prevent the outbreak of war. Japan should be in a position to undertake a series of coordinated measures—economic, diplomatic, and military—aimed at the avoidance of armed conflict. The "economic diplomacy" pursued by a succession of Japanese premiers is one potential instrument for the avoidance of war. International conferences and exchanges may serve to foster a level of communication and mutual understanding that will make it possible to identify and deal with problems before tensions have reached the point where hostilities seem imminent. In the military field, Japan's exercise of self-restraint in the development of its own defense capabilities and its advocacy of arms control measures generally may help to dissuade other nations from adopting overtly a belligerent posture vis-à-vis Japan. At the very least, it minimizes the possibility of any Japanese military moves that might be construed as provocative by a potential aggressor. All of these measures aimed at the avoidance of war constitute a kind of *bonus deterrence* or, as the French put it, *dissuasion*. The emphasis is on offering positive incentives, or bonuses, to remain at peace, rather than on merely threatening retaliation. Of course, this dissuasive deterrence must be supplemented by the more conventional retaliatory deterrence represented by the U.S. military presence in Japan, which ensures that an aggressor cannot act against Japan without making a conscious decision to risk a direct confrontation with the United States.

No matter how hard Japan tries to avoid armed conflict, however, the possibility of war cannot be completely ruled out. In order to determine how Japan might develop a standard defense force to meet such a contingency, it is necessary to consider the kind of attack that seems most likely, should deterrence fail.

First, one can safely assume that no aggressor will resort to an open, large-scale armed attack on Japan so long as other means of coercion are available. Second, an aggressor may well be seeking to achieve relatively limited political or economic goals—for example, to force a change in certain Japanese policies. Rather than launching a frontal assault, an adversary nation would be tempted to exploit some of Japan's inherent vulnerabilities—its lack of adequate means of dealing with urban disturbances, heavy reliance on sea lines of communication (SLOC), which cannot easily be defended against a harassing force, and susceptibility to "quarantine" or blockade. Exploitation of these weaknesses would represent a kind of psychological warfare that the Japanese people are ill prepared to counter.

Only when these approaches have proven ineffectual or when internal disarray has escalated to crisis proportions might an aggressor turn to a direct attack on Japan. A direct attack would serve two purposes: first, even a limited invasion would intensify Japan's domestic disturbances; second, and most important, a sharply circumscribed military action might not elicit a strong reaction from the United States.

There is another plausible scenario that might lead to a direct attack on Japan. This scenario relates to the global context. A potential aggressor might be tempted to launch a probing attack against Japan if (1) Japan appears to be the weakest link in the defense structure of the noncommunist nations, and the aggressor does not think it necessary to commit a substantial portion of its military resources to carry out a successful attack on Japan; and (2) the United States is so preoccupied with problems elsewhere in the world that it is unable to counter effectively a probing action against Japan.

Thus, the most likely contingency for Japan is the following:

1. The aggressor nation has already created or exploited internal disturbances through indirect means.
2. It then launches an armed attack limited in scope, weaponry, and duration; it declares that this limited "deployment" (aggression) was "invited" by certain elements in Japan and that the United States should stay out of the conflict in order to avoid escalation.
3. The aggressor quickly attempts to establish a limited military fait accompli before the United States has time to respond.

To prevent the establishment of such a military fait accompli, Japan does not need any retaliatory capability; the goal is simply restoration of the status quo ante, not defeat of the aggressor in its homeland. Japan must have a denial and resistance capability, consisting of a standard defense force in a high state of readiness and a plan for diplomatic efforts, to be undertaken in conjunction with U.S. initiatives, to terminate the conflict on the most favorable terms. This denial and resistance capability would be designed to deny access to Japanese air and sea space and to prevent any sustained occupation of Japanese territory. Such a capability would function both as a "magnet" to bring about timely U.S. military intervention and as an indispensable means of persuading a potential invader that any aggression would be costly.

In concrete terms, an effective denial and resistance capability would require the following: (1) highly sophisticated defensive firepower, including precision-guided munitions (PGMs) for air defense, anti-submarine warfare (ASW), and anti-ship defense; (2) PGM platforms, such as vertical take-off and landing (VTOL) aircraft, which require fewer and smaller land bases; (3) efficient intelligence networks and data processing systems, including airborne radar and satellite-based intelligence systems; and (4) strong logistic and communications backup.

A limited buildup of Japanese defense capabilities within the framework of the standard defense force concept would not be a source of tension; rather, it would contribute to the maintenance of a stable balance of power in the Pacific. As already indicated, it would avoid offering a potential aggressor the temptation of a "weak link" in the non-communist world's security structure. Furthermore, efficient Japanese naval and air forces capable of surveillance and denial in Japan's immediate environs would alleviate the burden borne by the United States, freeing U.S. forces to maintain the security of sea lines of communication in the Indian Ocean and Persian Gulf, where Japan cannot make a direct military contribution.

However desirable such a limited buildup may be, it would entail high financial costs at a time when the defense establishment finds itself hard pressed to gain even a minimal slice of the budgetary pie. There are several possible solutions to this problem. The three armed services might be assigned responsibility for setting their own priorities and subdividing the defense budget. But given the prevailing climate in Japan, this might result in a proportionately smaller allocation to each item than is presently received, thus producing a very ineffective defense structure. Another possibility would be to overhaul the existing defense system, setting a temporary ceiling at existing or reduced manpower levels and streamlining the entire system by allocating more to such vital sectors as intelligence and logistics. This would be accompanied by the stepping up of diplomatic-economic measures (i.e., bonus offering) to facilitate the avoidance of war.

Conclusion: The United States and the Defense of Japan

As they consider how to plan effectively for the defense of Japan, Washington and Tokyo must recognize a number of basic facts. First, gone are the days when the security of Japan could be ensured mainly by retaliatory deterrence.

No longer can it be assumed that a bluff of direct military involvement on the part of the United States will deter or contain a "civil war" in an Asian context. Japan and the United States must coordinate and intensify their dissuasive deterrent efforts. The bonus Japan can offer a potential adversary to remain at peace could be significant in terms of technological, agricultural, and oceanographic cooperation.

Second, the time is ripe, given the changing climate in Japan, for the Japanese and the Americans to devise more effective means of communication on strategic matters, including a better understanding of how to define the most likely contingencies. Moreover, the two countries ought to refrain from making pronouncements on security affairs that are intended mainly for domestic political consumption. They must face up to certain realities. U.S. military power in Asia, especially naval power, will remain limited as long as situations elsewhere in the world demand more attention from the United States. Japan's defense buildup will also be limited. The expansion of Japanese naval forces will be slow, and Tokyo will remain reluctant to play a military role beyond its immediate periphery. The defense budget will probably not exceed 1 percent of GNP, which itself may not increase rapidly, as long as the cost of defense manpower and hardware continues to rise. In light of the constraints on both nations, it is essential that they cooperate more closely in order to ensure that they will be able to avoid the outbreak of war or, failing that, to limit any conflict and bring about a rapid termination.

Cooperation between Tokyo and Washington will be facilitated if the United States comes to view Japan's security less in protector-protégé terms and more as part of a global strategy in which the United States has an interest in ensuring the survival of Japan as a member of the family of democratic nations. The Americans presumably recognize that Japan's industrial potential is a major asset to the democracies as a whole. A drastic change in Japan's industrial-economic system would lead to a gradual collapse of the internal structure of many Pacific nations whose economies are closely interwoven with those of Japan and the United States. If, assuming the worst, Japan were coerced to change its system, the impact would be global and would inevitably affect the security of Europe, as well as that of the United States. Finally, Japan is geographically situated at critical choking points vis-à-vis the Soviet Pacific Fleet, whose unrestrained expansion might destabilize the balance of power in the Pacific.

Japan's overall strategic position may well remain vulnerable, even coercible. Japan probably will continue to be indefensible by military means alone, for the country's inherent vulnerabilities are not easily altered. There should be no illusions about this. The emphasis in Japan's defense strategy must remain on the avoidance of war through dissuasive or bonus deterrence, supplemented by the retaliatory potential of the United States. But Japan's defensive, or holding, capabilities can be strengthened through the gradual adoption of more sophisticated defense systems. Although military means have only a limited role to play in assuring Japan's security, that role is not an unimportant one. Once this is understood, it becomes clear that the only realistic alternative for the defense of Japan is to develop the means to prolong holding time and establish closer coordination with the United States in order to make U.S. mediation—military or diplomatic—more effective.

Notes

1. Katsumi Kobayashi, *The Nixon Doctrine and U.S.-Japanese Security Relations*, California Seminar on Arms Control and Foreign Policy Discussion Paper no. 65 (Santa Monica, Calif., 1975), p. 6.

2. *New York Times*, August 26, 1970, p. 1; and press release quoted by Kobayashi, *The Nixon Doctrine and U.S.-Japanese Security Relations*, p. 7.

3. To be sure, Mr. Kissinger may now be able to reveal his reasons for going along with President Nixon.

4. Makoto Momoi, *The Energy Problem and Alliance Systems: Japan*, International Institute for Strategic Studies, Adelphi Paper no. 115 (London, 1974), p. 25.

5. Ibid.

6. Speech by former Defense Minister Naomi Nishimura, Foreign Correspondents' Club, Tokyo, October 11, 1971.

7. Kobayashi, *The Nixon Doctrine and U.S.-Japanese Security Relations*, p. 6.

8. *Mainichi Shimbun*, December 8, 1975, p. 1.

9. Makoto Momoi, "Pax Russo-Americana and Its Theoretical Impact on Japan's Defense Concept," in *Contrasting Approaches to Strategic Arms Control*, ed. Robert L. Pfaltzgraff, Jr. (Lexington, Mass.: Lexington Books, 1974), p. 204. Makoto Momoi and Masataka Kosaka, eds., *Takyokuka-jidai no Senryaku* [Strategy in a multipolar era] (Tokyo: Nihon-Kokusaimondai Kenkyujo, 1973), pp. 469-475, elaborates on the difficulties Japan would face in any effort to exercise the nuclear option.

10. "Dokuritsu Minshu Nihon-no Boei Mondai" [Defense issues of independent, democratic Japan], in *Zenei* [Vanguard] (Tokyo: Japan Communist Party, Special Issue, 1972), p. 41.

11. See Momoi and Kosaka, *Takyokuka-jidai no Senryaku*.

12. Quotations from Minister Sakata's press conference are based on the author's stenographic memo, since he acted as official translator. There are certain differences of phraseology between this memo and the English translation of the Defense White Paper, entitled *Defense of Japan* (Tokyo: Defense Agency, 1976). The latter is a faithful, if literal, translation of the original, *Nihon-no Boei*.

13. Speech by Defense Minister Sakata, Foreign Correspondents' Club, Tokyo, June 3, 1976.

5

The U.S. Nuclear Umbrella and Japanese Security

Morton H. Halperin

Is the U.S. nuclear umbrella over Japan still credible? This question is now being asked with some frequency in Japan. It is not a new question. Indeed, both Japanese and American experts have been debating the answer for some years. Nor has the question been limited to Japan; it has often been asked about the NATO countries as well.

The first paper that I know of that raised the question of the future credibility of the U.S. nuclear guarantees to its allies was written at the Rand Corporation in 1954. This paper argued that the U.S. guarantee to its NATO allies would cease to be credible when the Soviet Union developed an intercontinental nuclear capability with bombers or missiles.

In fact, the European concern about the adequacy of the U.S. nuclear deterrent developed only slowly and mainly in response to U.S. proposals to deal with the problem. In the early 1960s European experts and their governments debated proposals for multilateral forces, European nuclear forces, and other devices to enforce the deterrent by giving "Europe" (really Germany) a finger on the nuclear trigger. As a substitute, the Defense Department proposed more candid discussions, and these have been held within the framework of the Nuclear Planning Group.

By the end of the 1960s, the question of the adequacy of the deterrent had almost ceased to be asked within NATO. The

American nuclear guarantee was again taken for granted. A free exchange of views among governments and experts and in public helped to sort out the issues and to persuade most Europeans that there was little cause for alarm. As long as the European-American relationship remained close and the common interests of the two regions were clear to any potential adversary, the nuclear guarantee would work. The NATO debate helped to show that the "question"of the credibility of the nuclear deterrent was not in fact a single question but rather a whole series of separate questions.

Now that the issue is being raised in some Japanese political circles, it is important that there be a full and frank exchange of views at the official, expert, and public levels. This chapter is meant to be a contribution to the exchange among experts from the two countries. The argument of this paper can be put very simply:

1. The United States has a nuclear commitment to Japan.
2. The U.S. commitment is sufficient to meet Japanese security requirements; in this sense the nuclear umbrella is still credible and will remain credible.

The credibility of the nuclear umbrella depends on a series of different questions:

1. In whose eyes does the umbrella have to be credible?
2. What U.S. nuclear response is necessary to make the umbrella credible?
3. How likely does a response have to be thought to be in order to make the umbrella credible?
4. Against what countries is the umbrella directed?
5. Against what acts of those countries is the umbrella effective?
6. What actions of the Japanese government is the umbrella designed to protect?

This chapter considers each of these questions in turn. It seeks to demonstrate that the answer to the question, "Is the U.S. nuclear umbrella credible?" depends on the answers to each of these separate questions. For example, at one

extreme, no one would argue that "the U.S. nuclear umbrella would be credible in the eyes of Japanese leaders in
that they would be certain that the United States would use
nuclear weapons against the Philippines if the Philippine
government was resisting by using conventional military
force a Japanese government attempt to seize a Philippine
island." At the other extreme, few would doubt that "the
American nuclear deterrent would be credible in the eyes of
the Chinese leaders in that they would attach a significant
probability to the likelihood that the United States would
carry out some form of nuclear retaliation against them if
they launched a nuclear strike against Japan because the
Japanese government refused to appoint a prime minister
friendly to Peking."

Both of these scenarios are unrealistic, but they are put
forward to demonstrate starkly that the question of the
credibility of the American nuclear umbrella depends critically on each of the elements described in the two cases.

It is my contention that for the full range of plausible
answers to each question, the deterrent is fully credible. I
turn then to the individual questions.

Credibility of the Umbrella: Six Questions

In Whose Eyes Does the Umbrella Need to be Credible?

The credibility of the U.S. nuclear umbrella depends on its
ability to deter actions by foreign governments that threaten
the interests of the United States or its allies. Thus the
credibility of the umbrella rests on the beliefs of the leaders of
the countries whose behavior is to be affected and not on
beliefs in the United States or Japan.[1]

The U.S. nuclear umbrella over Japan would be completely worthless as a deterrent if Japanese and Americans had
confidence in it but Soviet and Chinese leaders did not.

Conversely, doubts that Americans or Japanese might
have about the deterrent do not affect its credibility if Soviet
and Chinese leaders believe that the United States will act.
Thus one must focus on the potential adversary and ask
about his perceptions and interests.

Moreover, the government of a country is not a single

monolithic entity. It consists of conflicting bureaucratic entities and rival political leaders. The credibility of the deterrent depends on the beliefs of groups or individuals with sufficient power to order an action or sufficient power to veto it.

What American Nuclear Response is Necessary To Make the Deterrent Credible?

It is sometimes assumed that the credibility of the deterrent depends on the willingness of the United States to launch an all-out nuclear strike against a country threatening Japan. Such a reaction is sometimes said to be incredible because it would very likely mean a nuclear response against the United States. In many situations, however, the threat of a much more limited nuclear response will be more than sufficient to deter an attack.

For example, the nuclear capability of a single U.S. aircraft carrier armed with nuclear weapons could do enormous damage to any country. A single submarine armed with nuclear missiles could do even more damage.

In short, the threatened U.S. response could be limited and still be an effective deterrent. A country might well hesitate before running the risk of limited nuclear retaliation.

How Likely Does a Response Have To Be Thought To Be?

This brings us to the third question of how likely the U.S. nuclear response has to be. Certainty is by no means necessary. In considering the likely consequences of any contemplated action, decision-makers rarely can be certain of anything. What they must do is weigh the probability of various responses and the consequences of each.

Japanese may ask themselves, "Can we be sure?" that the Americans will respond. Leaders of a country contemplating an attack on Japan must ask, "How likely is the U.S. response and how costly would that response be?"

Given the great destructive power of nuclear weapons and the devastation that even a limited nuclear strike would cause, even a low probability of U.S. nuclear response is likely to be sufficient to deter an action against Japan.

Uncertainty rather than certainty will be the key factor. A foreign leader asked to approve an action that could bring the U.S. deterrent into play will want absolute assurances that the Americans will not in fact be involved. It will not be enough to say that the odds are low or that it appears unlikely. Opponents of an action will be able to oppose it by asserting that there is some risk of a U.S. nuclear response. No one will be able to say for certain how high that risk is, but that very uncertainty is a powerful deterrent.

The most credible deterrent is a high probability, if not a certainty, that there will be a U.S. response sufficient to deal with the threat and including the commitment of substantial U.S. forces. Whether this intervention will initially be nuclear or conventional is less important than that a potential aggressor believe that the United States will not stand idly by.

One can sum up the contrast between the way the issue is often argued and the way this chapter suggests it should be, in relation to the first three questions, with two contrasting propositions:

1. For the nuclear umbrella to be credible, *Japanese* leaders must be *certain* that there will be a *total* U.S. nuclear response; and
2. For the nuclear umbrella to be credible, *foreign* leaders must be *uncertain* about whether there will be at least a *limited* U.S. nuclear response.

Against What Country is the Umbrella Directed?

I have already suggested that the credibility of the nuclear umbrella depends on the perception of those to be deterred and not on the perceptions of Japanese or American leaders. Thus, one must ask what country is to be deterred.

Clearly, the nuclear umbrella would only come into play against nuclear powers. Japan would not want the United States to threaten the use of nuclear weapons against non-nuclear powers whose actions might be threatening American interests. Apart from moral, political, and nonproliferation considerations, there are no non-nuclear countries that could conceivably pose a security threat to Japan that could not be deterred or defeated by the conventional military forces of Japan or, if necessary, of Japan and the United States.

Thus, the nuclear deterrent need only be credible against the People's Republic of China and the Soviet Union. Questions and doubts thus should be discussed in the specific context of these two countries. This brings us to the fifth question.

What Actions of the Specific Country Are To Be Deterred?

Not only must one focus on a specific country, but one must also ask what acts of that country are to be deterred.

One key question is whether the nuclear umbrella can be confined to nuclear threats or whether it needs to function against conventional threats as well. I would argue that the nuclear umbrella can and should be limited to nuclear threats.

The case of China is relatively easy. China's capability to launch a conventional attack against Japan is extremely limited. Chinese military forces are designed for the defense of Chinese territory, primarily against Soviet threats. Most analysts have concluded that the People's Republic could not capture Taiwan against the defense that the Nationalists could mount on their own. An attack against Japanese islands would be even further beyond their capability.

The possibility of limited military clashes between China and Japan over oil drilling, fishing rights, or other matters cannot, of course, be ruled out. However, one cannot expect the U.S. nuclear umbrella to be of any relevance in such cases, at least as long as China does not seek to bring its own nuclear capability into play. The British experience with Iceland over fishing rights demonstrates very vividly the irrelevance of even a national nuclear capability (as well as conventional superiority) in resolving such disputes.

The situation with regard to the Soviet Union is different in some ways. The Soviet military capability is greater than that of China, and the Soviets could, if they chose to do so, mount a conventional attack on Japan. However, it is extremely difficult to conceive of the circumstances in which the Soviets would mount the necessary military deployments to make such a threat even remotely credible. Moreover, U.S. conventional power would be brought into the area to balance the Soviet buildup. Japan has relied and can continue to rely on U.S. conventional power to deter or defeat any possible Soviet conventional threat against Japan.

The situation in central Europe is quite different. There Soviet military forces already in place could quickly seize some German territory. The military balance in the center of Europe has traditionally been a matter of great concern to European and world powers; two world wars have been fought over the territory. The military balance directly affects political developments in many central European countries. Both NATO and the Warsaw Pact countries maintain substantial ready forces facing each other across the line.

Given these circumstances and the widely shared, if incorrect, view that the Warsaw Pact countries hold a decisive conventional advantage, the NATO countries have seen the nuclear deterrent as necessary to deter Soviet conventional threats. The credibility of that deterrent has been seen to depend on the stationing of large numbers of U.S. troops and nuclear weapons on the central European front.

None of these circumstances exist in East Asia. The Soviet-Japanese conventional military balance along the Soviet-Japanese "border" is simply not an important political fact, and a Soviet conventional threat is extremely implausible.

If this argument is correct, then the U.S. nuclear umbrella can be limited to nuclear threats by the Soviet Union or the People's Republic of China. The purpose of the U.S. nuclear umbrella then is to prevent the Soviet or Chinese leaders from successfully employing nuclear blackmail or from actually dropping nuclear weapons on Japan.

Returning to our early questions, the objective is to persuade Soviet and Chinese leaders that the probability of various U.S. responses combined with the damage to their security likely to result from each possible response is sufficiently high to deter the use or threatened use of nuclear weapons.

If the nuclear umbrella need only work for cases of nuclear actions by the Soviet Union or China, then considerations beyond those of U.S.-Japan relations come into play. U.S. security interests throughout the world and the credibility of all of its commitments would be seriously undermined if the United States permitted either China or the Soviet Union to engage in nuclear blackmail successfully. Resistance to nuclear threats throughout the world has been and remains a key element of U.S. nonproliferation policy.

Moreover, "nuclear blackmail" has always been an elusive concept. It has seldom been tried and with the possible exception of Sino-American relations has never been successful.[2] The problem is that the threat is generally disproportionate to the ongoing dispute and extremely difficult to make credible. The issuance of a nuclear threat by any nuclear power makes it very likely that another nuclear power will enter the dispute on the other side.

Beyond that, the credibility of U.S. commitments in Europe and elsewhere would be truly undermined if the United States permitted the Soviet Union or China to engage in successful nuclear blackmail or nuclear attacks on Japan. Certainly, no one could convince leaders in Peking and Moscow that such action did not run an unacceptably high risk of U.S. nuclear retaliation.

What is "unacceptable" depends on what the consequences of not using nuclear threats are. This brings me to the last question, which is at once the least asked and the most important.

What Actions of the Japanese Government Is the Nuclear Umbrella Designed To Protect?

Doubts about the U.S. nuclear umbrella cannot be assessed unless one focuses on what is happening when the nuclear threat arises. One aspect of this question has already been discussed: namely, what threats or actions are to be deterred. It was argued that in the case of Japan, at least, this could be limited to threats to use nuclear weapons. The nuclear umbrella could not, but need not, deter lower-level threats.

Equally important is the question of whether Tokyo is taking actions that raise the possibility of nuclear threats against Japan.

It is precisely Japanese foreign policy that makes the question of the credibility of the U.S. nuclear umbrella so easy to answer. Japan simply does not pose a threat to Chinese or Soviet interests (or for that matter the interests of any other country) to raise even remotely a threat of nuclear retaliation.

A Japan that had thrown off its antiwar constitution and rearmed substantially and that was controlled by an expansionist group bent on military adventures might well find the U.S. nuclear umbrella unreliable. If, for example, Japan sought to capture the northern islands by military means or to reoccupy Taiwan to keep it from coming under the control of the mainland government, the Soviet Union or China might resort to nuclear threats. In such a situation, the costs of permitting Japan to gain its objective might seem unacceptable. Moreover, the Soviet or Chinese leaders might conclude that the United States would not intervene. Other forms of Japanese adventurism would be equally without U.S. protection.

But Japan does not contemplate any such actions. Its foreign policy eschews threats to use force against others. Japan does not take diplomatic or economic actions that threaten important interests of other nations. The U.S. nuclear umbrella must be sufficiently credible only to persuade China and the Soviet Union not to seek to coerce Japan into taking actions that would serve Soviet or Chinese interests. Is there anything Japan could do that would be so important to Chinese or Soviet leaders that they would run the risk of U.S. nuclear retaliation in order to get Japan to act?

The only conceivable possibility is an attempt to persuade Japan to expel U.S. forces stationed in Japan or to break the security tie with the United States. China now seeks to persuade the United States to maintain forces in East Asia and has no interest in such threats. Soviet interests, as defined in the Kremlin, are less clear, but it seems unlikely that the Soviet leaders value the breakup of the U.S.-Japanese alliance highly enough to risk a nuclear confrontation. In contemplating such an effort, they would know that a U.S. response is most likely when the threat is directed specifically at U.S. interests.

Forward Deployment and the Role of Tactical Nuclear Weapons

An element of deterrence not discussed thus far that could affect the credibility of the nuclear umbrella is the role of tactical nuclear weapons. Closely related is the question of forward deployment.

Tactical nuclear weapons can be thought of as a way to fudge a credibility gap by making it easier to understand how a conventional attack could lead to nuclear retaliation against the aggressor and ultimately to a nuclear attack on the aggressor's homeland. In the absence of tactical nuclear weapons designed for use on the battlefield, the United States would have to make credible its intention to launch a strategic nuclear attack as its first nuclear strike.

If tactical nuclear weapons exist, the threat can be more moderate and credible: the United States will employ nuclear weapons on the battlefield either in response to enemy use or, if necessary, to meet an apparently successful conventional attack.

The use of nuclear weapons on the battlefield is fraught with great danger and uncertainty. The existence of such weapons and their presence in the battlefield area has the advantage of creating uncertainty in the mind of an attacker. He may, for example, be reluctant to concentrate his forces for an attack, particularly for an amphibious assault, for fear that they will present an irresistible target for a tactical nuclear strike. On the other hand, the actual use of such tactical weapons against an opponent similarly equipped may not be to the benefit of the defending side. Such use is likely to lead to very substantial casualties on both sides, and the possibility of further escalation would be very great.

Each side would seek to target the nuclear delivery systems of the other, and to do so each would be tempted to use longer-range systems of its own. Hence, a tactical nuclear war is likely to escalate very quickly to a strategic exchange. This potential for escalation makes tactical nuclear weapons a credible bridge to the strategic deterrent, but at the same time reduces their value as an independent option.

A U.S. pledge not to use nuclear weapons first would reduce somewhat the contribution of tactical nuclear weapons to the deterrent. Such a pledge would not, of course, rule out the use of nuclear weapons in response to a nuclear threat or nuclear blackmail. It would appear to make a nuclear response to conventional attack less likely, but it would not preclude the possibility. A country launching a major conventional attack would recognize that a U.S. no-first-use pledge might not hold up if the United States were losing a major conventional war. An agreement forbidding the first use of nuclear weapons would make nuclear blackmail less likely and would encourage the development and deployment of adequate conventional forces by the United States and its allies. It would also contribute to nonproliferation.

It is in this context that the issue of deployment of tactical nuclear weapons in Northeast Asia needs to be considered. The situation in Japan, which does not permit nuclear storage or transit, is, of course, very different from that in Korea, where the United States now admits nuclear weapons are stored.

U.S. nuclear weapons have been kept in Korea for many years. The original policy stemmed from the decision made in the 1950s that the United States would use nuclear weapons in any major military conflict. Thus, it was assumed that if the United States engaged in combat in Korea, it would immediately use nuclear weapons. Once that policy was abandoned in the early 1960s, the storage of nuclear weapons in Korea could no longer be justified, but no fundamental reevaluation of the policy was ever undertaken, and the weapons remain on the peninsula.

Although the United States has not adopted a no-first-use policy, it has sought to structure its forces so that it would not be necessary to use nuclear weapons in response to a conventional attack. No U.S. president would want to use nuclear weapons in the opening hours of a war on the Korean peninsula. He would want first to see if the attack could be contained by conventional means or to see the status quo ante restored by diplomatic measures. Given that policy, the stationing of nuclear weapons in Korea becomes unnecessary and dangerous. The time it would take to move nuclear weapons to Korea from U.S. territory (measured in hours) would be far less than the time needed to decide whether to use the weapons; the logistic effort would hardly be noticed amid the requirements of a conventional war.

Having the weapons in Korea poses several risks. First, even though the weapons are reportedly no longer stationed near the demarcation line, there remains the danger that they will be overrun and captured by the North Koreans. A U.S. force in danger of being overrun might use nuclear weapons without authority. Alternatively, a president might feel obliged to authorize a nuclear strike if the alternative were the capture of the weapons and the destruction of the unit. South Korean forces might be tempted to seize nuclear weapons and seek to use them, bypassing the safety devices. All of these problems would be compounded by a substantial U.S. troop withdrawal that left the weapons in place.

Even if the United States decided to use nuclear weapons in Korea, it would not necessarily want to fire them from Korean territory. Nuclear strikes could be launched from carrier-based aircraft, from long-range bombers, or from missiles launched from submarines. The same would be true of Japan. If Japan were under conventional attack, it would not make much sense to move nuclear weapons into crowded and vulnerable Japanese airfields.

The development by the United States of tactical nuclear weapons and the possibility of delivering them from sea or air add something to the credibility of the U.S. nuclear umbrella. There is no need, however, for deployment in Asian territory.

Conclusion

The argument of this chapter can be restated. The U.S. nuclear umbrella is sufficiently credible in the eyes of Japan's potential opponents to deter nuclear threats. The credibility of the deterrent does not depend on the stationing of U.S. nuclear weapons or even conventional forces in Japan. The deterrent will remain credible as long as Japan and the United States maintain common interests and an alliance relationship, and as long as Japan does not pose a military threat to its neighbors. Moreover, as Kiichi Saeki and others have argued persuasively, it is more credible than an independent Japanese nuclear capability.

Notes

1. The nuclear umbrella needs also to be credible to allies if it is to deter them from actions contrary to U.S. interests. If Japan is to refrain from developing a nuclear capability of its own, Tokyo must be persuaded that the U.S. umbrella is credible.

2. The Eisenhower administration believed that nuclear threats helped to end the Korean War and to persuade the Chinese not to press the use of military force in the Taiwan Straits in 1954 and 1958.

6
The Meaning of the U.S. Nuclear Umbrella for Japan

Takuya Kubo

Japan's Defense and Nuclear Policies

Defense Buildup Plans and Reliance on the
U.S. Nuclear Deterrent

For twenty years, beginning in 1958, the development of Japan's Self-Defense Forces (SDF) was guided by a series of defense buildup plans. The last of these, the Fourth Five-Year Defense Plan, came to an end in March 1977. Since then, the defense buildup has been based on a "Defense Plan Outline" adopted in October 1976, which set forth long-term goals. Initially, there was not much awareness of the nuclear factor in these defense plans. But as nuclear strategy came to encompass the globe, Japan's dependence on the U.S. nuclear deterrent was recognized. The Third Defense Plan accepted nuclear dependence on the United States as part of the basic structure of national defense. Subsequently, in accord with Japan's "defense concept" as stated in the Fourth Defense Plan and the 1976 Defense Plan Outline, it was asserted that "Japan will depend on America's nuclear deterrent against nuclear threats."

In June 1976, a Defense White Paper was issued, setting forth guidelines for the further development of the SDF. According to this white paper, Japan has confidence in the effectiveness and credibility of the U.S. nuclear deterrent. There is no need, from either a military or a political viewpoint, for Japan to develop its own nuclear weapons.

Moreover, it is recognized that Japan's nuclear armament would create serious apprehension on the part of other nations, especially neighboring Asian countries.

Given the public's strong "nuclear allergy," which is reflected in Diet deliberations, discussions that touch on the question of nuclear weapons have been treated as something of a taboo even within the ranks of the military. To this very day, there has been virtually no study of nuclear strategy or nuclear weapons in terms of defense considerations. The Japanese people have, of course, been exposed to public discussion of a number of nuclear-related issues: the implications of advances in China's nuclear development; the removal of U.S. nuclear weapons from Okinawa upon its reversion to Japan; the alleged presence of nuclear weapons at U.S. bases elsewhere in Japan, especially following the assertion in 1974 Senate testimony by a retired U.S. naval officer, Rear Admiral Gene R. LaRocque, that U.S. ships do not off-load nuclear weapons before entering Japanese ports; the port calls of the nuclear aircraft carrier Enterprise and of nuclear submarines; and security guarantees for non-nuclear nations in connection with ratification of the NPT. Although a public airing of these issues, many of them highly controversial, may have raised the level of popular awareness concerning nuclear matters and may even have reduced somewhat the intensity of the nuclear allergy, the strong opposition to public discussion of nuclear issues remains virtually undiminished. As long as these attitudes persist, there appears to be little likelihood that nuclear questions will be examined in any greater depth in the future.

By its very nature, however, national security cannot be discussed realistically without reference to the nuclear context. The logic of nuclear questions ought to be vigorously pursued, if only so that Japan might reaffirm as a result of thoughtful strategic analysis its rejection of nuclear weapons and its commitment to world peace. But, as indicated, a willingness to permit such discussions is not as yet widespread.

The Three Non-Nuclear Principles

The most celebrated statement of Japan's nuclear policy is contained in the so-called three non-nuclear principles. The origin of these principles dates back to 1959. Nobusuke Kishi, then the prime minister, stated in Diet interpellations that Japan would neither develop nuclear weapons nor permit them to be brought into the country. The policy of "not possessing, manufacturing, or allowing the introduction of nuclear weapons" was spelled out explicitly by Prime Minister Eisaku Satō during Diet questioning in late 1967. This formulation was incorporated into the text of his administrative policy speech early the next year, and it then became known officially as the three non-nuclear principles.

During the 1968 Diet session, the opposition parties applied pressure on Prime Minister Satō to support adoption of the three non-nuclear principles as a Diet resolution, rather than leaving them merely a policy asserted by the LDP-controlled government. In the face of these pressures, the prime minister declared that Japan's nuclear policy had four pillars, and he came out against a Diet resolution that focused on the three non-nuclear principles. He argued that such a resolution would destroy the integrity of the larger four-pillar policy. The four pillars consisted of:

1. The three non-nuclear principles.
2. Efforts at nuclear disarmament.
3. Reliance on the U.S. nuclear deterrent for Japan's national security and maintenance of the U.S.-Japan security relationship.
4. Development of nuclear energy for peaceful purposes.

The debate between the government and the opposition parties on this issue did not reach any conclusion at the 1968 Diet session. It was not until the 1971 Diet deliberations that the matter was resolved. At that time, the government ceased its advocacy of the four-pillar policy in order to win Diet approval of the agreement by which Okinawa reverted to Japan. Following this concession by the government, the three non-nuclear principles were approved by the House of Representatives as part of a resolution concerning the non-nuclear status of Okinawa and the reduction of U.S. bases there.

The NPT and Japan's Security

Notwithstanding its strong commitment to the non-nuclear principles, Japan did not move to ratify the NPT immediately after signing it in 1970. The government announced that formal ratification would hinge on the satisfactory fulfillment of three conditions: progress in nuclear arms reductions on the part of those states now possessing such weapons, guarantees concerning the security of non-nuclear-weapon states, and equal rights for all nations with respect to the peaceful uses of nuclear energy. Initially, the principal objections to the treaty had to do with economic and technological matters—specifically, the inequality of provisions for inspection of peaceful nuclear facilities and the potential leakage of industrial secrets. These objections were overcome in February 1975, however, when an agreement was signed providing for the same kind of inspection of Japanese facilities as that required of the EURATOM nations.

Nevertheless, opposition to the treaty within the LDP continued to mount during 1975. The basis for this growing unwillingness to ratify the NPT now focused on questions relating to national security. These were the principal arguments advanced:

1. It was to Japan's future advantage to maintain a free hand concerning the nuclear option.
2. The third of the non-nuclear principles, forbidding the introduction of nuclear weapons into Japan, needed to be reexamined.
3. The U.S.-Japan security structure needed to be strengthened.
4. Although there was no reason for adamant opposition to ratification, there was no need to rush into it.

As LDP leaders indicated that they would support ratification only if it were accompanied by a strengthening of the

U.S.-Japan security relationship, the opposition parties, which previously had been favorably disposed toward the treaty, now began to voice reservations. Indeed, the opposition parties decided to oppose ratification and, as a result, no action was taken on the treaty in 1975.

In 1976, however, the government took a strong position favoring ratification. Prime Minister Miki stated clearly to the Diet that the government would not allow the introduction of nuclear weapons under any circumstances, even in the event of an emergency. The opposition parties once again supported the treaty, and the number of stubborn opponents within the LDP diminished. All parties except the Communists voted to ratify the treaty in May 1976.

Recent Trends in Public Attitudes toward Nuclear Weapons

On the NPT question, four of the national dailies supported ratification, while one was somewhat critical of the treaty. Roughly the same pattern holds with respect to the three non-nuclear principles. The "big three" daily newspapers endorse the non-nuclear principles unconditionally, and two smaller dailies are slightly critical, expressing doubts about the desirability of a blanket refusal to allow the introduction of nuclear weapons even in an emergency.

Public opinion polls administered in 1975 produced the following results:

Do you think Japan will go nuclear in the future? (Sankei Shimbun)

	1973	1974	1975
I think so	28%	27%	25%
I don't think so	42	36	30
I cannot judge	29	33	40
I don't know	1	4	5

Do you agree with the three non-nuclear principles?

	Sankei Shimbun	Asahi Shimbun
Agree	67%	77%
Oppose	23	10
Don't know	10	9

Do you think the principle of not allowing nuclear weapons to be brought into Japan is being observed? (Asahi Shimbun)

Is being observed	11%
Is not being observed	67
Other answers	4
No answer	18

In considering these polls, which indicate the continuing strength of public opposition to nuclear weapons, it is worth noting that a growing majority are unwilling to predict that Japan will refrain indefinitely from acquiring nuclear armament. Moreover, although an overwhelming majority support the three non-nuclear principles, there is still a minority that strongly opposes the third principle, which forbids the introduction into Japan of nuclear weapons. And there is, in any case, very substantial doubt in the public mind as to whether that principle is being observed.

It is hard to say how public attitudes with respect to nuclear weapons will develop in the future. But there is certainly no reason to assume that public opinion will permit Japan to acquire its own nuclear weapons at any time in the foreseeable future. Besides, from a geopolitical standpoint Japan is highly vulnerable to nuclear attack; it is almost impossible for Japan to develop an effective and credible nuclear deterrent capable of coping with the major nuclear powers. Possessing a nuclear capability that is inadequate carries with it certain risks, even if such weapons could conceivably offer some military advantages. In any case, Japan's nuclear armament would seem to be ruled out not only by domestic and international political considerations but by calculations of military feasibility as well.

U.S. Forces in Northeast Asia and Nuclear Deterrence

The U.S. Nuclear Deterrent in Korea

Following the Korean War, the United States announced that it would not hesitate to use nuclear weapons if they were needed for the defense of South Korea. It can be assumed that nuclear weapons were deployed in Korea and Okinawa during the 1950s. In June 1975, as is widely known, former Secretary of Defense James Schlesinger officially confirmed the presence of U.S. tactical nuclear weapons in Korea.

When they were first deployed to South Korea, U.S. nuclear weapons were intended to help deter a massive military invasion from China and to limit potential American casualties. Today, in the 1970s, there is a military balance on the Korean peninsula, if one takes into account the role of the U.S. presence there. It is now probable, thanks to the large-scale concentration of U.S. conventional firepower, that an invasion from North Korea could be deterred without having to resort to nuclear weapons. Secretary Schlesinger acknowledged this in his August 1975 press conference. It is anticipated that the military balance on the peninsula will be maintained by complementary measures and that the deterrent will function effectively, even if U.S. ground combat forces withdraw as scheduled.

Admiral LaRocque has laid stress on the dangers of stockpiling nuclear weapons and has urged the removal of nuclear weapons deployed outside the United States. During the 1976 presidential election campaign, Mr. Carter and other Democrats insisted on the pullout of nuclear weapons deployed in South Korea; the issue is still the subject of consultation between the two governments. If indeed these weapons are dangerous to stockpile and are not absolutely essential for South Korea's defense, should the United States withdraw them? The answer is probably no. These are some of the reasons:

1. Maintaining its nuclear weapons in Korea enables the United States to keep open a broader range of options to deal with all contingencies, even though it is unlikely that nuclear weapons would actually be needed to defend South Korea.
2. The withdrawal of nuclear weapons may lower the certainty of America's defense commitment to South Korea in the eyes of other countries, including North Korea. The removal of U.S. nuclear weapons could

only increase the confidence of the North Korean side while reducing that of the South Korean people. In this respect, an analogy might be drawn to the demoralized condition of the South Vietnamese government forces at the end of the fighting.

3. The Defense Department's 1976-1977 white paper indicates that the U.S. military presence in Northeast Asia, including Korea, should be viewed with reference to the global context. In the event of a crisis in Europe, U.S. nuclear weapons, along with aircraft and other components of the U.S. presence in Northeast Asia, are meant to discourage the transfer of Soviet forces currently deployed in Asia to positions west of the Urals. These U.S. forces thus may play a potentially significant role in helping to hold the USSR and China in check. Now that nuclear weapons have been removed from Okinawa, the importance of those nuclear weapons still deployed elsewhere in Asia may have increased. Moreover, the forward deployment of these weapons offers an intrinsic flexibility that cannot be duplicated by nuclear-armed submarines.

If the United States keeps its nuclear weapons in South Korea, they will constitute a deterrent of high credibility. This credibility derives from the expressed willingness of U.S. leaders to use nuclear weapons, if necessary, and from the existence of adequate means of delivery; the effectiveness of nuclear weapons as a deterrent to conflict in Korea is enhanced by the conventional capabilities the United States retains in Korea itself and elsewhere in the region. Of course, given the situation prevailing on the Korean peninsula, the likelihood that nuclear weapons would actually be used is quite low.

Should the United States decide to remove its nuclear weapons from Korea, the impact of this step would depend on what other measures it might take in conjunction with nuclear withdrawal. Although the withdrawal of U.S. nuclear weapons might not lead to a North Korean invasion of the South, it could, as already indicated, present problems not only for South Korea but for other U.S. allies as well. The announcement of a date for the withdrawal of U.S. ground combat forces has increased the potentially destabilizing impact of removing U.S. nuclear weapons from Korea. The negative effects could be minimized, however, if the United States were to take the following steps:

1. Reconfirm the U.S. commitment to the defense of South Korea and, at the same time, issue a clear statement as to why that country's defense is important to the United States.
2. Withdraw gradually and deliberately U.S. ground forces with regard for the maintenance of stability on the peninsula.
3. Persuade North Korea to make some concession equivalent to the removal of U.S. nuclear arms from South Korea, rather than withdrawing them unilaterally.
4. Utilize the removal of nuclear weapons as a basis for promoting discussions among countries concerned about the stability of the Korean peninsula.

Some people argue that it is enough for the United States, if it withdraws its nuclear weapons from South Korea, to say that it will reintroduce them in an emergency. Such an argument may be understandable in military terms, but the problem is a political and psychological one. Accordingly, if nuclear weapons are withdrawn, appropriate measures should be taken to compensate for this. At the very least, it is better to refrain from speaking of the withdrawal in public, as Mr. Carter did during the campaign.

U.S. Forces in Japan and the Nuclear Deterrent

Although no nuclear weapons have been deployed in Japan since their removal from Okinawa, the Third U.S. Marine Division on Okinawa is equipped with howitzers capable of firing 155-millimeter or eight-inch nuclear shells. The 313th U.S. Air Force Division on Okinawa and the 1st Marine Air Division at Iwakuni have F-4s, A-4s, A-6s, and other airplanes capable of carrying nuclear warheads. Since these forces are meant not only for the defense of Japan but also for the broader purpose of helping to maintain military equilibrium and political stability in Asia, it is only natural that they should have nuclear delivery capabilities.

Because no nuclear weapons are deployed in Japan, as they are in other countries protected by the U.S. nuclear umbrella, questions have been raised about the effectiveness of the umbrella for Japan. A segment of the LDP and other Japanese believe that the policy of keeping U.S. nuclear weapons out of Japan even in an emergency reduces the credibility of the nuclear deterrent. Indeed, they have argued that this policy, based on the third of the three non-nuclear principles, is fundamentally inconsistent with the idea of reliance on the U.S. nuclear umbrella. I believe, however, that although adherence to the non-nuclear principles may diminish slightly the credibility of the U.S. nuclear umbrella, it will still be sufficiently effective in an emergency even without the deployment of nuclear weapons to Japan itself.

Although the deployment of nuclear weapons to a particular country is generally thought to heighten the credibility of the nuclear umbrella for that country, the case of Japan is different. Unlike the European countries or Korea, Japan lacks contiguous borders with foreign countries, which means that the kinds of military conflicts that can be expected to occur will also differ from those projected elsewhere. Thus, certain types of nuclear weapons, the development of which may be important for Koreans or Europeans—for example nuclear land mines and surface-to-surface missiles—are unnecessary; indeed, the very need to deploy nuclear weapons is obviated by Japan's geostrategic position.

The capability of U.S. forces in Japan to deliver nuclear warheads, which, as noted, is linked to the larger effort to deter war in Asia generally, contributes to the credibility of the nuclear umbrella by introducing an added element of ambiguity. Potential adversaries must calculate that these delivery systems may be equipped with nuclear warheads during a crisis, notwithstanding Japan's present insistence that it will never permit the entry of nuclear weapons.

Furthermore, the widespread deployment in the Pacific of U.S. naval and air forces, including B-52s, together with the stockpiling of nuclear weapons in numerous locations in the region, makes it possible for nuclear weapons to be utilized against any attacking country. This is something that must be taken into account by any country that might contemplate attacking Japan. The impressive array of U.S. nuclear forces deployed in the Pacific thus provides ample nuclear deterrence from Japan's standpoint, even though nuclear weapons are not deployed in Japan itself.

This means, of course, that the U.S. military presence in the Pacific, particularly that of the Seventh Fleet and the B-52 bombers based at Guam, assumes great importance for Japan. The military balance in Northeast Asia is such that if the U.S. forces were to be withdrawn, the ramifications would be extremely unfavorable for our side. It should be pointed out, however, that because the geopolitical situation and military circumstances in Asia are so different from those in Europe, the relative weight assigned to nuclear weapons as a component of the overall military posture is substantially lower in Asia. One can expect many more cases in Asia than in Europe where the use of nuclear weapons would not be appropriate.

Consequently, if U.S. conventional capabilities in Japan or Korea were to be reduced on the assumption that one could always fall back on the U.S. nuclear deterrent, there would be a considerable sacrifice of flexibility to respond to diverse situations. Under certain circumstances, this loss of flexibility could conceivably lead to an unnecessary lowering of the nuclear threshold, a prospect that would hardly be desirable for either the United States or its allies.

The Nuclear Transit Issue

As indicated in the earlier reference to the testimony of Admiral LaRocque, there has been considerable controversy surrounding allegations that nuclear weapons have entered Japanese territorial waters and ports aboard U.S. naval vessels in transit. The record of port calls made by U.S. ships entering Sasebo and Yokosuka reveals that there were 125 port calls by nuclear submarines from 1964 to 1976, as well as a visit by the nuclear-powered aircraft carrier *Enterprise*. Since 1964, opposition party spokesmen have claimed that these vessels had nuclear weapons aboard when they entered. They have repeatedly argued that this blatantly violates not only Japan's non-nuclear principles but the agreement undertaken in 1960 through an exchange of notes stipulating that the United States would consult Japan in advance concerning any "major changes" to be made in the equipment of U.S. forces in Japan. The Japanese government's response, each time these charges have been raised, has been as follows: "The United States government has stated that it has not violated Japan's basic policies. The introduction of nuclear weapons is cause for prior consultations, to be sure, but as the United States has not yet sought to have prior consultations, it is inconceivable that nuclear weapons are being brought into Japan."

One could argue that the "major changes" referred to in the 1960 exchange of notes should have been interpreted to cover only the deployment or stockpiling of weapons brought into Japan for the purpose of equipping the U.S. forces there, but such an interpretation was never adopted. In the course of Diet debates, it became clear that naval vessels entering Japanese harbors with nuclear weapons aboard fell within the agreed-upon interpretation of "major changes" requiring prior consultations; the U.S. government also has appeared to operate on the basis of this understanding.

Government statements in the Diet concerning the passage of nuclear-weapons-carrying vessels through Japanese territorial waters have tended in the past to be somewhat confused. Today, such passage is regarded as requiring prior consultations. If, however, maritime laws are established creating international straits, then free passage may be recognized, at least as far as certain delineated areas are concerned.

Speaking generally, any restriction on the movement of vessels carrying nuclear weapons will impose restraints on the maneuverability of U.S. forces. For military men, who always seek to maximize freedom of movement, such restraints may be more than a minor inconvenience. But inasmuch as there is not, in Asia, the same need that exists in Europe to maintain a capability for instantaneous nuclear response, existing constraints on the movement of nuclear weapons through Japanese waters are probably permissible from a strategic standpoint; they do not significantly diminish the effectiveness of the nuclear deterrent.

Given Japan's dependence on the U.S. nuclear umbrella, there may be some room for inventiveness in interpreting and implementing the security treaty, should the security of Japan clearly require it. At the present time, however, the intensity of the nuclear allergy does not permit much latitude in these areas. The United States, for its part, must take these popular attitudes into account in determining what use it will make of its bases in foreign countries. If it pays attention to the domestic circumstances prevailing in countries where bases are maintained, the United States is likely to develop a sharper sensitivity to what is politically feasible. In the long run, this will be to the benefit of the United States itself.

Japan's Defense and Evaluation of the U.S. Nuclear Deterrent

Military Threats to Japan and Nuclear Deterrence

Under current world conditions, a military clash between nuclear powers, even one limited to conventional weapons and a restricted geographical area, is extremely dangerous because of the risk that it will escalate to a nuclear war between these countries. Each nuclear power will therefore take special care to avert any confrontation that may lead to war with another country armed with nuclear weapons. According to U.S. military strategy, the avoidance of conflict in Asia depends on the maintenance of an interrelated system of deterrence consisting of conventional and nuclear capabilities in the region and operating against the backdrop of the global strategic balance.

Japan's neighbors, especially the Soviet Union and China, possess overwhelming military power, including nuclear arms. But so long as the security treaty remains in effect, a large-scale military invasion is exceedingly unlikely. Potential aggressors are aware that a direct conventional attack on Japan will immediately encounter a response from U.S. conventional forces and, under certain circumstances, may lead to the use of U.S. tactical or strategic nuclear weapons. Though it is doubtful that the United States would move to raise the conflict to the nuclear level, no country can afford to discount the possibility.

In Europe and Korea, large-scale conventional deployments are required in order to prevent the lowering of the nuclear threshold. But Japan, as an island nation, would not appear to need such massive conventional capabilities so long as U.S. forces can be mobilized speedily. The nuclear threshold can be kept at a high level without any large-scale deployment of conventional forces.

Massive conventional air attacks or naval blockades probably could not force Japan to surrender in a short span of time; if the fighting persists for a long time, it will merely invite the United States and other countries to intervene. A nuclear attack on Japan would not only destroy any spoils of war; it would probably prompt the United States to retaliate with a limited nuclear counterattack. Since this would lead to an asymmetrical situation in which America's homeland does not receive direct damage while the homeland of the other country does, this option would not appear to be very advantageous for the other country. If a land invasion of Japan were attempted, it would require massive troop movements, which would be exposed to U.S. nuclear strikes; if, in order to avert such attacks, invading troops scatter, then they will become vulnerable to counterattack even from conventional forces.

In short, as long as Japan has a reliable and effective conventional capability and the U.S.-Japan security relationship remains in effect, a structure of deterrence based ultimately on the nuclear umbrella and the global strategic posture of the United States will function effectively for Japan.

Conditions for the Use of Tactical Nuclear Weapons in Asia

Apart from the question of whether tactical nuclear weapons ought to be used, I would like to discuss specific conditions relating to the use of nuclear weapons as they affect the credibility of the nuclear deterrent.

It is noteworthy that most countries debating the pros and cons of possessing nuclear weapons are either nonaligned or uncertain about the ultimate reliability of their alliance commitments. These countries also tend to be located in regions where, from a geostrategic point of view, tactical nuclear weapons can be used. In many parts of Asia, however, this is not the case. Vietnam was, on the whole, not well suited for the use of tactical nuclear weapons. Still, it is said that General Westmoreland considered using nuclear weapons to defend Khe Sanh when that marine outpost was surrounded by Vietnamese troops in 1968. If North Korea should launch a full-scale invasion of the South, a major thrust against Seoul may be anticipated. But given the dense concentration of population to the north of Seoul, how could nuclear weapons be used to repel the attacking force?

Although it is generally assumed that nuclear weapons would be utilized for defensive purposes, one would be hesitant actually to resort to such weapons against an invading army that could hide out in vast mountains and forests or melt into the indigenous population, especially when population concentrations are such that severe civilian casualties would be unavoidable. And if the other side should suspect such hesitancy, the deterrent power of nuclear weapons would be weakened. On the other hand, in those areas where the terrain is more suitable for the use of nuclear weapons, the credibility of the deterrent would obviously be higher.

Since any invading force must approach Japan by sea, where nuclear weapons can be used with relative ease, the conditions governing the use of nuclear weapons might seem to enhance the credibility of nuclear deterrence for Japan. But once the invaders land on Japanese soil, nuclear arms cannot easily be fired at them without incurring very high civilian casualties. Moreover, even if the sea offers an environment suitable for the use of tactical nuclear weapons, it would have to be assumed that their actual use would provoke a nuclear response by the enemy. Given the likelihood that the invaders would thus be tempted to employ nuclear weapons against the Japanese islands, which are highly vulnerable to nuclear attack, there would in fact be real constraints on using nuclear weapons at sea.

In order to maintain the credibility of the nuclear deterrent, however, it is necessary to demonstrate a willingness and capability to use nuclear weapons, whatever the circumstances; at the very least, the matter of use must be left unpredictable. In the final analysis, of course, the problem is not military but political, and the necessary judgments will have to be made by political leaders.

Nuclear Deterrence and the Non-Nuclear Principles

The nuclear umbrella of the United States thus has an important role to play in deterring both conventional and nuclear threats, as well as the danger of nuclear blackmail. Quite apart from the question of whether nuclear weapons would actually be used in response to a conventional attack and the related question of whether the use of nuclear weapons would be feasible in light of the prevailing geostrategic conditions, the mere possibility that a conflict may escalate to the nuclear level should serve to give pause to a potential aggressor. As pointed out earlier, it should not be necessary to bring nuclear weapons into Japan to fulfill this function.

Although some may criticize this view as naive or overly optimistic, Japan's dependence on the nuclear umbrella and its continued adherence to the three non-nuclear principles should not be seen as contradictory. Rather, holding to these principles should be viewed as a way of maintaining the security relationship with the United States that benefits both countries, and, at the same time, as a way of respecting popular sentiments in Japan. Even though port calls by nuclear-armed vessels may be substantially different from the deployment of nuclear weapons to Japanese soil and even though there are potential military costs in prohibiting such calls, unless those costs are such as to undermine the effectiveness of the deterrent I believe it is reasonable to pay heed to these domestic political concerns.

Moreover, the fact that Japan has become a non-nuclear sanctuary with no bases from which nuclear strikes might be launched may constitute a form of military force disengagement that could provide some diplomatic leverage in negotiations aimed at furthering détente. In the Cuban missile crisis of 1962, it was understood that the removal of MRBMs from Cuba by the Soviets and Jupiter missiles from Turkey by the Americans contributed to the rapprochement that subsequently developed between Washington and Moscow. It is conceivable that the international recognition of Japan's three non-nuclear principles, together with the withdrawal of U.S. nuclear arms from the Korean peninsula, could, if reciprocated by conciliatory moves by the other side, contribute to a future agreement among the major powers concerned to stabilize the situation on the Korean peninsula.

The Credibility of the U.S. Nuclear Umbrella

Security Guarantees for Allied Nations

In France, doubts about the credibility of America's nuclear umbrella are long-standing and well known. The gist of the French criticism is that the United States would not be willing to jeopardize Washington or New York by retaliating against a nuclear power that had assaulted its ally; in any case, the ally, if attacked, would already be beyond rescue.

There are, however, a variety of ways in which the United States can respond to nuclear threats against an ally: diplomatic protests, nuclear counterthreats, limited use of nuclear arms, massive nuclear retaliation, and others. Moreover, since appropriate responses may differ according to the particular circumstances of the threat and international conditions at the moment, one cannot give a clear and simple response. The level and form of the U.S. reaction to a nuclear threat aimed at an ally will depend on many factors, including the following: the illegality of the threatening country's behavior, the repercussions of the threat for other countries, the strength of the threatened ally's will to resist, and the importance of that country in the scheme of U.S. national interests.

There is no doubt that the French criticisms have brought to light some essential points. America's nuclear retaliation after an allied nation has sustained a large-scale attack will not have much meaning to that ally. But it should be pointed out that these criticisms are based on rather extreme scenarios; real situations are likely to be more varied and complex, and there are effective means of reacting to these situations at all the various levels of nuclear response. It is possible, for example, to answer nuclear coercion with countercoercion, or limited nuclear use with limited counteruse.

A U.S. declaration to use all means at its disposal, including massive nuclear intervention, in order to protect an allied nation, would be effective in making potential adversaries hesitate before taking so great a risk—quite apart from the question of whether they actually believe the United States is likely to make such an extreme response. In this sense, the U.S. nuclear deterrent seems to be functioning effectively in spite of variations in its strength and content as perceived by different countries. Indeed, given the basic policy of détente between nuclear weapon states and given current conditions that work to discourage adventurism, it can be said that the U.S. nuclear umbrella appears to be working adequately. But if the U.S. nuclear umbrella is sufficiently credible for Japan, it may well be that a more difficult problem will concern the kind of guarantees that the United States, and other nuclear powers, can give to nonaligned, non-nuclear-weapon states.

Security Guarantees for Non-Allied, Non-Nuclear Nations

In connection with the NPT, discussions of security guarantees for non-nuclear-weapon states faced with nuclear threats have progressed. The question of security guarantees is a particularly serious matter for those non-nuclear nations that are nonaligned. In anticipation of these concerns, the United States, the Soviet Union, and Great Britain issued a declaration at a June 1968 Security Council meeting to the effect that they would provide immediate assistance, in accordance with the UN Charter, to any non-nuclear-weapon state threatened with nuclear attack. At the same time, the Security Council adopted a resolution concerning the security of non-nuclear-weapon states. The resolution stated that the Security Council "recognizes that aggression with nuclear weapons or the threat of such aggression against a non-nuclear weapon state would create a situation in which the Security Council and above all its nuclear weapon state permanent members would have to act immediately in accordance with their obligations under the United Nations Charter."

Generally speaking, it would probably be undesirable for the United States to respond with nuclear weapons on behalf of nonaligned nations with which it has no formal defense commitments, if only because of the costs that this would incur. But if the area involved is vital to America, then any response—from diplomatic protests to limited nuclear retaliation—might be undertaken by the United States.

If these nonaligned nations have a potential capability to develop nuclear weapons and if they are unable to secure adequate guarantees in the face of threats from nuclear powers, they may very well refuse to adhere to the NPT. The unwillingness of China or France to join the NPT complicates the problem. For nuclear weapon states that regard nuclear proliferation as a grave danger to international security, the question of how credible a guarantee they can provide to these non-nuclear states is a serious matter indeed.

7

The Post-Vietnam Strategic Context in Asia

Franklin B. Weinstein and John W. Lewis

Responses to the War's End

Through the long years of debate over America's involvement in Vietnam, critics and defenders agreed that Vietnam itself held little intrinsic significance for the United States. The case for involvement did not rest on the assumption that communist control of South Vietnam's people or resources in itself posed any direct threat to U.S. interests. Rather, Vietnam's importance, it was argued, derived from the likely impact of a communist victory on other noncommunist countries. Above all, defending South Vietnam would affect U.S. security because Washington had made a commitment there. The war was a test of America's perseverence in fulfilling its commitments; the fact of the commitment rendered irrelevant the question of whether it ought to have been made.

The assumed interdependence of commitments has underlain the entire security structure established by the United States in the postwar era. Successive U.S. leaders have asserted that a failure to meet any commitment would imperil all other commitments and inevitably the United States itself. Negotiated during the 1950s, these commitments were undertaken primarily with reference to a global threat. Washington, perceiving an essentially monolithic communist menace under Moscow's direction, determined that communist expansion in Asia could be blocked or turned back by convincing Soviet leaders that the cost of aggression anywhere would be unacceptably high. Inevitably this determination became linked to the deterrence of nuclear assaults and other threats aimed directly at the United States. The logic of deterrence dictated, moreover, that even a commitment made in error—or without due recognition of the potentially high costs to the United States—had to be honored in order to preserve the total strategic structure.

U.S. Commitments and Reactions of America's Asian Allies

From Dulles to Kissinger, U.S. secretaries of state asserted that U.S. security was only as strong as its weakest link.[1] Thus the collapse of Saigon amid charges by President Thieu that the United States had betrayed its commitments to his government understandably raised questions among some of the other countries whose security rested on U.S. guarantees. The South Koreans, for example, were obviously alarmed at the possible implications of America's Vietnam debacle for their survival, and Kim Il-sung's provocative statements in Peking in late April 1975 intensified their fears. Tokyo, too, expressed considerable unease about the possibility of intensified hostilities on the Korean peninsula. In the wake of Saigon's collapse, Foreign Minister Miyazawa indicated that he would seek additional reassurances concerning the U.S. security guarantee to Japan.[2] Apprehension that the United States might now renege on its Asian commitments beyond Vietnam was also evident in President Marcos's sharp questioning of the value of the U.S. commitment to the Philippines.[3] An unidentified "top official" in the Philippines declared: "We are disturbed by an emerging view that commitments made by U.S. Presidents are nothing more than statements of intent that do not bind the American people or Congress. . . . We have to ask ourselves whether we can continue to be involved in conflicts and animosities engendered by policies not our own."[4] Even leaders of countries not formally aligned with the United States openly doubted Washington's dependability. Singapore's Lee Kuan Yew termed the Vietnam defeat an "unmitigated disaster" and questioned the United States' ability to defeat aggression in the future.[5] And Indonesia's Foreign Minister Malik chided the United States for failing to honor its commitments.[6]

These initial reactions of dismay were diluted by muted expressions of relief and, in some cases, by a barely concealed gloating over the embarrassment suffered by the United States. Many Asians also believed that the U.S. withdrawal from Vietnam, whatever the circumstances, might enhance security in Asia and even add to the credibility of some U.S. commitments. Washington's Asian allies could feel a special sense of relief that the war had finally ended and that the United States had at last extricated itself from a quagmire that had drained its energies and threatened to push its people toward isolationism. For the Japanese and South Koreans, the war's conclusion promised a restoration of priority to Northeast Asia, an area strategically far more vital to U.S. interests than Vietnam. Besides, America's allies, for the most part, had never truly regarded Vietnam as the ultimate test of U.S. power. They feared, however, that if the United States considered Vietnam to be such a test, then a U.S. defeat could precipitate an abrupt U.S. abandonment of Asia, thrusting nations that had relied on Washington into an uncertain future.[7] And even Asian leaders who reproved the United States for its unreliability observed that Saigon's fall was mainly its own doing; its inability to mobilize its own people had led to excessive and eventually self-defeating dependence on an outside power.[8]

The United States moved quickly to ease the anxieties of its allies by reasserting an undiminished determination to keep its remaining commitments. Even before the final collapse of the Saigon government, Washington had begun the process of reassuring its allies that the United States would stand by its commitments to them, regardless of the outcome in Vietnam. This process was intensified after the communist victory in May 1975. The conspicuous display of U.S. military power in freeing the *Mayaguez*, the reassurances given Prime Minister Miki in his August visit to Washington, Defense Secretary Schlesinger's summer visit to Japan and Korea and his declaration of America's readiness to use tactical nuclear weapons in defense of Korea, and President Ford's enunciation of a Pacific Doctrine in December 1975 were all part of the effort to persuade those still tied to U.S. commitments that the United States remained a reliable ally.

Soviet and Chinese Reactions

The immediate Soviet and Chinese public reactions to the communist victory in South Vietnam were, given the magnitude of the event, cautious and ambiguous.[9] There was no indication that either Moscow or Peking expected any direct payoffs; neither power could be sure how the victory would affect its overall position vis-à-vis the other in Indochina. Chinese military forces remained in northern Laos, but the North Vietnamese and Soviets reportedly were gaining influence elsewhere in the tiny state.[10] The Chinese had the most pervasive contacts, if not real influence, with the new Cambodian leaders, who were, in general, quite cool toward the Soviet Union and all other foreign states.[11] Moscow appeared to be in the stronger position among the Vietnamese, though the possibility of acquiring military bases that might serve Soviet interests against China or the United States would have to be weighed against probable Vietnamese fears of provoking China and Hanoi's quest for costly reconstruction support from China and the U.S.

Despite the military developments associated with major Soviet naval exercises in April and the *Mayaguez* incident in May, Moscow's reactions struck a distinctly political note, particularly after the end of the Helsinki conference in Europe.[12] Soviet leaders more actively promoted the idea of an Asian collective security system and denounced as Peking propaganda any suggestion that such an arrangement could be threatening to Asians.[13] The meager results produced by Soviet overtures for closer ties with Japan were probably the best evidence that, on balance, the Soviet strategic position in Asia had not been visibly enhanced by the American loss in Indochina. Nor did the noncommunist states of South and Southeast Asia appear to perceive any measurable increase in the Soviet threat to their security, despite rumors of Soviet military moves in the area.

China's official reaction to the communist victory in Saigon, while certainly supportive, struck a public note of reconciliation.[14] Peking celebrated the victory by completing negotiations for diplomatic relations with the Philippines and Thailand and by giving assurances to Americans, Japanese, and others that it wished the United States to maintain its presence in Asia, particularly its alliance relationships. The Chinese leaders seemed to evaluate ongoing developments in Asia in a global context and pressed the United States to challenge Soviet power with greater force and will. The secretary of state reportedly stated that the Chinese attributed Washington's failure in Vietnam to its pursuit of unrealistic goals, thus calling into question its capability to block Soviet threats in other arenas.[15] The United States was now a "wounded tiger," and China seemed willing to help it recuperate so that it could more effectively counter Soviet power.

This sentiment was echoed in Peking during the December visit by President Ford. There, at a press conference on December 4, 1975, the secretary of state noted that if war should occur and "should there be military expansion, I believe that the United States would see the problem quite similarly [with the PRC]."[16] He cited U.S.-Japan relations as an example of parallel policies being pursued by Peking and Washington and said that such policies "consist of the perceptions of what is needed to maintain peace and equilibrium." In an autumn interview, a senior Chinese leader had made the identical point about common interests and remarked that key issues are viewed "from the level of global strategy." By comparison, he said, lesser matters "are only trivial, 'like chicken feathers and onion skin.'"

Evidence of the limits to the parallelism in the strategic thinking of Washington and Peking emerged in their assessment of the Korean problem. In reaffirming Washington's intent to defend the Seoul government, Secretary of Defense James Schlesinger indicated that the United States was not only holding firm on the positioning of its forces near the truce line and on its right to use tactical nuclear weapons, but was also opposed to any fundamental rethinking of its Korean position, for fear that this would play into the communists' hands.[17] The Chinese recognized American and Japanese uneasiness about Korea and, by their initial reluctance to help allay those fears, seemed to confirm Washington's estimate that the danger of armed conflict in Korea was great. Two U.S. congressional delegations to China in the late summer of 1975 concluded that the Chinese had found it necessary to support the North Koreans as the sole legal sovereign state on the peninsula both out of fear of losing influence over Korea to the Soviets and because continued tensions in Northeast Asia could put pressure on the Japanese in ongoing negotiations between Tokyo and Peking on a peace and friendship treaty.

Indirectly, however, the Chinese downgraded Korea's significance and its potential for conflict in contrast to Washington's view. Chinese leaders told the congressional delegations that "as long as [South Korea's] Park does not wage a war there will be nothing significant happening" in the area. The Chinese argued that the real problems were in Europe "because Soviet moves in Asia are secondary,"[18] a line reflected in the Chinese slogan that Moscow "is making a feint to the East while attacking to the West."[19] In the end, the Chinese assessment, rather than the more pessimistic initial American view, seemed to have validity.

Southeast Asia

Although the end of the Vietnam war toppled no dominoes in Southeast Asia, civil strife, often abetted by communist forces, did continue. The victory of the Khmer Rouge in Cambodia, of course, preceded the collapse of the Saigon government; the Pathet Lao's subsequent accession to power was abetted by the events in Laos's neighbors, though the outcome can hardly be said to have been determined by those events.

Beyond Indochina, the initial effects of the communist victory in Vietnam were minimal.[20] In Thailand, bandits, Muslim separatists, and communist insurgents reportedly became more active along the Thai-Malaysian border. Thai military officials speculated that additional weapons might have become available to the insurgents from Vietnam, but since these rebels had long received arms and training from Hanoi, no major change in the situation was indicated.[21] U.S. intelligence analysts reported increased infiltration into Thailand from Laos and warned of a possible massive rise in such infiltration in late 1976 or early 1977.[22] The Thai situation did grow more precarious after the coup of October 1976, which brought about a sharp polarization within the country and increased the danger that a major civil war might develop. But the predicted increase in infiltration did not occur, and the problems Thailand faced were largely of its own making.

Malaysia's rebellion, clearly growing more serious, had an even more tenuous link to the Vietnam war's end than Thailand's. Insurgent terrorism had been increasing in Malaysia before the communist victory in Vietnam, though the insurgents, operating from sanctuaries in southern Thailand, reportedly numbered no more than 2,000 and were nearly all ethnic Chinese.[23] The largest insurgency active in Southeast Asia in 1975 was the Moro National Liberation Front, a separatist Muslim movement in the southern Philippines. With an estimated 16,000-20,000 men under arms, it had no connection with communism in Vietnam or elsewhere. Its principal supplier of weapons was Libya. The New People's Army in Luzon, consisting of 1,800 armed men, represented no immediate threat but was reported to be building up its strength.[24]

More important than the possibility that Thai or Malaysian insurgents might have taken some small measure of encouragement from the communist victory in Vietnam was the intensification of steps to normalize relations with Peking and other communist governments. In November Thailand established diplomatic relations with Cambodia, and the way was cleared for diplomatic relations with Hanoi pending resolution of the Vietnamese demand that airplanes flown to Thailand in the last days of the former Saigon government be returned.[25] Thailand also indicated a readiness to support Malaysia's call for creation of a zone of peace and neutrality in the ASEAN region,[26] as did Indonesia's Foreign Minister Malik.[27] And the Philippines in early May called for a nonaggression pact in Southeast Asia and the expansion of ASEAN, possibly to include the new communist regimes of Cambodia and South Vietnam.[28] By 1976, all of the ASEAN nations had agreed to establish diplomatic relations with the unified Socialist Republic of Vietnam.

The shift toward accommodation became a hallmark of Southeast Asian policies in 1975, and perhaps the sharpest break with the past was the acceleration of the process of dismantling the Southeast Asian security structure of the 1950s and 1960s. In early March, the Thai government, bidding for political support from liberal and left-wing elements, set an eighteen-month deadline for the withdrawal of U.S. forces from Thailand.[29] Following the *Mayaguez* incident, Thailand and the United States agreed to cooperate in meeting that deadline.[30] In July 1976, the last U.S. troops left, except for 250 advisers operating under the military aid agreement.

In late April 1975 the Philippines formally notified the United States of its decision to discuss changes in the agreements covering U.S. bases. President Marcos suggested that the U.S. Congress's unwillingness to authorize aid to America's allies might make the bases of doubtful value. In July he further declared that his government would seek control of all U.S. bases in the Philippines, while allowing the United States use of certain facilities.[31] Senior officials accompanying President Ford to Manila in December indicated that Washington was not prepared to yield to Marcos's demands but might accept an arrangement under which the American flag would be lowered at the bases to provide what one official called "a cosmetic form of sovereignty that would improve his [Marcos's] standing among third-world nations of Asia."[32] The issue continued unresolved into 1977.

Viewing Southeast Asia as a whole, Arthur W. Hummel, Jr., then assistant secretary of state for East Asian and Pacific affairs, testified in late 1976 that the initial post-Vietnam fears among the ASEAN nations had "largely subsided." In Hummel's words, "Since the fall of Saigon, we have not seen a major increase in the level of Communist insurgent activity in Southeast Asia." He added that "none of the insurgencies represents a threat to the existence of the central government of the country in which it operates."[33]

Impact of the War's End on U.S.-Japan Relations

What did these developments mean for the U.S.-Japanese alliance? With the exception of their fears about Korea, the Japanese expressed little concern about direct or immediate threats to their security in the post-Vietnam era. In September the Japanese Foreign Ministry's annual diplomatic blue paper stressed Japan's role as a stabilizing force and urged cooperation in the economic as well as the military area to ensure security.[34] The following month Japan Defense Agency Director-General Michita Sakata announced that Japan's new defense plan would be based on the assumption that the next ten years would be a time of peace for Japan, and the plan accordingly was to be scaled down to account for the reduced level of threats and for continuing economic constraints.[35] From the Japanese standpoint, Vietnam had long been considered a remote land of peripheral interest, and the Southeast Asian developments taking shape in the wake of the U.S. defeat seemed of limited strategic significance. By early August Japanese leaders had stated that the basic situation remained "much as before."[36] Sakata declared in a November interview that the communist victory in Vietnam had had "very little" impact on Japan's defense strategy; if there had been any influence on Japan at all, it had been "purely psychological."[37]

Japan's principal concern was how the United States would continue to ensure the security and stability of Northeast Asia. Considerable doubt was also expressed about what Washington expected of Japan in the building of a defense structure for the new era. And these concerns inevitably led many Japanese to wonder whether they should not, in reassessing their relationship with the United States, prepare to do more to provide for their own defense.

Perhaps the greatest significance of the post-Vietnam debate over Japan's potential defense role lay in the fact that it took place at all. Though the discussion of Sakata's plan for modest military development produced few signs that Japan would depart from its military reliance on the United States, the question of Japan's defense role had now become an open subject for serious public discussion. Although few Japanese judged the end of the Vietnam war as the beginning of a more menacing era for Japan, Tokyo had to consider the limitations on U.S. power in planning for the future. The Japanese argued that Japan might have to defend itself at some later date. In a speech in December, Sakata noted the continuing importance of military security and urged his countrymen to "have a strong will to resist aggression and an unbending spirit to defend the country."[38] The Japanese seemed reluctant, however, to assume any major new military posture, resisting any substantial increase in "burden sharing" and any commitment to defend neighboring countries.[39] Thus the debate about defense strategy continued within the framework of assumed military dependency on the United States.

Indeed, the principal new theme in U.S.-Japan relations in the months after the end of the Vietnam war was toward closer consultation. This emphasis in part reflected the reaffirmation of long-standing Japanese ties with the United States and assumed the essential viability of the relationship. In the summer of 1975 both parties discussed the creation of a "consultative mechanism" that would give the Japanese a greater degree of confidence in their defense ties to the United States. Tokyo, for its part, wished to create a forum to clarify how U.S. bases in Japan would be used in an emergency; to keep it informed with respect to U.S. planning, and to provide an opportunity for Japanese officials to express their views and requirements to their American allies.[40] As a result, Secretary Schlesinger and Director-General Sakata initiated planning for the formation of a top-level staff committee to coordinate defense planning and operations. The closeness in U.S.-Japan relations signified by this agreement found expression as well in Secretary

Kissinger's speech before the Japan Society in June. In that address, Kissinger pledged that the United States would not "turn away" from Asia and asserted that the United States, having "learned from experience," had managed to overcome the strains in its relations with Japan evident several years earlier.[41] The emperor's visit to the United States in October, reciprocating President Ford's trip to Japan a year earlier, also served to symbolize the strength of the United States–Japan relationship in the post-Vietnam era.

The War's End and the Strategic Context in Asia

A striking characteristic of Asian international affairs since the war's end is how little the strategic context appears to have been altered by the Indochina denouement. A major reason for the unexpectedly modest impact of Vietnam's fall is that the fundamental strategic context had been changing for the previous fifteen years in ways that had made the war far less significant and relevant. Between 1960 and 1975, several major developments had transformed the relationships among the major powers and become the basis for a new strategic context.

First, the Sino-Soviet dispute had grown more serious and had increasingly assumed military as well as political dimensions. Second, the U.S. dominance in strategic weapons and more recently on the high seas had ended. Parity and, in some cases, an alleged U.S. inferiority had prompted greater independence on the part of states that had previously linked their futures and survival to the United States. Third, these changes in basic security patterns were coupled with the increasing economic power of previously dependent states, particularly Japan and the oil-producing countries. The combination of the oil crisis and the American recession called into question continued economic reliance on the United States and challenged countries such as the United States and Japan to work out new modalities of economic cooperation consistent with the changes in basic security patterns. This challenge took on a particularly urgent cast in 1971, when the United States and China ushered in ping-pong diplomacy and upset a fundamental assumption of the previous strategic context (and one of the rationales for the Vietnam war itself)—namely, that Chinese power presented the greatest challenge to the stability of Asia.

These several shifts in power and the resultant alignments were enshrined in the Nixon Doctrine, which stated:

> First, the United States will keep all of its treaty commitments. . . . Second, we shall provide a shield if a nuclear power threatens the freedom of a nation allied with us or of a nation whose survival we consider vital to our security. . . . Third, in cases involving other types of aggression we shall furnish military and economic assistance when requested in accordance with our treaty commitments. But we shall look to the nation directly threatened to assume the primary responsibilities for providing the manpower for its defense.[42]

Such a formal expression of the new strategic context when coupled with the staged withdrawal of U.S. forces from Vietnam and détente with China and the Soviet Union helped offset the impact of the war's end in Indochina.

A central result of these long-developing changes in the strategic context was a diminution of the U.S. capacity to structure political relationships in Asia by the direct application of military or economic power. This trend also reflected an altered domestic political context in the United States, where support for overseas military operations had dwindled. The new situation conformed to the reality of diverse and hostile relationships among the communist states and their inability to act in concert, which contributed to a diminishing sense of any need for the United States to project its military power into various Asian situations.

The war's end brought to a conclusion what had seemed an interminable search for a way to avoid humiliation in fulfilling a commitment to an ally whose long-term prospects had always remained bleak. Once the "sourest contingency" had come to pass, the years of striving to avoid failure appeared to have been far more painful than the failure itself. Now it is apparent that the war's end and the subsequent changes of government in Washington, Tokyo, and Peking have provided the United States and its Asian allies a good opportunity to reassess their security policies and fit them to a basic strategic context that has changed considerably. So long as the war persisted and old leadership prevailed, it was very difficult for the United States to undertake such a reassessment.

The collapse of America's allies in Indochina need not be viewed merely as a defeat for U.S. foreign policy. If the words of both American and Asian leaders are to be taken seriously, the accelerated trend toward self-reliance on the part of America's Asian allies can only be viewed as a favorable result of the war's end. For the first time in more than four decades, policy-makers have been presented with an opportunity to develop concepts of security for an Asia that seems likely to remain at peace. The question is: will the initial reaffirmation of U.S. military strength and commitments after the Indochina debacle inhibit or assist that process of rethinking old concepts and adapting them to the changed strategic context? We now turn to some questions that might be considered as part of that process of rethinking.

The Need for Change in Prevailing Concepts of Security

Old Policies for a New Strategic Context?

Recent studies of Asian security, and especially those focusing on U.S.-Japan security relations, have produced an anomaly: they elucidate the changed strategic context, but then make policy recommendations that call for perpetuation of the status quo. In the case of U.S.-Japan relations, the only recommendation for a significant change of policy is for the intensification of consultation.[43] More generally, the promise of a new look under both the Ford and Carter administrations has yet to yield any fundamental change. Is it not curious that security policies that were formulated in response to a strategic context markedly different from the one prevailing today should still be deemed appropriate?

There are reasons for thinking that significant changes may be needed. In the first place, the commitments that constitute the heart of U.S. security policies in Asia were made in the strategic context of the 1950s. these commitments, as we have noted, assumed the dominant power of the United States and the implacable hostility of relationships with presumed adversaries, especially the People's Republic of China. The reduced capacity of the United States to project its military power unchallenged and the possibilities of constructive interaction with the Chinese raise questions about a defense policy based on contrary assumptions. For one thing, public opinion cannot be expected to support all of the commitments recently reaffirmed by the United States when those pledges are based on such outmoded assumptions about the nature of the strategic context.[44] The fundamental questions, we believe, concern the feasibility and the wisdom of perpetuating America's Asian commitments in their current form. As will be seen, we raise these questions in order to bring commitments into line with attainable objectives on the assumption that this would bolster, not shatter, Asian security.

The questions of feasibility and wisdom are not merely a matter of determining whether conditions have changed with reference to particular commitments. Many U.S. commitments, if examined individually, probably were never feasible to implement. Most of those commitments were undertaken as part of a global bargaining process with the Soviet Union, a fact well known to at least some of America's allies.[45] The United States adopted what Hans Morgenthau has called a "collector's approach" to alliances, signing up members and making commitments in the belief that the more countries it could persuade to be its allies and accept its commitments, the greater its success in competition with the Soviet Union. Many of these commitments, such as the one in Vietnam, were undertaken haphazardly and without agreement on the intrinsic importance of the area concerned or the feasibility of defending it against all dangers. Because U.S. policy-makers in the 1950s regarded communist movements as surrogates for Soviet power, they assumed that any threat would lead to a confrontation with the Soviet Union, with the matter resolved at that level. In the era of massive retaliation and "no more Koreas," Washington undertook commitments on the assumption that it was unlikely to be called upon to implement them. Few seriously contemplated how the United States might actually conduct any limited wars to fulfill those commitments.

By the 1960s, this approach to commitments had become wedded to the logic of deterrence theories, which explicitly separated the act of commitment from the substance of the commitment. Herman Kahn's phrase "the rationality of irrationality" points to the advantages of making a commitment in order to establish a general principle, such as the unwillingness to permit the communists to take any Western area by force, even though it would not serve the national interest to carry out the course of action prescribed by the particular commitment.[46] Again it was assumed that commitments probably would not have to be implemented at lower levels of threat because neither side was likely to risk the final escalation to nuclear war. The logic of deterrence theories led inescapably to the conclusion that all commitments, although not of the same weight in U.S. interests, were interdependent and would have to be honored with equal zeal. Where deterrence logic was intended to free non-strategic interests from nuclear threats, the reverse in fact occurred. Commitments of all kinds became less conditional, more crucial, and more subject to global criteria.

Vietnam, of course, demonstrated the basic fallacy of attempting to apply deterrence logic to all commitments, especially those tied to ambiguous situations. Although the downgrading of counterinsurgency was already anticipated in the Nixon Doctrine, the suddenness of South Vietnam's collapse forcibly convinced many military planners that a commitment to contain insurgents was unattainable in most places and that any linkage of such an effort to strategic deterrence was undoubtedly unwise as well. In the aftermath of the Vietnam debacle the United States apparently began to detach counterinsurgency warfare from its list of "strategic" commitments, curtailing training programs for that contingency. Yet the Nixon Doctrine and President Ford's Pacific Doctrine reaffirmed all U.S. commitments, even though the real threat in some of the countries concerned, such as the

Philippines, Thailand, and perhaps even South Korea, was likely to come from insurgent movements. The question is: at what point will U.S. commitments be activated? In the past the United States has sought to clarify its commitments by asserting that their interdependence made it essential to implement them all. In light of the Vietnam experience and Washington's decision not to fight the kinds of wars that seem most likely in the countries the United States is obligated to defend, one might question the wisdom of that response. It may well have been necessary for Washington to give reassurances to its allies after the fall of Saigon in order to provide a breathing spell of stability, but it would be most unfortunate if those reassurances should prevent the United States and its allies from undertaking a serious reappraisal of the meaning and extent of all existing commitments.

Close consultation between the United States and its allies is desirable as the reappraisal proceeds. This is bound to produce a new relationship between the United States and Asian countries, reflecting the surfacing of demands and grievances. Yet this two-way relationship is needed, not only so that all parties can be confident that they are being kept informed of their allies' plans and the intelligence estimates on which those plans are based. If a commitment is worth retaining, then it ought to be made clear under what conditions and with what forces it is to become operational; it is also important to establish a decision-making mechanism through which all partners can participate in determining the policies on which their security rests.

There is, however, need for caution lest increased consultation be viewed as an end in itself and as a substitute for a serious reappraisal of all policies and their underlying premises. New mechanisms for consultation and decision making provide a framework within which to search for ways of accommodating conflicting interests, but they do not resolve those conflicts. For example, the contradiction between Washington's desire for flexibility in using its Japan-based forces outside Japan and the Japanese desire to determine, or at least influence, decisions concerning the deployment of any forces based in Japan will not disappear with the creation of a new consultative mechanism. Nor does increased consultation speak to the problem of formulating security policies that can muster enough public support to be politically viable. It serves little purpose if the U.S. and Japanese governments in consultation agree on policies that they may for domestic reasons be powerless to implement. Indeed, an emphasis on consultation in the absence of a rethinking of how commitments fit the strategic environment *and* domestic political realities may only raise false expectations, leading subsequently to bitterness and frustration.

Need for a Broader Concept of Security

The need for rethinking extends beyond the question of commitments to the concept of security itself. Suggesting new policies, as we have discovered in our own efforts to answer the questions we have posed, is an extraordinarily complex task. This may not be merely a reflection of the fact that it is easier to pose questions than to answer them. It may well be that analyses of strategic change have tended to lead back to existing policies because of the narrowness of the prevailing U.S. concept of security and the breadth of its notion of threats.

The United States, in its preoccupation with the credibility of its commitments, has tended to view the security of Asia as dependent mainly on its firmness in standing by pledges. The determination to demonstrate the credibility of U.S. commitments in simple "yes" or "no" terms, however, has sometimes precluded serious consideration of alternative approaches to security and has produced a somewhat simplistic notion of what constitutes security.

To begin with, it may be necessary to recognize, as many now do in Washington, that there is no such thing as "the security of Asia." In the present strategic context, there is little basis for assuming that all Asian "security situations" are linked. It would be more useful to think of the security of various Asian countries (and in some cases parts of countries) rather than "the security of Asia." Nor does security necessarily mean the same thing to all Asian and U.S.

leaders. To Washington, it may mean curbing the influence of particular communist countries or of communism in general; to some Asian leaders, it may mean the suppression of ethnic separatist movements or of other domestic political opponents. U.S. leaders tend to conceive of security in narrowly military terms; some Asian leaders, among them many Japanese, are inclined to perceive policies dealing with trade and energy, or foreign economic aid and investment, as critical components of a security policy.

Within the United States itself, the government's tendency to place heaviest emphasis on the military dimensions of security has come under increasing attack as security issues have grown more politicized. Clearly, security has come to mean different things to different domestic groups. Some U.S. leaders speak of the maintenance of Asian security through U.S. commitments, but many Americans have questioned whether aiding a narrowly based regime merely because it is anticommunist really adds to U.S. security and, if so, just what security means. It is hard to say how generalized or ambiguous challenges from the Soviet Union, China, or North Korea are likely to be interpreted. An example is the question of how to assess the further increase of Soviet naval forces in the western Pacific. Nor can anyone predict with confidence how the U.S. Congress would vote if a significant threat of insurgency were to arise in South Korea.[47]

Assessing the likely effect of any given measure taken in the name of security has grown still more difficult as strategic issues have become politicized. As Henry Rowen has noted, confusion even about the meaning of the concept "strategic" has sometimes made debates on U.S.-Soviet arms control negotiations fruitless or misleading.[48] Consider, for example, the controversy over the "strategic" implications of precision-guided munitions (PGMs). Many arms control specialists view these weapons with alarm, principally because they can increase the accuracy of nuclear-tipped missiles and thus threaten fixed land-based systems. But other specialists have suggested that the introduction of PGMs, say in South Korea, could stabilize the situation, enhancing Korean security while facilitating the removal of U.S. tactical nuclear weapons from the peninsula and making it unnecessary for Seoul to seek an independent nuclear capability.[49] If the introduction of PGMs did lead in these directions, then some arms control proposals (for regional no-first-use or nuclear-free zones in Northeast Asia) might come to warrant a second look.

Finally, the debate on security has grown still more confused as the likelihood of hostilities has diminished. How is the concept of security affected by the assumption that peace will probably prevail? What kinds of armed forces and weapons systems are needed, and can be politically supported, under these circumstances? What levels of U.S. guarantees are needed in the future to prevent, say, Taiwan or South Korea from acquiring nuclear weapons?

There are no easy answers to all of the questions we have raised about the adequacy of existing concepts of security. But some hints as to new ways of thinking about security issues, especially as they affect U.S.-Japan relations, have come from the writings of Japanese specialists on security affairs. In contrast to the tendency among Americans to propose old policies for the new strategic context, these Japanese have observed that key changes in the strategic context are likely to demand policies of a different order. Fuji Kamiya, for example, has noted that the emergence of China as a global force means that the United States and Japan must now view Asian affairs in a different context, with inevitable differences in their interpretation of various issues. Kamiya thus calls for a "new concept" to replace the "complacent partnership" that existed in the 1960s.[50] Kiichi Saeki has noted that in a multipolar world it is neither desirable nor possible for Japan "to depend decisively on the United States for any length of time."[51] He points out that some vital security needs, such as access to sea-lanes, can better be achieved by economic and diplomatic means than by military action. Building on an earlier proposal by Shinkichi Eto,[52] Saeki calls for a multilateral approach to security, with the U.S.-Japan Security Treaty supplemented by nonaggression pacts with China and the USSR and by economic and cultural cooperation. He suggests that "the most effective way to maintain friendly relations with the United States is to improve relations with the Soviet Union and China."[53] A strategic environment in which the United States continues to engage in simultaneous negotiation and rivalry with the Soviet Union and China may be to Japan's advantage, since it "could heighten the relative attractiveness of Japan to all three countries."

This line of thinking runs counter to the basic notions underpinning the security relationship established in the 1950s—namely, that security can best be secured by a close relationship with the United States and the maintenance of political distance from the Soviet Union and China. By taking a broader view of security, such an approach moves the discussion outside the continuing military dependence on the United States and into an arena in which Japan, and other U.S. allies, possess a greater range of independent options. If Saeki's proposals are followed to their logical conclusions, they could lead to a conception of security in which questions about the credibility of U.S. commitments are no longer central.[54]

Security in Post-Vietnam Asia: Concepts and Policies

Emphasis on Nonmilitary Approaches

We have suggested that a realistic adaptation to the post-Vietnam era requires a conception of security that goes beyond the previous preoccupation with military alliances and commitments. Given a strategic context that permits Japanese defense planners to assume a decade of peace, security appears to depend less on military arrangements and more on a range of economic, diplomatic, and military measures aimed at preventing dominance by either Moscow or Peking. Of considerable importance are the political steps that Moscow and Peking themselves can be expected to take in order to curb each other's influence.

In the current international environment, economic incentives that give a potential adversary nation a positive interest in cooperation may not only be as effective in maintaining peace as a military alliance; they would also appear to have the important added advantage of countering the implicit assumption of enduring hostility that underlies a military alliance. This obvious and often overstated point still lacks salience in what policy-makers do as opposed to what they say. As perceived military threats recede, security is likely to be sought increasingly through policies aimed at ensuring sources of raw materials, market outlets, and access to sea-lanes, which, as Saeki has pointed out, can much more easily be attained by economic and diplomatic means than by military ones. Indeed, many Japanese have already come to evaluate their security from this perspective, and Americans might consider its relevance to the United States. Japan's nonmilitary approach to security may well be an effort to make a virtue of necessity, but the virtue is no less real. Although the Japanese obviously have felt freer to play down the military aspects of security because they have been able to rely on U.S. defense guarantees, the United States, without abandoning its determination to maintain a position of military strength, has the opportunity to place greater emphasis in its security policies on economic co-operation. To the Japanese, how the United States responds to its request for assured supplies of nuclear fuels and for equality of access to sensitive enrichment and reprocessing technology will indicate how far the United States is prepared to go in changing this emphasis.

The policies of the United States and its Asian allies have in fact already begun moving toward a broader concept of security. But they could go much further; one reason why they have not is that conceptualization about security has lagged behind policies. The prevailing emphasis on the credibility of military commitments as the underpinning of the U.S. security structure, with its assumption of a continuing enemy relationship with the communist powers, imposes severe restraints on economic and political interaction.

If allowed to develop freely, that interaction could give old adversaries a vital stake in continued amicable relations with one another. For example, Japan's energy needs for both fossil and nuclear fuels could lead to commercial arrangements between Japan and the People's Republic of China in oil development and between Japan and the Soviet Union for natural gas and enriched uranium. Of course, any dependence by Japan on these powers could conceivably make it subject to blackmail. This risk could be greatly reduced if the United States were to develop a coherent national energy policy with due regard for the vital needs of its allies. In any case, given the magnitude of the Japanese economy, Moscow and Peking might well find that develop-ment of their energy exports to Japan creating a stronger interest in Japan's stability and continued economic viabil-ity.[55] This would be even more likely if the relationships were to become more interdependent, with China and the Soviet Union relying on Japanese technology, capital, and trade.

Economic measures taken with the new security possibil-ities in mind could help blunt any aggressive impulses harbored by the communist leaders of Indochina or North Korea. Although it is naive to believe that wars are caused or prevented by economic considerations alone, those con-siderations can and do play a major part in the events leading to conflict or cooperation. Japan has taken the lead in developing economic relations with these states.[56] The PRC's trade with Japan and the West has already become a major factor influencing China's international outlook. The further development of Japanese economic relations with North Korea, for example, can eventually have an important moderating effect on Pyongyang; a desire to avoid jeopardizing those relations could become a significant obstacle to any aggressive actions vis-à-vis South Korea. U.S. economic relations with North Korea could accelerate this process. And there is certainly much that the United States could do in Southeast Asia to give its former adversaries a stake in the preservation of peace. Washington, which has been generous in aiding its defeated enemies in the past, could consider responding positively to the overtures from Hanoi for economic aid.[57] Congressional reluctance to support such aid may well diminish as relations between Washington and Hanoi improve. In any case, trade relations provide a place to begin. The point is not that these economic relationships will work wonders, but that a revised concept of security could make some economic policies relevant and effective for security purposes.

Encourage Multialignment

Closely related to the emphasis on nonmilitary approaches to security is the concept of multialignment. The multipolar strategic context of the 1970s makes it possible for the United States and its allies to develop relations with their presumed communist adversaries without jeopardizing their basic relationship with one another. Saeki's suggestion that Japan might best ensure the cordiality of its relations with the United States by seeking improved relations with China and the Soviet Union is a general principle that fits the new strategic context well. A diversity of crosscutting relationships linking communist and noncommunist nations on different issues means that conflict, when it arises, is likely to be fragmented along numerous lines—with less danger that polarization would lead to hostilities.

The creation of crosscutting alignments on specific issues would tend to lessen dependence on the United States without resulting in dependence on any other single power. It offers the noncommunist nations of Asia a greater possibility of working out an accommodation of interests with their communist neighbors without merely moving out of one orbit and into another. And the process of diversifying alignments is itself likely to strengthen further the multipolarity of the system and to generate added opportunities for alternative relationships. Here we do not give counsel on what other states should or should not do but on what the attitude of the U.S. government and Congress should be.

The cost of this diversification, which is already under way, is a diminished sense of solidarity among the former members of the American-guaranteed alliance system. Clearly, each country will have its own perception of its interests and will feel freer to manifest divergencies with the United States. But the lessened degree of dependence on U.S. power could have advantages for the United States as well. Although the U.S. strategic deterrent obviously retains an important role, multialignment would probably reduce further demands on U.S. military power, which seems appropriate for an era of diminished U.S. capacity to project its military power in Asia. It could give Asian nations a greater political capacity to provide for their own security by placing them in a position to balance and even on occasion manipulate their relationships with the more powerful. This approach, which shifts priorities from the maintenance of alliance solidarity to the working out of an accommodation of interests between America's Asian allies and their communist neighbors, holds out more realistic prospects for making Asian problems manageable over the long run than does a policy that rests on America's will to intervene and on the readiness of nations to remain frozen in alignments created at a time when the probability of military conflict appeared high.

Once again, policies have to some extent outrun conceptualization. The United States has moved further than anyone might have expected at the start of the 1970s toward rapprochement with China, and so have America's allies. Yet some of Washington's Asian policies, especially those pertaining to Korea, reflect the persistence of conceptions of security that, as already indicated, do not appear consistent with the post-Vietnam strategic context.[58] This inconsistency not only raises the danger of America's perpetuating a conflict that might otherwise be significantly ameliorated; it also needlessly impedes the laying of a foundation for long-term security through multialignment.

Perhaps the most important step that can be taken toward multialignment lies in Japan's relations with the communist powers. Since the defense of Japan must be the ultimate concern of U.S. (and Japanese) security policies in Asia, improvement of relations between Japan and the communist countries can have a substantial impact on the full range of U.S. policies in Asia. As already noted, some Japanese have proposed that Tokyo supplement its security treaty with the United States by negotiating nonaggression treaties with China and the Soviet Union. The United States might well lend encouragement to that endeavor, especially by making it clear that the U.S. nuclear umbrella would remain effective.

As Japan explores the possibilities of balanced relations with Moscow and Peking, the United States might now consider the extent to which it should seek to foster a more balanced relationship with Peking.[59] Given the more forward thrust of Soviet policies at this time, the greatest opportunities would seem to lie in relations with China. There have been serious proposals for greater normalization of relations with China while maintaining the Taiwan defense treaty[60] and for exploratory arrangements to sell China defense-related technologies.[61] The transition from the Ford to the Carter administration, however, postponed any early decision on these and other controversial proposals even though some administration specialists agreed that greater flexibility vis-à-vis China would be an effective way of bringing U.S. policies into line with the strategic context. A more active U.S. relationship with the PRC might expand further the scope for initiatives by Japan and other Asian nations. Of course, frequent and frank consultation would be essential to keep such policies from being misinterpreted, but a China fully independent of and somewhat antagonistic to Moscow clearly appears essential to the stability and peaceful development of East Asia.

Washington has already taken a number of other steps to promote the diversification of relationships. It has responded positively to bids from the Vietnamese for the establishment of more normal relations and to moves by noncommunist states of Southeast Asia to seek normalization of relations with both Peking and the communist states of Indochina. Going further, the United States might also consider moving toward less hostile relations, perhaps even diplomatic ties, with North Korea, though maintaining close liaison with the South. In the effort to normalize diplomatic relations with both Vietnam and North Korea, Japan is in a position to take a leading role. In the case of North Korea, Tokyo may be able to play the sort of pioneering role that many people anticipated it might play in U.S.-China relations prior to the first Nixon shock.

Undoubtedly Seoul would oppose such a course, at least at the outset. Two considerations might be mentioned here. First, Washington and Tokyo must determine the extent to which they wish to permit their own priorities to be set by President Park and whether his opposition could in itself destroy their initiatives toward the North. It should be noted in this regard that although the United States and Japan share some interests in common with South Korea, their interests sometimes differ. Second, U.S. and Japanese leaders could make sustained efforts to persuade Seoul to explore the normalization of relations with Pyongyang (begun abortively in 1972). None should have illusions about the prospects for Korea's peaceful reunification, for it may well be that differences between the two sides are fundamentally irreconcilable, short of reunification by force as in Vietnam. But culture and history are not negligible forces, and, especially back in 1972, there seemed to be a real basis for hoping that important steps could be taken at least to reduce tensions and diminish the prospect of war. The establishment of diplomatic relations with Pyongyang by Washington and Tokyo could spur a revival of Kim's earlier interest in talks with Park. Caution would obviously be in order, but caution need not equal inaction.

Whatever strains there may be in U.S. relations with Seoul, an effort by Washington to develop relations with North Korea and with other communist states of Asia, accompanied by encouragement of America's Asian allies to do the same, might give the smaller communist states added flexibility in their efforts to reduce their dependence on either Moscow or Peking. This independence would have its dangers (such as a diminished capacity to "restrain" Kim Il-sung), but the more flexible, constructive relations with noncommunists that the new strategic context makes possible could, in the long run, reduce their incentives to assault their neighbors.

Make Commitments Conditional

Ultimately, the critical change in the view of security, if conceptualization is to fit the strategic context of post-

Vietnam Asia, involves the way security commitments are made and interpreted. There seems to be reasonably broad agreement on the need for a more selective view of commitments. Secretary Kissinger noted that "we must be very careful in the commitments we make, but . . . we should scrupulously honor those commitments that we make."[62] But what of commitments already made? If we allow ourselves to be bound indefinitely by commitments made under circumstances that have drastically changed, we invite disaster. If, as Mr. Kissinger says, we must be more selective in the commitments we make, does not the same logic lead us to be more discriminating concerning commitments already made? The pursuance of interdependent and equal commitments, based on the assumption that all such pledges are part of a bargaining process with a monolithic adversary, has led U.S. policy-makers to undertake "firm" commitments where there may otherwise have been small justification for such an undertaking. By treating de facto all commitments as equally critical and striving to make them all equally credible, Washington has only managed to raise doubts about the credibility of those commitments that are truly vital.

In the more complex and fluid strategic context of the post-Vietnam world, it would be appropriate to refrain from viewing commitments as abstractions or as absolute, open-ended promises. The notion that untenable or obsolete commitments must be kept simply because they have been made ought to be discarded. In the multipolar world of the 1970s, commitments can be separated from one another; there is no reason to assume that disavowal or redefinition of U.S. commitments that no longer serve U.S. interests must jeopardize obviously vital commitments, unless Washington asserts that it will do so. Many nations, such as France, have long taken a much more situational view of commitments, regarding them as an expression of a government's view of its national interests at a particular time and for concrete political purposes. From this perspective, a commitment acquires a compelling credibility and an aura of permanency not because of promises made, but because of strong mutual interests.[63]

Furthermore, the credibility of each commitment rests not on the firmness of will in the abstract or on the sanctity of promises but on confidence in the attainability of that commitment in specific crises. Such confidence is enhanced by clarity concerning the limits of each commitment. For these reasons, the United States, for its part, would increase its credibility by seeking an unambiguous understanding with its allies (and its adversaries) on the specific conditions under which commitments are to be met—on the specific hows and whys of implementing its commitments in Asia. By thus "conditionalizing" U.S. commitments, it may be easier to distinguish between commitment and obsession, between actions that enhance mutual security and actions that temporarily support particular ruling groups.

The idea of conditionalizing commitments is, of course, by no means new. For example, the initial U.S. commitment to South Vietnam in October 1954 was made contingent on certain reforms to be undertaken by the Saigon government.[64] Yet such conditions were never seriously applied, because doing so ran counter to Washington's view of commitments as instruments in the global competition with Soviet power, rather than as mutually agreed responses to specific situations.

It misses the point to assert, as some do, that no commitment has ever been completely unconditional and that the United States has, since the advent of the Nixon Doctrine, grown more selective in its view of commitments. The Nixon Doctrine and Ford's Pacific Doctrine both pledged unequivocally that the United States would uphold all of its Asian security commitments. Neither Nixon nor Ford, nor for that matter Carter, has asserted as a matter of principle the right of the United States to modify a commitment because of changed circumstances or to put aside a pledge if certain conditions are not fulfilled. The inconsistency between continuing reaffirmation of unconditional commitments and what policy-makers see as a more selective approach to those pledges may make it much more costly to move away from unneeded or infeasible commitments. The public repetition of unconditional promises, even if made with implicit reservations, limits U.S. flexibility in modifying a commitment and reduces Washington's leverage in helping to ensure that necessary conditions are fulfilled.

The assertion that the implementation of commitments is contingent on the fulfillment of certain conditions by no means constitutes a license for the United States to interfere in the affairs of other countries. It simply sheds the veil of sanctity that past secretaries of state have cast over U.S. security commitments; perhaps more important, it draws attention to the fact that unless the American people believe that a given commitment serves American interests, as those interests are interpreted at the time the commitment is to be implemented, not when it was made, the commitment cannot be successfully carried out.

The process of reconsidering commitments and clarifying the conditions under which they may be applicable obviously involves difficult domestic and international negotiations. Each commitment must be dealt with individually on its own terms, but doing so in most cases will encourage new inputs from the Congress and new demands from our Asian partners. These may complicate the process. A U.S. readiness to reopen questions of commitments, if done incautiously, may intensify fears and could, in fact, preclude fruitful negotiations. These are real dangers, not to be underestimated, but we believe that the process is essential if the United States is to build a clear understanding of its commitments abroad and a viable base of support for them at home.

This is not the place for a discussion of the specific conditions that ought to be attached to each U.S. commitment. That process, as noted, will be complex and delicate. But some general observations might set the terms of the agenda. A distinction should probably be made—perhaps in all cases—between the nuclear and non-nuclear components of U.S. commitments. The U.S. nuclear umbrella is directed principally against the Soviet Union; its relation to China is somewhat less clear, since to some degree it protects even the Chinese. It affords a kind of defensive security that no non-nuclear nation currently can provide for itself. If Moscow (or Peking) were to pose a nuclear threat to a non-nuclear nation allied to the United States, that nation would expect the U.S. to act. Here a high degree of confidence is vital, though the specification of precise U.S. actions should probably be left ambiguous.

A non-nuclear response to a conventional attack might depend on how U.S. interests in the situation are calculated at the particular time; some areas of uncertainty add to the deterrent and account for the variability of local warfare. The degree of Soviet (or Chinese) involvement would obviously be a major factor, but on balance any commitment to future U.S. conventional involvement should be kept to a minimum; the distinction between aid, air-sea power, and ground troops should be carefully studied and determined. Explicitly acknowledging the possibility that a U.S. commitment might not be activated under certain circumstances would appear to diminish the credibility of some commitments, but in reality this is merely a matter of acknowledging what all sides have suspected for a long time.

Leaving open the possibility of saying that a commitment does not apply in certain circumstances could not only prevent the United States from becoming imprisoned by its own rhetoric and from deciding that it must keep commitments merely because they have been made. It would also make it easier for Washington to use commitments to bargain with allied governments in ways that may avert the conditions for a crisis in the first place. There would be risks for the United States, but they would be more manageable than the political trauma of failing to meet unattainable commitments. An allied government that dislikes the conditions imposed can decide to forego U.S. assistance, or it can decide to go along. Conditionalizing commitments may discourage nations from relying on the United States, but is this necessarily to be viewed with concern? There are good reasons to consider abandoning the 1950s notion that committing the United States to the defense of as many nations as possible is desirable as a counterweight to Soviet power. Perhaps a more appropriate measure of success, given the strategic context in post-Vietnam Asia, would be the number of nations that decide they no longer must rely on any American guarantee except for the nuclear umbrella.

In considering a commitment to defend a nation against a conventional attack, the serious risks inherent in any security commitment to an underdeveloped country should be recognized. Where it is necessary to make a commitment to such a country, it should be most highly conditionalized. Instability is probably an inevitable part of the development process, and challenges to their governments from "subversive" elements are difficult to avoid.[65] Many of the states that gained independence after World War II embrace ethnic groups that have little sense of loyalty to a state whose boundaries mirror the extent of a particular colonial power's holdings; even as they enter the fourth decade of their independence, such states continue to face armed rebellions on the part of ethnic minorities. As U.S. government officials have increasingly come to recognize, there is a great danger that unconditional commitments to such governments will involve the United States in supporting a particular regime against legitimate domestic adversaries. For example, few U.S. policy-makers would see any U.S. interest served by aiding Manila or Bangkok against Muslim separatist movements.

Even where insurgent movements are clearly identified as communist, it is worth asking just how important it is, given the multipolar strategic context, to extend commitments for the purpose of sustaining anticommunist governments. Anticommunist governments may be more open to commercial and political relationships, but given the tensions that arise where there is economic domination by outside powers, how healthy in the long run is that kind of economic relationship? Where a government's political base is narrow, does a conspicuous foreign economic presence not provide a convenient rallying point for antigovernment forces to develop a nationalist appeal? This seems especially likely in Korea, where nationalism has traditionally had a strong anti-Japanese component. And does the promise of foreign economic and military support not encourage a government to refrain from seeking the sort of political accommodation with its domestic adversaries that would be essential were it to follow a more self-reliant course? The Vietnam experience certainly suggests that intervention in the name of anti-communist stability may actually stimulate and abet pro-communist challenges.

For that matter, it would be well to consider the more fundamental question of how instability in the under-developed lands of Asia influences the security of the United States or Japan. Instability that threatens to bring the major powers into conflict obviously affects their security, but they could avoid this danger by agreement to remain neutral, except under very limited circumstances. Will U.S. aloofness not increase the prospects for communist success? In the first place, we now have considerable evidence that the path of self-reliance may be a more powerful obstacle to communist success than dependence on outsiders. Even assuming communism gains in certain areas as a result of U.S. neutrality, would the addition to the list of communist nations strengthen the strategic capabilities of the USSR or China? Might not an increase in the number of communist governments among the underdeveloped countries widen the field of Sino-Soviet confrontation and impose on the communist powers demands that would weaken, rather than strengthen, them in their capacity to threaten U.S. or Japanese security, whether interpreted narrowly or broadly? The assumption, so easily made in the bipolar 1950s, that each nation that "goes communist" adds to the power of Moscow and Peking, must be demonstrated, if it is to be accepted as valid today.

We raise this possibility not because we believe the limitation of U.S. military commitments will yield further communist takeovers, but to suggest that even this eventuality might not have such dire consequences. In fact we believe that few governments would be seriously endangered. In any case, alternative, nonmilitary forms of commitment are likely to be far more critical. The energy, food, and monetary crises will continue to pose a greater threat to U.S. and Japanese security than the small bands of communist rebels or the propaganda boasts of Moscow and Peking.

The overriding U.S. security interest in Asia is the preservation of a viable, closely allied Japan. In adjusting U.S.-Japan relations to the post-Vietnam strategic context, the potential nuclear threat to Japan requires Tokyo's high confidence in the nuclear umbrella and in the readiness of the United States to come to Japan's defense if threatened by direct conventional attack or blackmail. Japan's role in such an arrangement and the level of the U.S. contribution to Japan's defense are considered elsewhere in this book. Here we would only point to the obvious need for agreed political objectives and compatible defense policies capable of attracting wide domestic support in each country. In this regard the new consultative mechanism established by the U.S. and Japanese governments could play an important role not only in defining the specific military responsibilities of each party in emergencies and the procedures for making decisions, but also in seeking ways to achieve this broader compatibility.[66]

If preserving the security of Japan is a prime goal, then the United States' other Asian commitments must be assessed, at least in part, from the standpoint of their impact on Japan. This brings us back to Korea. Although war by no means seems imminent, the Korean peninsula is still the place in Asia most likely to erupt in armed conflict involving the major powers. Those powers, especially Japan, therefore view Korea as the critical security problem in post-Vietnam Asia. It is here that we need to examine most closely the appropriateness of existing policies in light of the changed strategic context. Thus, the remaining chapters of this book undertake a detailed consideration of the Korean situation and the policy alternatives for the United States and Japan.

Risk-taking and the New Strategic Context

Any proposal for change must confront the fact that there is something reassuring about holding to past policies and concepts, even where there may be doubt about their efficacy and appropriateness in a changing situation. This reluctance to abandon the conventional wisdom of the past is especially apparent in the security field, where the potential stakes are so high.

A new course always contains uncertainties, and caution is never inappropriate. But in considering the risks of de-emphasizing military aspects of security and conditionaliz-ing commitments, we might take into account not only the dangers of the "worst case," but also the "opportunity costs" exacted by excessive caution. If efforts to prepare the way for an accommodation of interests between potential adversaries involve risks, there are also dangers in assuming the worst and foregoing opportunities for progress.

In the strategic context of post-Vietnam Asia, the calcula-tion of risks and opportunity costs may be changing. As we contemplate a decade of peace, the risks of redefining and narrowing commitments seem lower. On the other hand, there is more to be lost from missed opportunities for progress toward a long-term accommodation of interests, since such opportunities have grown more real and more numerous. As we contemplate the post-Vietnam era, a bit more boldness in seizing the opportunities before us and shedding outmoded conceptions may be in order.

Notes

1. In Dean Rusk's words: "the integrity of . . . [America's] alliances is at the heart of the maintenance of peace, and if it should be discovered that the pledge of the United States is meaningless, the structure of peace would crumble and we would be well on our way to a terrible catastrophe." U.S., Department of State, *Depart-ment of State Bulletin* 56, no. 1454 (May 8, 1967): 725; and ibid. 56, no. 1456 (May 22, 1967): 771. See also Secretary Dulles's assertion that a failure to defend Quemoy and Matsu would "threaten peace everywhere," quoted in Robert W. Tucker, *The Just War: A Study in Contemporary American Doctrine* (Baltimore: Johns Hopkins Press, 1960), p. 186; and Secretary Kissinger's statement that "peace is indivisible," *Department of State Bulletin* 72, no. 1868 (April 14, 1975): 461.

2. *New York Times*, May 2, 1975. It has been noted, however, that the Japanese government's interest in having such reassur-ances from Washington may have been motivated not by any real doubts on Miyazawa's part concerning U.S. reliability but rather

by a political need to cover the government's flank against attacks by certain Diet members. Ibid., April 4, 1975.

3. Ibid., April 19, 1975. Later the Filipino leader accused the United States of having written off Southeast Asia. See ibid., April 26, 1975, and May 10, 1975.

4. Ibid., April 13, 1975.

5. Ibid., May 10, 1975.

6. Ibid., March 27, 1975.

7. Ibid., April 13, 1975.

8. Ibid. There were numerous examples of this reaction in the Indonesian press.

9. A reasonably complete summary of communist responses to events in Indochina can be found in *Trends in Communist Propaganda* 36, nos. 18, 19, 21 (May 1975). This is a U.S. government publication.

10. *New York Times*, December 24, 1975.

11. Ibid., May 12, 1975.

12. The extent and objectives of the Soviet naval buildup have been the subject of continuing debate. According to the *Chicago Tribune* (November 14, 1975): "In April, when most of the world's attention was focused on the collapse of South Viet Nam and Cambodia, the Soviet Pacific fleet, estimated to number in excess of 300 ships compared to the United States' 75, launched the biggest naval exercise in Soviet history."

13. *New York Times*, August 28 and September 14, 1975; *Washington Post*, August 14, 1975.

14. Numerous unconfirmed reports suggested that China was far from satisfied about the communist victory in Indochina. For example, see *New York Times*, August 15 and September 30, 1975 (on Peking-Hanoi talks); and *Baltimore Sun*, December 23, 1975. For a general article on how the Sino-Soviet dispute may have limited damage to U.S. influence in Asia after the fall of Saigon, see *Washington Post*, August 17, 1975. The Soviets, of course, expressed worry about China's turning its attention from Vietnam to other Asian countries such as Japan and Thailand. See, for example, *New York Times*, June 19 and 24, August 7, and October 9, 1975.

15. *New York Times*, October 24, 1975.

16. White House Press Release, December 4, 1975, p. 4.

17. Schlesinger said on August 27, "There has been no change in Kim Il-sung's scheme to reinvade South Korea." *Haptong* (Seoul), August 27, 1975. See also *Kyodo*, August 29, 1975.

18. U.S., Congress, *The United States and China* (Washington, D.C.: U.S. Government Printing Office, 1975), p. 14.

19. Prime Minister Miki at the Seventy-Sixth Extraordinary Diet session seemed to take the opposite view: "the focus of attention is shifting . . . from Europe to the Middle East and Asia." Tokyo, JOAK-TV, September 16, 1975.

20. For a country-by-country rundown on insurgency in Southeast Asia, see the article by Robert Shaplen in *Boston Globe*, December 20, 1975.

21. *New York Times*, November 2, 1975.

22. *Palo Alto Times*, August 12, 1975, and Shaplen, *Boston Globe*, December 20, 1975.

23. *Far Eastern Economic Review*, October 3, 1975; *New York Times*, May 11, 1975; and Shaplen, *Boston Globe*, December 20, 1975.

24. *New York Times*, May 11, 1975, and Shaplen, *Boston Globe*, December 20, 1975. Shaplen, however, wrote that the Muslim rebels numbered "at least 9000."

25. Interview with Premier Kukrit Pramoj, *Far Eastern Economic Review*, December 12, 1975.

26. Ibid.

27. Weinstein conversation with Malik, San Francisco, September 9, 1975.

28. *New York Times*, May 10, 1975.

29. Ibid., March 4, 1975.

30. Ibid., June 5, 1975.

31. Ibid., July 8, 1975.

32. Ibid., December 7, 1975.

33. Department of State News Release, "Southeast Asia and U.S. Policy," September 28, 1976.

34. *Kyodo*, September 12, 1975.

35. Ibid., October 21 and 29, 1975. The news agency on the latter date wrote:

The Defense Agency cited the following factors, both domestic and global, as major reasons for the scale down into a peacetime defense structure:
- The global trend toward détente, including improvement of U.S.-Soviet and U.S.-China relations, will continue in the future.
- The Japan-U.S. mutual security treaty is effectively working as a strong deterrent force.

•The Defense Agency is faced with difficulties in recruiting personnel and securing military bases under the current severe economic situation.

Agency officials estimate that the completion of the redeployment under the new plan will take some 10 years. The new well-balanced and qualitatively improved peacetime buildup plan, backed by the deterrent provided by the Japan-U.S. security pact, will contribute to a stable balance of power in Asia, the new defense plan said. It also said that Japan's new balanced defense strength would help effective functioning of the Japan-U.S. pact. . . .

Under the new defense plan, the agency plans to set a clear maximum limit on the SDF's quantitative strength. In studying the maximum limit, the agency is aiming for the tentative defense power limitation in peacetime presented to the Diet in 1973. The 1973 peacetime limitation consisted of 180,000 men for the ground force, 250,000 to 280,000 tons of naval ships for the maritime force and some 800 planes for the air force.

The new defense plan also cited as possible armed aggression against Japan in the form of (1) indirect aggression, air space intrusion, other menacing demonstrations and guerrilla activities, and (2) small-scale direct aggression including surprise attacks.

The English-language version of the full white paper is *Defense of Japan* (Tokyo: Defense Agency, 1976).

36. *The United States and China*, p. 6.

37. *Far Eastern Economic Review*, November 14, 1975.

38. *New York Times*, December 7, 1975.

39. Some Americans, however, hoped otherwise. As a panelist at the 1975 American Political Science Association discussion of Japanese defense issues put it, the Japanese are finally "getting more realistic about their own defense" and are likely to cooperate in constructing "a genuine alliance."

40. Sakata noted that it was "rather strange" that there had never been any top-level consultations with the United States concerning the use of U.S. air bases in Japan in an emergency. *Far Eastern Economic Review*, November 14, 1975.

41. *Department of State Bulletin* 73, no. 1880 (July 7, 1975).

42. *United States Foreign Policy 1972: A Report of the Secretary of State* (Washington, D.C.: Government Printing Office, 1973), p. 332; and Richard M. Nixon, *U.S. Foreign Policy for the 1970s; Shaping a Durable Peace* (Washington, D.C.: Government Print-

ing Office, 1973), pp. 109-110. Quotes from the latter source.

43. This anomaly is found, in greater or lesser degrees, in Fred Greene, *Stresses in U.S.-Japanese Security Relations* (Washington, D.C.: Brookings Institution, 1975); Martin E. Weinstein, "Japan's Foreign Policy Options in the Coming Decade," National War College, *National Security Affairs Conference Proceedings* (July 8-10, 1974), pp. 169-179; "Framework for an Alliance: Options for U.S.-Japanese Security Relations" (A Report by Task Forces of the United Nations Association of the U.S.A. and the Asia Pacific Association of Japan, August 1975); and Ralph N. Clough, *East Asia and U.S. Security* (Washington, D.C.: Brookings Institution, 1975).

44. See below, note 47.

45. Japanese Vice Minister of Defense Kubo, for example, noted that the United States was likely to keep its forces in Korea indefinitely because they were there as part of a global mission, not just for the defense of South Korea and Japan. *Kyodo*, September 13, 1975.

46. For further discussion of this, see Franklin B. Weinstein, "The Concept of a Commitment in International Relations," *Journal of Conflict Resolution* 13, no. 1 (March 1969):   See also Herman Kahn, *On Escalation: Metaphors and Scenarios* (New York: Praeger, 1965), pp. 57-58; and Thomas C. Schelling, *Arms and Influence* (New Haven: Yale University Press, 1966), chap. 2 ("The Art of Commitment").

47. A Harris survey released on July 31, 1975, stated that only 39 percent of Americans would support helping South Korea if it should be attacked by the North. According to another poll, only 14 percent would approve of U.S. intervention in a new Korean war, while 65 percent went on record as opposed. *New York Times*, May 6, 1975.

48. Testimony by Henry S. Rowen on the Vladivostok Agreement before the International Security and Scientific Affairs Subcommittee of the House Committee on International Relations, June 25, 1975.

49. National War College, *The Second National Security Affairs Conference Proceedings* (July 14-15, 1975), p. 140.

50. Fuji Kamiya, "Summit Talks in Retrospect," in *United States–Japanese Relations in the 1970s*, ed. Priscilla Clapp and Morton H. Halperin (Cambridge, Mass.: Harvard University Press, 1974), p. 146.

51. Kiichi Saeki, "Japan's Security in a Multipolar World," in

Clapp and Halperin, *United States–Japanese Relations in the 1970s*, pp. 189, 200-201.

52. Shinkichi Eto, "Japan and America in Asia during the Seventies," *Japan Interpreter* 7 (Summer-Autumn 1972): 248-249.

53. Saeki, "Japan's Security in a Multipolar World."

54. It is interesting that the proposals of the task forces of the UN Association of the U.S.A. and the Asia Pacific Association of Japan, though reaffirming many existing security policies, call for a broader approach to security. See "Framework for an Alliance."

55. C. G. Jacobsen, "Japanese Security in a Changing World: The Crucible of the Washington-Moscow-Peking 'Triangle'?" *Pacific Community* 6, no. 3 (April 1975): 352-365.

56. Trade between Japan and North Korea increased from $36 million in 1967 to $131.2 million in 1972. Gordon White, "North Korean Chuch'e: The Political Economy of Independence," *Bulletin of Concerned Asian Scholars*, April-June 1975, p. 52.

57. For example, see *New York Times*, June 4 and 5 and November 23, 1975.

58. The United States has, of course, called for negotiations by all parties in Korea. See the statement made by the United States during the UN debates in October and November 1975 in *Department of State Bulletin* 73 (December 8, 1975): 817-823. Though one cannot rule out a positive response at some point, such a call might have better prospects of success if it were accompanied by other policies aimed at reducing tensions.

59. See Victor H. Li and John W. Lewis, "Resolving the Chinese Dilemma: Advancing Normalization, Preserving Security," *International Security* 2, no. 1 (Summer 1977): 11-23.

60. Proposal by Senator Adlai E. Stevenson in U.S., Congress, *Congressional Record* 121, no. 162 (November 4, 1975): S19115-S19117.

61. Secretary of Defense James R. Schlesinger's final press conference transcript, October 20, 1975, p. 16. For a discussion of the military implications of the $200 million Rolls-Royce jet engine deal with China, see *New York Times*, December 15, 1975, and *Christian Science Monitor*, December 16, 1975.

62. News conference of April 29, 1975, *Department of State Bulletin* 72, no. 1873 (May 19, 1975): 629.

63. For a discussion of alternative ways of viewing commitments, see Weinstein, "The Concept of a Commitment in International Relations," pp. 39-56.

64. It is worth noting that the *New York Times* article reporting

President Eisenhower's letter to Ngo Dinh Diem offering aid carried the headline: "Eisenhower Asks Vietnam Reforms."

65. See Introduction to John W. Lewis, ed., *Peasant Rebellion and Communist Revolution in Asia* (Stanford: Stanford University Press, 1974), for a comparative analysis of these challenges.

66. On the importance Japan attaches to this, see the Sakata interview in *Seikai Orai*, July 1975.

8

The Prospects for Peace in Korea

Fuji Kamiya

Coincident with the collapse of Saigon in April 1975, North Korean President Kim Il-sung revisited Peking after a fourteen-year absence. His belligerent rhetoric, together with generally heightened insecurities in the aftermath of the communist victories in Indochina, gave rise to the notion of "imminent crisis"—namely, the imminent threat of another military attack by North Korea against the South. For some months, that notion gained currency in both the United States and Japan. Anxieties subsequently abated, but rose again for a time following the 1976 tree-cutting incident at Panmunjom.

Much of the present apprehension about the future of South Korea stems from a belief that there are important similarities betwen Korea and Vietnam. Indeed, the two peninsulas share some basic traits. Both are situated on the periphery of China's cultural sphere. There are historical parallels worth noting. Both peninsulas recovered their independence after the end of the Pacific war, and both found themselves divided into two separate states, North and South, which were caught up in an intense military confrontation. The communist governments in both Korea and Vietnam for more than a decade have been wary of leaning too strongly in one direction or another in the Sino-Soviet split; both adopted a policy of self-reliance while holding to the political objective of "liberating" the South. In each case, the southern state ultimately came under the domination of authoritarian army elements, pursuing policies that restricted civil liberties and democratic practices. In light of these similarities, it may not be illogical to fear that the factors that led America to abandon South Vietnam to its fate may produce the same result in Korea.

It is dangerous, however, to embrace the "imminent crisis" thesis for the Korean peninsula on the basis of inferences from the Vietnamese experience. There is need for self-restraint in spreading the notion of "imminent crisis." It is incumbent on us to clarify fully the similarities and differences between Korea and Vietnam, taking into account all of the variables, both external and internal, that bear on the current situation. In spite of the superficial similarities of the two peninsulas, I am inclined to reject the "imminent crisis" thesis because I feel that there are great differences in the two peninsulas as well as in the relevant international contexts.

Although one can never be certain about the long run, there is, in my view, no danger that the Korean peninsula will be engulfed in war in the near future. I base this conclusion on an analysis of the situation in the two Koreas as well as in China and the Soviet Union.

Of course, it scarcely needs saying that the prospects for peace in Korea will be significantly influenced by U.S. policy concerning the peninsula. There is no denying that the fall of South Vietnam gave rise to serious doubts about the viability of America's commitment to the defense of South Korea. But those doubts were short-lived. In the months after the end of the Vietnam war, various top-level leaders of the U.S. government reiterated on numerous occasions America's intention to maintain its commitment to South Korea. Moreover, the Congress, which only a year earlier had seemed to be moving toward reducing aid to and disengaging from South Korea, has been more willing since the spring of 1975 to go along with the government's Korea policy, at least for the time being. This includes many of those who had been doves on the Vietnam war issue. The same trend may be observed in the mass media. There were, of course, some prominent exceptions, but I believe that the fall of South Vietnam was a catalyst for the revival of a widespread consensus in the United States on the importance of maintaining the commitment to South Korea. The scandal surrounding South Korean lobbying practices in the United States has raised some new uncertainties, but there has been no evidence to date of any congressional move to abandon Seoul. And even though President Carter has indicated his intention to withdraw U.S. ground forces from Korea, he has been unequivocal in his reaffirmation of the U.S. intention to stand by its commitment. I proceed, therefore, on the assumption that the United States will, for the foreseeable future, continue to support the Seoul government.

I also assume that the Japanese government will continue to take a stand supportive of the South Koreans. To be sure, Japan's attitude toward Korea has undergone some trying moments in recent years: (1) hostile reactions in Japan to the "renovation" of the South Korean government structure after November 1972; (2) the controversy surrounding the abduction of a Korean opposition leader, Kim Dae-jung, by Korean CIA agents while he was in Japan; and (3) concern about the danger of war, and the reliability of the U.S. commitment, at the time of South Vietnam's collapse. But these doubts and concerns were not allowed to get out of hand, and the Japanese government has held to the position that cooperative relations with Seoul are important. The Diet, mass media, and public opinion also have come to recognize, more strongly than ever before, what was first specified in the Satō-Nixon Joint Communiqué in 1969 and reaffirmed by Prime Minister Miki and President Ford in 1975—namely, that the security of Korea and maintenance of peace on the peninsula are essential to Japan's own security.

I shall, therefore, consider the likelihood of another war in Korea on the premise that both the United States and Japan will support the Seoul government. Afterwards, I shall speculate briefly on prospects for a longer-term settlement of the Korean problem.

South Korea and South Vietnam: How Much Similarity?

In South Vietnam, the success of the National Liberation Front (NLF) was in part attributable to its ability to establish and maintain a number of "liberated areas." These areas, sometimes referred to as "leopard spots," were spread across the countryside. It is, of course, well known that the Ho Chi Minh trail not only crisscrossed South Vietnam but also cut through Laos and Cambodia. The Ho Chi Minh trail brought to the liberated areas a constant flow of additional supplies from North Vietnam. Furthermore, the Vietnamese communists were able to create sanctuaries running along the Cambodian and Laotian borders and into those countries. In order to wipe out those sanctuaries, the U.S. and South Vietnamese government forces moved into Cambodia in April 1970 and Laos in February 1971, but the benefits of these invasions were short-lived. The deeply rooted "leopard spots" were not removed by the Paris Accords, and in the end these areas served as the bases from which the spreading communist forces moved to bring down the Saigon government.

In the case of Korea, the question arises as to whether a national liberation front based in liberated areas can emerge as it did in Vietnam. In explaining how the unification of Korea is to be brought about, Kim Il-sung has stressed the "three great revolutionary capabilities." At a congress held in 1968 to celebrate the twentieth anniversary of the establishment of the Democratic People's Republic of Korea, Kim stated: "In order to finish the great task of liberating the Korean people, capabilities in three areas need to be readied: namely, strengthening of socialist capabilities in the Northern half of Korea, and stimulating and accumulating revolutionary capabilities in South Korea; pushing forward the international revolutionary movement; and solidifying the links between the two." This idea of a three-pronged revolutionary effort had been expressed as far back as December 1955, in a speech Kim gave entitled "To Abolish Revisionism and Formalism in Ideological Activities and Establish Independence." In short, the theme of promoting the unification of Korea by consolidating the socialist base in the North and cultivating revolutionary potential in the South has been consistently advanced for more than two decades. This theme is quite similar to the pronouncements made by the North Vietnamese after 1956 with respect to their strategy for reunifying their country. In connection with the development of revolutionary capabilities in the South, Pyongyang hailed the Revolutionary Party for Reunification as "a reliable political general staff in [the South Korean people's] revolutionary battle for freedom and liberation"; a manifesto and program, issued in the name of the Party's Central Committee in Seoul during August 1969, was said to embody the true aspirations of the South Korean people for the overthrow of the existing Seoul regime and reunification of the country, to be followed ultimately by the establishment of a socialist and communist society. Much as the North Vietnamese continually broadcast the achievements of the NLF, the North Koreans have reported through broadcasts and other means of transmission the progress of the Revolutionary Party for Reunification.

But in spite of these similarities, the fact is that a Korean version of the South Vietnamese National Liberation Front does not exist. Moreover, it is inconceivable that a South Korean NLF, formed as an explicitly anti-Park force, will take shape in the foreseeable future. In order to understand why this is so, it is necessary to consider the following factors.

First, there are important differences in the character and level of maturity of the South Korean and South Vietnamese governments. South Vietnam was never a modern nation-state in the sense of having concentrated in the hands of the central government powerful mechanisms of control reaching out effectively to all corners of the country. South Korea, on the other hand, has clearly established a centralized and modern governmental structure. To be sure, the government headed for so long by Syngman Rhee was known to be a police state. In the name of anticommunism, President Rhee squashed all domestic opposition in order to keep himself permanently in power. Such tactics deserve to be criticized, of course, but if one leaves criticism aside for the moment and looks at it from a slightly different slant, one must conclude that Rhee's success in extending his repressive rule across the country indicated that the mechanisms of state control had been developed to a high level. It need hardly be mentioned that South Korea's state machinery for control has grown even stronger in the decade and a half since Syngman Rhee. In contrast, the government of Nguyen Van Thieu, and those of his predecessors in Saigon, completely lacked such control capabilities. The outlying areas of South Vietnam were always promising seedbeds for the development of NLF strongholds.

Second, although the NLF in South Vietnam had its greatest strength in the rural areas, these areas on the whole support the government in South Korea. Indeed, the pattern of past elections reveals that Seoul, Pusan, and other large metropolitan areas tend to show opposition party leanings and that the rural areas seem inclined toward the government party. It has been observed that in South Vietnam, the people in the large urban areas did not once rise against the government, not in the Tet offensive of 1968, nor in the spring offensive of 1972, nor even in the final assault leading to the fall of Saigon in 1975. What this suggests is that it is not easy in the present era for urban dwellers to rise up suddenly and overthrow the government. Moreover, although urban residents in Korea may be said to lean toward the opposition parties, the plastic bombs and other terrorist tactics that were so rampant in Saigon have not been employed in Seoul. The absence of such tactics in the rural areas of South Korea provides an even more striking contrast with South Vietnam. Some Korean revolutionary "fish," to use Mao Tse-tung's terminology, have found it hard to find a "sea" in which to swim.

The third difference relates to geographic conditions— namely, the richly verdant jungles of South Vietnam and the barren mountains of South Korea. This has a significant bearing on the ease wth which guerrilla activities can be carried on. Moreover, it is highly unlikely that a Korean version of the Ho Chi Minh trail could be created in a peninsula surrounded by the ocean.

Fourth, one must consider the powerful anticommunist feelings found among the South Korean people. These sentiments, which developed as a result of the bitter experiences of many South Koreans during the 1950-1953 war, have been manifested on a number of occasions recently. Despite the intense animosity between the government and the opposition parties, especially since the "renovation" of the government structure in November 1972, there has been a positive response among broad segments of the population to calls for all-out mobilization of the people at those times when the danger of war seemed high. After the fall of Saigon, for example, President Park appealed to the country for support, stating his readiness to "defend Seoul to my death with six million fellow citizens." Rallies were held in every part of the country. It is reported that on May 10, 1.4 million people took part in a rally in Seoul to express their support for the government in the face of a potential threat from the North. It is difficult, of course, to know the motivations of those who attended. Perhaps those who joined the rally did not do so entirely because of their anticommunism or fear of the North. But even if one makes allowances for other motivations, there still seems to be a remarkable degree of unity among the citizenry in their opposition to communism.

The display of anticommunism and national unity in defense of South Korea seemed to emerge largely, if not entirely, as a spontaneous response of the people to the uncertainties created by the collapse of the Saigon government. Yet President Park took this situation as an opportunity to bring forth in May 1975 a new set of restrictive "emergency measures," which seemed to reflect the government's weakness rather than its strength. But even though they recognized that the new measures might be aimed as much at bolstering the political position of President Park as at mobilizing the country against a possible invasion from the North, the New Democrats, Seoul's principal opposition party, decided to support the new "Domestic Stabilization Law."

For some years now, as the government has enacted

various measures to limit opposition activities and make
secure its own political position, criticism of the oppressive-
ness of the present leadership of South Korea has been on the
rise. There may be many things wrong with the Park
government, but we must recognize that he has been able to
maintain a stable and efficient system. Critics vigorously
attack the policies of the Park government, but they tend to
look only at one aspect of his regime. It is also important to
take into account the remarkable economic advances in
South Korea during the last five to six years, not only in the
cities but in the rural areas, too. Kim Dae-jung once said that
people in the rural areas were suffering economic hardships.
Such a situation has now almost disappeared. At the end of
the 1960s, people in South Korea said they still had some
distance to go in order to catch up with the North economically; now, nobody denies that the South is far ahead in that
field. Thus, although Park sometimes uses power in a crude
way, his economic policies have been successful enough to
become an important force for stability. Moreover, it is very
hard to imagine who among the present South Korean
leaders might replace Park in the near future. Thus, despite,
the growing criticism of Park's repressive policies, his
government's ability to exercise control over the country has
also increased significantly. From the standpoint of a variety
of domestic factors, then, one can see that there are crucial
differences between South Korea and South Vietnam.

North Korea: Radicalism and Restraint

Although the basic posture of the Workers' Party and the
Pyongyang government toward the problem of reunification has been quite consistent over the last twenty years, it is
possible to discern alternating cycles of moderation and
radicalism. Considering just the past decade, the following
pattern emerges: the last five years of the 1960s were a period
of radicalism; from 1970 to the first half of 1973 North
Korean attitudes swung toward moderation; from then until
now there has been a swing back toward radicalism.

The original statement of North Korea's more radical
approach to reunification in the late 1960s came in a report,

entitled "Current Conditions and Our Party's Mission," made by Kim Il-sung at the Workers' Party conference held in November 1966. This conference is generally known for its decision to extend by three years the Seven-Year Plan for economic development then being implemented. But what is especially noteworthy about Kim's report was the strong emphasis he placed on military, not economic, matters. Although Kim treated the extension of the Seven-Year Plan as unavoidable, he stressed the need for "parallel construction of the economy and national defense," rather than directing efforts at economic development alone. This, he said, was necessitated by the rise in international tensions. Presumably he was referring to the escalation of the Vietnam war the year before, the normalization of diplomatic relations between Japan and South Korea, the deepening Sino-Soviet conflict, and other matters. When the party adopted in 1966 a set of policies calling for "modernization of the military, arming of all the people, and fortification of the whole country," it was inevitable that this more militant posture would come to be reflected in the Pyongyang government's treatment of the reunification problem. Previously, the North Koreans had always been careful to attach the adjective "peaceful" to any reference to the peninsula's reunification. In this period, however, that adjective was often dropped in favor of an emphasis on resolution of the problem without any outside interference. The typical formulation was: "The unification of Korea is an internal problem for the Korean people." At the same time, rhetoric on the development of revolutionary capabilities in the South grew more militant. For example, Pyongyang declared, "We want to see in today's situation the revolutionary forces of south Korea developed quickly and the People's Democratic Revolution of Liberation pushed forward powerfully." Another typical statement was: "Through the noble struggles of the Korean people, spreading throughout south and north Korea, and the patriotic struggles of Korean citizens abroad, the day of unification for our motherland is drawing near."

A number of incidents during the late 1960s may be

interpreted as ways of expressing this more militant attitude. These include the attack on the Blue House in January 1968, the seizure of the *Pueblo* in the same month, guerrilla incidents at Uljin and Sampo in October, and the shooting down of an off-course U.S. EC-121 aircraft. In the end, however, these actions and the generally more radical policy of the North Koreans probably did more to strengthen the position of President Park than to foster the development of revolutionary forces in South Korea. Previously, Park had been hampered by constitutional restrictions against a third term. Pyongyang's militance provided Park with a pretext for revising the constitution in order to maintain himself in power.

At the Fifth Congress of the Workers' Party in November 1970, North Korea returned to a more moderate policy. The adjective *peaceful* was restored to statements on reunification. Compared to Kim's report four years earlier, the tone of Pyongyang's pronouncements was now noticeably soft. In Kim's words, "Needless to say, the South Korean revolution is a struggle of the South Korean people themselves . . . the South Korean revolution must, in all situations, be made by the South Korean people on their own initiative. But it is the obligation and responsibility of the people in the Northern half, as part of the same nation, to actively support the South Korean people in their revolutionary struggle." Kim even went so far as to say that "we have made it clear time and again that if democratic figures with a national conscience come to power in South Korea and demand the withdrawal of U.S. troops, release political prisoners and guarantee democratic freedom, we are ready to hold negotiations with them any time and any place on the question of the peaceful reunification of the country." This speech was a response to President Park's Liberation Day statement in August 1970 urging a "competition for good will between north and south." It paved the way for the dialogues that followed, beginning with the North-South Red Cross conference on reuniting separated families in August 1971 and leading to the North-South Joint Communiqué of July 4, 1972, and subsequent discussions.

People in Seoul were excited by the July 4th communiqué, in which the two sides agreed to work toward reunification, to refrain from slanderous attacks and armed provocations, to establish a "hot line" between the two capitals, and to create a North-South Coordinating Committee to oversee implementation of the agreements and related matters. The word *unification* even danced across the pages of Japanese newspapers. But the distance separating the two countries was simply too great. After twenty years without any dialogue between the two Koreas, they could not move so abruptly into full-scale talks on reunification. It may be that the two countries, spurred on by the spectacular strides toward détente in U.S.-China and U.S.-Soviet relations, rushed too quickly into these discussions without adequate preparations within their own governments and among their own people. The preparations that did occur, however, probably were not productive from the standpoint of creating an atmosphere conducive to successful talks. On the grounds that South Korea needed to "renovate" its constitutional structure in order to strengthen its position in the forthcoming dialogue with North Korea, Park declared a state of martial law, suspended portions of the constitution, and dissolved the National Assembly. Subsequently, he enacted a new constitution, which made it possible for him to remain as president indefinitely through indirect elections. North Korea also undertook constitutional revisions at roughly the same time. The result of all these measures taken "in preparation" for reunification talks was to heighten the disharmony of the discussions.

President Park's statement on June 23, 1973, and President Kim's response dashed whatever hopes remained that the talks might prove fruitful. In actuality, Park's statement, in which he indicated that he would support simultaneous admission of the two Koreas to the United Nations, was a sharp reversal of Seoul's long-standing policy. That night, in a speech welcoming a delegation from Czechoslovakia, Kim rejected Park's proposal as one that would make the division of the country permanent; according to Kim, if the two Koreas desired to enter the UN prior to the reunification of the country, they should enter it "as a single state under the name of the Confederal Republic of Koryo," leaving the "two existing social systems in the north and south as they are for the time being."

From this point on, North Korea swung back to a more radical posture. Pyongyang seized upon the controversy over the Kim Dae-jung kidnapping as a basis for severely criticizing the Park government. In a statement released in connection with the September 1974 convening of the UN General Assembly, North Korea abandoned self-restraint. Although the statement was entitled "Toward the Autonomous and Peaceful Unification of Korea," it referred to the North Korean state as the only legitimate Korean state and called the government in the South a puppet regime. With respect to domestic policies, the period beginning in 1974 was one of militance and intense mobilization as if for war. Strident rhetoric reminiscent of the late 1960s was invoked by Kim and other leaders. Adding to the atmosphere of tension between the two Koreas were the discovery of tunnels dug by the North Koreans across the DMZ and an incident involving the "five western islands."

Viewing the swing from moderation to radicalism, one cannot rule out completely the possibility that Pyongyang will undertake a military solution to the problem of reunification. North Korea's move back toward a militant stance preceded the collapse of South Vietnam; the defeat suffered by America's ally there probably reinforced this trend. Certainly the sense of threat felt by the South Koreans cannot be dismissed even for the period prior to South Vietnam's fall. Indeed, given the reports coming in from North Korea during 1974 and 1975, it must have been difficult for people in the South to remain calm.

Yet, even if one acknowledges that there was some basis for the South Koreans' perception of threat, I cannot agree with the idea that the situation ever reached the point of "imminent crisis," as was believed to be the case in the period following the Saigon government's defeat. Pyongyang may have drawn encouragement from Hanoi's success in accomplishing the reunification of Vietnam by military means. It is not hard to imagine that the North Koreans were strengthened in their determination to reject the idea of indefinite peaceful coexistence with Seoul. But this does not mean that the North has failed to examine carefully the points of difference between Vietnam and Korea. Pyongyang is probably not so naive politically as to take impetuously the same military action it undertook twenty-seven years ago. No matter how strident their rhetoric and no matter how strongly they may feel impelled toward forceful reunification, the North Koreans would have to recognize that such a course would be an enormous gamble. As long as they are aware of America's continuing support for Seoul and of the real strength of the South Koreans themselves, it is unlikely that they will be tempted to take such a gamble.

If the North Koreans were to move against the South, they would place in jeopardy the whole foundation for national development it has taken them many years to build up. They would also sacrifice their international standing. Twenty-five years ago, the only countries that recognized North Korea were communist bloc states. Pyongyang was completely isolated from the UN, its specialized agencies, and other international organizations. Today, eighty-five countries recognize North Korea, ninety-three recognize South Korea, and forty-six recognize both countries. Pyongyang now enjoys the same status as Seoul in certain UN specialized agencies and in most other international organizations. It is unlikely that the North will readily embark on some wild adventure that could negate in one stroke all that Pyongyang has achieved diplomatically over the past twenty-five years.

Nor do domestic conditions in North Korea lend much support to the notion that Pyongyang is likely to attack the South in the near future. At the heart of the "three revolutionary capabilities" is a strong North Korea as a foundation from which the revolutionary forces in the South might draw assistance. But North Korea is presently beset by serious problems. Economically, North Korea has been shown to be much more vulnerable than the South. There is evidence that the Six-Year Economic Plan undertaken in

1971 did not proceed on schedule. Kim's policy of *juche* ("self-reliance") is very attractive in many ways, but some of the weaknesses of this policy are now becoming apparent. North Korea has found itself without the foreign exchange needed to meet its international obligations. The debt to Japan alone is $60 million. Indeed, the situation in North Korea seems so serious that Pyongyang may need to consider a basic change in its policy. There are two options: (1) to return to a closed society, autonomous but poor; or (2) to open up the country and promote greater economic exchange with the outside world, including Western countries, in order to raise the economic growth rate and remain at least somewhat competitive as an economic rival to the South. One problem with the second course is that North Korea has very little to export.

All of these constraints need to be taken into account in interpreting the radical rhetoric of the North Koreans. Although Pyongyang will probably continue, through its words and actions, to attempt to intensify feelings of psychological unrest and instability in the South, this is not likely to amount to more than intermittent harassment at most. Although such provocations can be irritating, their significance should not be exaggerated. It is more important to note that for the foreseeable future, North Korea's main efforts will continue to be directed toward internal development.

China and the Soviet Union: Forces for Restraint

It is hard to believe that either China or the Soviet Union will actively support North Korea's invasion of the South at any point in the foreseeable future. This judgment is based on inferences drawn from a wide variety of materials and indicators. The *Economist* (London) observed in May 1975 that if a new war were to erupt in Korea, it would lead to a number of undesirable consequences for the Chinese: (1) it could lead to the inflicting of significant physical damage on China itself; (2) it would bring about the end of China's détente with the United States, resulting in Peking's loss of leverage and protection vis-à-vis the Soviet Union; (3) a war would probably prompt the Soviet Union to become North Korea's major supplier of arms and adviser on military strategy; (4) it could conceivably lead to removal of the restraints that presently keep Japan from undertaking heavy rearmament and the acquisition of nuclear weapons. Even if all of these possibilities do not materialize precisely as suggested here, there is no doubt whatever that a second Korean war, no matter which direction it might take, would have undesirable consequences for China. Certainly, if the North were to go down in defeat, China would face a confused and dangerous situation; but even if Pyongyang were to succeed in reunifying the peninsula by military means, the consequences would be difficult for China to handle. A reunified communist Korea might prove to be a powerful neighbor, or it might enter a period of great instability, with more territory under its domain than it could actually control. Either eventuality would be less desirable for China than the current situation.

There is little doubt that China's decision to enter the Korean War was stimulated by Peking's fear that the North Korean state might be totally destroyed and the UN army might press beyond the Yalu River. This, of course, posed a serious threat to China's own security. If the same situation were to arise again, the Chinese would probably make the same response. But barring that very unlikely contingency, China's chief interest would appear to lie in the preservation of the status quo in Korea. Ever since the rapprochement between China and the United States and the normalization of relations between China and Japan, Peking has accepted the existence of the U.S.-Japan alliance. No longer does China protest the presence of U.S. forces in Japan. The Chinese now even exchange military attachés with Japan's Self-Defense Forces. Moreover, given the problems of economic development and political succession that China currently faces, Peking's concerns are likely to be focused on internal affairs, rather than external. And among China's concerns in the external realm, the Taiwan question is far more important than that of the Korean peninsula.

If one considers the problems China faces in consolidating

its political order and setting an economic strategy for a new era, the situation prevailing today, both internally and externally, bears certain similarities to the situation that existed at the outbreak of the Korean War. That conflict, and China's involvement in it, exacted a high cost from the Chinese. As is well known, President Truman had stated at a press conference held on January 5, 1950, that the United States would not intervene in China's affairs, even if Peking decided to invade Taiwan. In short, the external environment at that time posed no obstacles to the achievement of the external goal carrying the highest priority—namely, the absorption of Taiwan. But the outbreak of hostilities in Korea, and China's involvement in it, caused the United States to change its policy concerning Taiwan from one of nonintervention to one of military commitment. As a consequence of the Korean War, China found that its primary external goal had to be delayed at least twenty-five years; indeed, no one knows when, if ever, it will be accomplished. Judging by the high costs for Peking of North Korea's invasion of the South in 1950, one would have to expect the Chinese to be exceedingly wary of another war on the Korean peninsula. Whatever public posture China may feel compelled to adopt from time to time, its real policy will almost certainly be aimed at maintaining the status quo in Korea.

There has been a lack of clarity in the Soviet Union's policies toward Korea. Following his April 1975 visit to Peking, Kim attempted to go to Moscow. He was unable to do so because of Secretary-General Brezhnev's illness; although Brezhnev was in fact ill, there were also indications that the Soviets may have been looking for a convenient excuse to avoid meeting with the North Koreans at that time. But whatever ambiguity may exist with respect to Moscow's relations with Pyongyang, it seems certain that the Soviet Union, like China, prefers the perpetuation of the status quo on the Korean peninsula.

The Soviets have much to lose from another war in Korea. For the Soviets, even more than for China, détente with the United States represents the central axis of its foreign policy.

The fact that North Vietnamese troops relied on Soviet tanks for their final assault on Saigon contributed to doubts within the United States about the effectiveness of détente. In May 1975, in a speech he gave in St. Louis, Secretary Kissinger acknowledged these doubts: "We must be cautious about charges that détente is a trap and a one-way street in which America unilaterally makes all the concessions. We must free ourselves from the notion that all steps back are advantageous to the Soviet Union and all problems caused by the Soviet Union." In defending détente, Kissinger warned that should the Soviets exploit détente as a basis for taking "selective advantage of beneficial opportunities," then U.S.-Soviet relations would enter a dangerous stage; this may be interpreted as an indirect but clear warning to the Soviets not to misuse détente to initiate a limited clash. Given this expression of America's attitude, the Soviets are not likely to try to "misuse" détente in Korea. Even if the Soviets were persuaded that the local situation in Korea was favorable for a Moscow-backed thrust by the North Koreans, they would be constrained by the broader aspects of their relationship with the United States in such vital areas as the nuclear balance and economic relations, especially with respect to food.

Moscow has, of course, a strong interest in discouraging Pyongyang from drawing too close to Peking. This leads the Soviets to give at least nominal support to North Korean aspirations for reunification and to stress the importance of allowing the Korean people to resolve their own problems without the involvement of external powers. The Soviet Union, which has followed a meandering course toward Korea since the war, recognizes that due to racial, cultural, historical, and geographic circumstances, North Korea feels closer to China than to the Soviet Union. Indeed, for the past few years relations between Moscow and Pyongyang have been chilly. Given all of these considerations, one cannot conceive of Brezhnev's lending support to an adventurous action by North Korea that, in the end, would probably strengthen the hand of Korean advocates of cooperation with China. Thus, for both the Soviet Union and China, their strong interest in détente and their rivalry with each other would seem to preclude support for any major North Korean military move against the South.

A Longer-Term Basis for Peace: Cross-Recognition

In 1970 I proposed that Japan and the United States recognize North Korea and that China and the Soviet Union simultaneously extend recognition to South Korea. The proposal was made on the assumption that this would make it easier for the two Koreas to recognize one another and that none of these arrangements would preclude peaceful re-unification of Korea at some point in the future. Indeed, cross-recognition, by easing tensions and facilitating a broader range of relationships for each of the existing Korean states, would in the long run help in a practical way to prepare the way for reunification. It thus seemed to me that these steps not only would help to strengthen stability and enhance the prospects for maintaining peace on the peninsula, but would also help to create an atmosphere conducive to reunification by reducing feelings of mutual insecurity and hostility between the rival Korean states.

Over the past several years, some indications of potential support for this concept have gradually emerged. State Department officials first mentioned the cross-recognition proposal to President Ford on the eve of his visit to Korea in November 1974. The United States has since indicated publicly its willingness "to reciprocate moves by North Korea and its allies to improve their relations with the Republic of Korea."[1] In the summer of 1975 I went to Moscow, where I broached the idea with the Soviet partici-pants in a Soviet-Japanese conference of specialists in international affairs. The official response was a predictable "nyet," but several months later I had an opportunity to meet privately with one of the Soviet conference partici-pants. He stated, "The idea of cross-recognition is unaccept-able officially, but unofficially it will constitute one subject for discussions."

The relevant question at this stage is what Japan and the United States can do to improve the chances that the communist side will accept the concept of cross-recognition as a basis for moving toward a longer-term solution of the Korean problem. Probably the most important thing is to promote a feeling of confidence on the part of both Koreas that neither is about to be abandoned by its friends or placed in a disadvantageous position as a result of cross-recognition. Without this kind of confidence, nobody can expect any meaningful dialogue to take place between the two Koreas. The immediate target of this dialogue should be peaceful coexistence, with reunification as a long-term goal. Unfortunately, Kim maintains that peaceful coexistence is harmful to the prospects for ultimate reunification of the Korean nation. He wants to move more rapidly to reunification, but this is clearly not feasible. Park has shown his flexibility in abandoning South Korea's version of the Hallstein doctrine, which would have had Seoul breaking its ties with any country that established relations with Pyongyang. But no real progress will be possible until Kim changes his attitude. It is very unlikely that China and the Soviet Union will accept the idea of cross-recognition until North Korea indicates a willingness to go along.

It is important, then, that assurances be given to both Koreas. From the standpoint of the South, this means that the basis of American and Japanese interests in the security of Korea should be made clear. Both countries have a strong interest in the maintenance of stability and tranquillity on the Korean peninsula. Seoul should be made to understand that Korea is not important to the United States merely for the sake of Japanese interests but because the United States itself has interests that are affected by what happens on the peninsula. Of course, the security of Japan and Korea are indeed closely intertwined. Some American analysts, like professors Reischauer and Cohen, have contended that Japan and Korea are separable; if the United States wants to ensure the security of Japan, it need look only to the Tsushima Straits as the periphery of the area to be secured and not beyond to the Korean peninsula. Physically, it may be accurate to say that the security of Japan need not be jeopardized by what happens in Korea, but if one approaches the problem at the psychological level, Japan and Korea may not be so easily separable. If the entire Korean peninsula were to come under Pyongyang's control, one would have to take seriously the possibility that Japan might undertake major rearmament, including nuclear weapons.

The best policy for the United States would be to avoid any major changes in its current posture. So long as Park's position on peaceful coexistence remains reasonable and Kim's unreasonable, there is no reason to change U.S. policy. But, assuming that the United States is planning to remove its forces from Korea, Washington should be cautious regarding the kind of commitment to be left on the peninsula after U.S. forces have been withdrawn. The weakest part of South Korea's defense is its air force. If the United States helps South Korea build up its air force, then a withdrawal might well be possible, leaving a certain balance on the peninsula between North and South. Up to now, the United States has been reluctant to build up South Korea's air force, because Seoul might be tempted to attack the North. A weak South Korean air force permits the United States to control the danger of South Korea's going North. The Soviet Union has apparently taken a similar attitude toward the North, at least with respect to naval capabilities. If North Korea has a strong naval capability, including LSTs, it might intrude by sea against South Korea. The Soviets have been very cautious to ensure that the North has only limited sea power. Both the United States and the Soviet Union therefore have indicated some desire to keep their respective Korean allies from acquiring capabilities that would encourage offensive actions.

What can Japan do? Diplomatic relations with North Korea appear unlikely for the time being, but Japan may have an economic role to play vis-à-vis the North. Economic relations with North Korea depend on how the debt problem is handled, but I think it is in Japan's interests to help North Korea surmount its present economic difficulties. It is unwise to let the North Koreans get pushed into a situation where they may begin to feel desperate. If this happens, they may adopt unreasonable policies. In order to encourage

Pyongyang to take a more reasonable stance, Japan should do what it can to keep the economic situation of North Korea from deteriorating too far. This means that the Japanese government should play an active role in helping to overcome obstacles to the further development of Japanese trade with North Korea. Of course, the overall emphasis in Japan's economic relations with the peninsula would continue to be on South Korea.

As the United States considers how to reduce its military presence in South Korea and Japan seeks to work out problems in its economic relations with North Korea, the central consideration should be the fostering of a sense of self-confidence on the part of both Korean governments. This is an essential ingredient not only for cross-recognition but also for longer-term arrangements for the preservation of peace and, perhaps, the eventual reunification of the peninsula.

Notes

1. Philip C. Habib, assistant secretary of state for East Asian and Pacific affairs, testimony before the Subcommittee on Foreign Assistance and Economic Policy of the Senate Foreign Relations Committee, April 8, 1976.

9

The United States, Japan, and the Future of Korea

Selig S. Harrison

Twenty-five years after the North Korean invasion, it is increasingly apparent that the meaning of the Korean War has been widely misunderstood. The original assumption underlying U.S. intervention was that the North had served as a pawn of the Soviet Union in the opening gambit of a worldwide communist expansionist offensive. This led to an image of the conflict, in turn, as a mere extension of the superpower rivalry, with its civil war aspects correspondingly obscured. As a variety of observers have demonstrated, however, there is considerable reason to doubt that Moscow either instigated the Northern attack or supported it with larger military objectives in mind.[1] On the contrary, it now appears that Kim Il-sung took the initiative himself, calling on his allies to support a unification attempt inspired by nationalist as well as communist dictates. In one suggestive analysis, Kim's desire to attack the South is explained in part as a response to an internal factional challenge from his Southern communist rival, Pak Hon-yong, later purged, who had fled North following the U.S. occupation. Having left his party base behind, it is said, Pak wanted to liberate the South in order to enhance his own power position and utilized the rallying cry of unification to challenge Kim for control of the newly formed Korean Workers' Party. Kim was compelled to outdo Pak as a nationalist by assuming the leadership of the unification cause himself.[2] The plausibility of this analysis is enhanced if one gives credence to Khrushchev's memoirs, with their detailed account of Kim's insistent pressures for help and a consistently skeptical, cautious Soviet response.[3] To be sure, the historical record remains inconclusive on many counts and may not be fully clarified, if ever, for many years. But despite these gaps, it now appears reasonable to conclude that there was never a clear dichotomy in Korea between a legitimate South and an illegitimate, "puppet" North controlled by Soviet and Chinese puppeteers. Since its inception, the Korean conflict has been a struggle between two equally Korean actors, a struggle basically governed not by external manipulation but by the self-activating nationalist hunger for reunification.

The Unification Issue

It is not our purpose here to evaluate the merits of U.S. intervention in the global context of 1950 or to review the tortured ups and downs of the subsequent Seoul-Pyongyang rivalry. Rather, it is to emphasize that a meaningful discussion of U.S. and Japanese policy options today should proceed from a sharpened recognition of the underlying character of the Korean conflict as internecine. Both of the Korean actors have been utilizing foreign support for their own local purposes, and both have acquired foreign entanglements as a legacy of the Cold War years. Still, as I have sought to demonstrate elsewhere, neither is so beholden to its foreign patrons that its victory over the other would represent more than a marginal triumph of foreign interests.[4]

The Free-Wheeling North

Even if one believes that Moscow manipulated Pyongyang in 1950, it is evident that the North has since established a free-wheeling relationship with both Moscow and Peking. The Pyongyang regime is best described not as a national communist regime but rather as a militant nationalist regime with a communist ideology. No other communist regime in the world has so explicitly and so defiantly repudiated the jurisdiction of a "guiding center" in international communism. With its central commitment to *juche*, or self-reliance, Pyongyang has consciously sought to diversify its foreign economic ties, and North Korean imports from communist countries declined from 83 percent of all imports in 1970 to 48 percent in 1974. Even militarily, Pyongyang has been gradually reducing its dependence by building a domestic munitions industry capable of making small arms, ships, and tanks. It is in the military sphere, however, that Pyongyang continues to have significant external dependencies. Just as Washington has its security ties with Seoul, so Moscow and Peking are linked with Pyongyang in security treaties under which each pledges military assistance "by all means at its disposal" in the event of an attack on the North. The North Korean treaty with Moscow must be renewed every five years and can be revoked by either party on a year's notice prior to the expiration of each five-year period, but Peking and Pyongyang must both consent to the amendment or termination of their agreement.[5] Significantly, given its *juche* emphasis, Pyongyang finds these treaties embarrassing and plays them down both domestically and in international forums, in contrast to Seoul's unabashed acknowledgment of its dependence on Washington.

For Kim Il-sung, nationalism is the psychological cement that holds together his rigid totalitarianism and gives his regime in the North its legitimacy. Historically, during the pre-1945 movement against Japanese rule, Korean communist factions failed to achieve the preeminent claim to nationalist leadership won by Vietnamese communism; and precisely for this reason, Kim has consciously attempted to compensate for the past with his *juche* policy, his anti-Japanese posture, and his commitment to unification. The ultimate rationale invoked to justify his Stalinist style is the need for national discipline in pursuit of unification or, at the very least, confederation. The strongest impression I gained during a five-week visit to the North in 1972 was that Kim could not abandon, or appear to abandon, the unification goal without seriously tarnishing his leadership image.[6]

Malaise in the South

The aspiration for some form of progress toward unification is a powerful, ever-present undercurrent continually
churning beneath the surface of events on both sides of the
thirty-eighth parallel. Koreans in North and South alike feel
that the vagaries of history have repeatedly cheated them of
their right to achieve and assert their national identity. The
trauma of division has been considerably more unsettling for
Koreans than for Germans, because Korea, despite its ancient
tradition of unity, has yet to win the recognition of its
identity in the community of modern nation-states that the
Germany of Bismarck achieved generations ago. As an Asian
country confronted by the challenge of Western dominance,
Korea has felt a special compulsion to win this recognition.
Yet Japanese colonialism intervened at the turn of the
century, just when Korea was defining its response to the
Western challenge, and then came the U.S.-Soviet partition.[7]

In the South, the embittered defensiveness toward the
North born in the Korean War has gone side by side with a
profound uneasiness over the prospect of indefinite division.
To be sure, open discussion of the unification issue has been
largely suppressed in the South by Park's sweeping "anticommunist law," especially since he began to solidify his
authoritarian rule in 1969. Every so often, however,
nationalist feeling bursts to the surface, revealing a broad-
based desire for a moderation of North-South tensions that
would enable Seoul and Pyongyang to reduce their external
dependencies and adopt a stronger, more concerted posture
toward other powers. One such occasion came in 1966 and
1967, when National Assembly hearings designed as a token
gesture to unification-minded groups released a flood of
pent-up popular sentiment.[8] Another indication of sub-
surface opinion in the South was the strong support for
Park's 1971 presidential opponent, Kim Dae-jung, who
stressed the issue of liberalized contacts with the North in his
campaign. In the controversial manifesto that led to their
arrest in March, 1976, Kim Dae-jung, former President Yun
Po-sun, and ten other opposition leaders not only attacked
Park for his political repression and for economic policies

that "foster corruption, foreign indebtedness and ever widening disparities of wealth," but they also strongly implied that he was partly to blame for the continued division of the country. "The tragic rupture of our land for the thirty years since liberation," they declared,

> has given an excuse for dictatorships in both north and south. . . . For the north and south to have a combined standing army strength of over a million men, and to maintain these forces with modern weapons, imposes an impossible burden on the economies of the Korean peninsula without foreign military aid. . . . Accordingly, "National Unification" is today the supreme task which must be borne by all the 50 million Korean people. If any individual or group uses or obstructs "National Unification" for its own strategic purpose, it will be impossible to escape the strict judgement of history. Depending on the attitudes of politicians, north or south, the opportunity for "National Unification" can either be brought closer or delayed. Those who truly believe in the nation and our common brotherhood, clearly perceiving the changing international situation, and seizing the chance when it comes, ought to have the wisdom and courage to deal with it resolutely. This is precisely what we must pursue as the goal of an independent foreign policy inspired by our own Korean interests.[9]

One of the explicitly stated themes of underground anti-Park propaganda is that he seeks to perpetuate tensions with the North for selfish political purposes, making conciliatory gestures, as in 1972, only to appease domestic and foreign critics. This is linked directly to the charge that he is mortgaging the country to Japan, an allegation that is particularly damaging to Park in view of his record as an officer in the Japanese colonial army.[10] In economic terms, the multiplying foreign indebtedness of the South and its heavy reliance on Japanese investment, in particular, provide short-term rewards for the Park regime in the form of jobs and profits for a Korean mini-*zaibatsu* sector. In political terms, however, the president's development program has had mixed results. Many politically conscious South Koreans believe that the extent of their external

dependence prolongs and reinforces the division of the
peninsula by continually increasing the vested interests with
a stake in the status quo. In this widely held view, Korea
would not only have increased hope for unification but more
to show for its economic efforts, in the long run, if it opted
for slower growth with greater equity and less control by
foreign investors who would like to see the peninsula remain
divided.[11]

De Facto or De Jure Coexistence?

To say that the aspiration for unification is a powerful one
is not to predict the early achievement of a formal union or to
suggest that the two Korean states are likely to leap overnight
from their present confrontation to confederal harmony. On
the contrary, any movement toward confederation or unification by peaceful means would no doubt have to come in
very gradual stages and would have to be preceded, in all
likelihood, by the emergence of more compatible regimes in
North and South that would be willing to take the risks
involved in cultural and political interchange. The most
that can be realistically expected in the foreseeable future is a
reduction of military tensions and a tortuous movement
toward de facto coexistence. In dwelling upon the strength of
nationalist feeling, our intent is to point up the critical
difference between a de facto coexistence that would leave the
door open for moves toward confederation or unification
and de jure "two Korea" arrangements that would appear to
freeze the division in its present form indefinitely. Just as it
would be unrealistic to overrate the chances for early
unification, so it would be a mistake to underrate the latent
force of nationalism and the depth of the desire in both
South and North to present a more concerted posture toward
other countries. So long as there is no sense of movement
toward confederation or unification, there will be a danger
of a military explosion in Korea, whether triggered by a frustrated North or, over time, by an increasingly well-armed
South. At best, even if military tensions can be reduced, it
will not be easy for external powers to promote "two Korea"
arrangements after the German model unless these are

clearly linked to projected steps in the direction of confederation or unification. In viewing Korea, in short, one should attempt to place the 1945 partition and the 1950 invasion in a long-term historical perspective, always bearing in mind that the resulting situation has been more comfortable for the other parties concerned than for the divided Koreans themselves.

The Japanese Role in the South

Against this background, it is now possible to embark upon an assessment of Japanese and U.S. interests and options in Korea. This is inevitably something of a circular exercise, for the Japanese debate over Korea policy hinges to a considerable extent on divergent assumptions with respect to the future U.S. posture, and conversely, the U.S. debate over whether to disengage from Korea has become to an even greater extent a debate over the nature of Japanese interests in the peninsula. Defenders of the U.S. presence contend that a U.S. withdrawal would lead to a militarized Japan, possibly nuclear-armed, and advocates of disengagement respond that a withdrawal in gradual stages would not critically affect Japanese defense or foreign policies. Both Tokyo and Washington, in varying degree, have tended to look on relations with Korea as ancillary to relations with each other.

Washington and the 1965 Treaty

Turning first to a consideration of Japanese interests in the peninsula, one is struck by the basic historical fact that the present asymmetrical Japanese involvement with the South came only after protracted and insistent U.S. pressures on both Seoul and Tokyo. Evidence is accumulating to indicate the severity of the differences between Washington and Seoul during the Syngman Rhee years over South Korean policies toward Japan. Washington wanted the normalization of relations between Seoul and Tokyo not only for military reasons but, above all, as an avenue for supplanting U.S. aid outlays with Japanese investment capital. Rhee, however, in the words of one of his closest associates,

sincerely believed that we could not afford to fall into the
Japanese lap economically or politically without perpetuating the division, without driving another big wedge into the
already existing national cleavage. And the Communists
would call us Japanese stooges . . . and that would develop
into a situation where the Southern Koreans would be driven
by force of circumstances toward the Communists. . . . Our
national survival requires that we do not get mixed up with
the Japanese pending reunification.[12]

Writing in 1964, on the eve of normalization, Professor
Hahm Pyong-choon, now South Korean ambassador to
Washington, belabored Americans for their

irksome, sermonizing attitude . . . in accusing us of being
narrow-minded and spiteful toward the Japanese. Our experience with the Japanese is something no other people can
understand. We fear that the inevitable outcome of economic
cooperation with Japan is that our economy will become an
appendage of the booming Japanese economy.[13]

Nevertheless, despite widespread opposition reflected in
serious riots, the new Park regime proved more malleable
than Rhee had been and ultimately concluded the 1965
normalization treaty.

Japan, for its part, had its advocates of normalization but
also had to be prodded into conclusion of the 1965 accord.
The Japanese objective of gaining economic access to the
South would have been satisfied by a joint declaration, as
against a formal treaty that was more likely to require at least
a partial bow in the direction of recognizing Seoul as the
exclusive sovereign in Korea. A simple declaration would
also have been less provocative to the broadly based Japanese
domestic opponents of normalization in any form, that is, to
those who wanted Japan to avoid involvement in the Seoul-
Pyongyang rivalry. Prime Minister Ikeda, after all, had often
emphasized that Japan could not disregard the de facto
existence of the Pyongyang regime, strongly suggesting on
many occasions that Japan would eventually deal with the
North. The treaty language finally chosen was deliberately
open-ended, lending itself to one interpretation on the part

of South Korea and another on the part of Japan. Article III declared that Seoul was the only lawful government in Korea "as specified in Resolution 195 (III) of the United Nations General Assembly." Thus, Japan could and did point to the resolution's reference to "a lawful government having effective control and jurisdiction over that part of Korea where the Temporary Commission was able to observe and consult and in which the great majority of the people of all Korea reside." Foreign Minister Shiina flatly assured the Diet on August 5, 1965, that "as far as this Treaty is concerned, the problem of North Korea is still in a state of *carte blanche*. The area of the treaty application is limited only to the area where the present jurisdiction of South Korea extends."

The Economic Stakes

Ironically, it was during the very years when the North was reaching the zenith of its long effort to maximize self-reliance that the Park regime opened the gates to its extensive dependence on Japan following the 1965 treaty. South Korean economic technocrats saw Japanese investment as a way of rapidly multiplying employment opportunities, and Park's political managers wanted slush funds from Japanese, American, and other foreign companies to help him consolidate his power. Gradually, Japanese economic involvement in the South has mushroomed, with official Japanese equity investment authorizations running nearly four times higher than U.S. authorizations at the end of 1974 and an even greater margin of advantage apparent in unofficial control of South Korean enterprises through dummy partners and technical assistance or licensing agreements. In American eyes, the Japanese presence in the South was less attractive after the fact than it had been in pre-1965 State Department position papers, not only because it grew so overwhelming in relation to the U.S. economic presence but also because the widespread use of the licensing pattern obviated major capital outlays and, to this extent, failed to relieve South Korean pressures for continuing U.S. military and economic subsidies. At the same time, Japan's governmental aid credits have clearly played a major role in stabilizing South Korean development budgets since 1965.

The Japanese economic role in the South has resulted in the growth of significant vested interests in the business sectors of the two countries as well as powerful political lobbies linked to the economic groups involved. Authoritative informal estimates indicate that Japanese parent companies control Korean enterprises with assets of nearly $1.7 billion, not to mention a volume of two-way trade that reached $4.9 billion in 1976 and the promise of offshore oil billions for leading South Korean, Japanese, and American interests if a projected program to develop part of the East Asian continental shelf should ever go forward. Given the size of the economic stakes acquired during the past decade, it is clear that the protection of existing vested interests in the South will be a major objective affecting future Japanese policy toward the Korean issue. However, this should be sharply distinguished from the larger national interests, which we shall now attempt to define.

Japan and Korea: Interests and Options

The governing Japanese interest in Korea at the present juncture would appear to lie in the reduction of North-South tensions and the prevention of a renewal of large-scale military conflict in which Japan could become directly or indirectly involved as an offshoot of the Japan-U.S. Security Treaty. This interest is directly linked to a broader Japanese interest in the preservation of regional stability and the avoidance of conflict with China or the Soviet Union. China, in particular, has been consolidating its ties with the North, and Tokyo's growing stake in close relations with Peking is increasingly intertwined with its stake in a reduction of tensions in the peninsula. Even if Korea could be completely insulated from the involvement of other powers, however, Japan would still have an overriding interest in a peaceful resolution of the North-South rivalry. Translated into policy terms, this would appear to rule out an alignment with either side that would tend to sensitize and polarize the division. History makes it peculiarly important for Japan to detach itself from the North-South struggle and to move toward harmonized relations with Seoul and Pyongyang that would help to moderate tensions in the peninsula.

A Difficult Encounter

Given the depth of the bitterness left over from the colonial period, the potential for future conflict between Japan and Korea would appear to be serious even under the best of circumstances. Colonialism aggravated what was, in any case, an endemically difficult sociocultural encounter between Japanese and Koreans, touching off a psychological cycle of challenge and response that still continues. By deepening its commitment to the Park regime, Japan would only magnify the potential for conflict and would alienate not only the North but also wide sections of anti-Park opinion in the South as well. As the instability of the Park regime grows, so do the tensions inevitably arising from its client status. On the one hand, Park clings more and more tenaciously to Tokyo and Washington; on the other, he resorts to anti-Japanese propaganda when it is convenient, as in the aftermath of his wife's assassination. Despite his spiraling indebtedness to Tokyo, Park is keenly aware that both sides have leverage in a patron-client relationship. Seoul has thus been able to violate Japanese sovereignty with a remarkable degree of impunity in the Kim Dae-jung affair, successfully bluffing Tokyo with its threat to break off relations. Tokyo, for its part, is indignant but bides its time, and anti-Seoul sentiment is submerged, for the present, by a generalized sense of exasperated irritation toward Koreans in general. The dangers inherent in the continuing growth of tension between Japan and the two Koreas are underlined by the magnitude of the Korean military and industrial establishments that have emerged on both sides of the thirty-eighth parallel. In their differing ways, Seoul and Pyongyang have both demonstrated that a unified Korea would give Japan significant economic compeition in certain spheres and would no doubt test Japanese forbearance, on many occasions, by adopting an assertive political posture commensurate with its newly consolidated strength.

It might be argued that the disadvantages of a unified Korea for Japan would make it logical for Tokyo to seek to keep the peninsula divided for as long as possible. This is superficially plausible, but it would be unnecessarily risky to pursue such a course by siding with Seoul against Pyongyang. Faced with the underlying nationalist attitudes in both North and South described earlier and thus the limited ability of outside powers to manipulate Korean events, Tokyo would be wiser to keep its options open by shifting to a symmetrical approach toward the two Koreas. If the Koreans themselves should come to terms with the continued division of the peninsula, a symmetrical Japanese approach would reinforce the process while in Korean eyes exempting Japan from blame for the division. In economic terms, such a peaceful North-South accommodation would enable Japan to enlarge upon its economic beachheads in the South by making limited but significant ties to the North. At the same time, when and if the division should ever come to an end, Japan would be on a sounder footing in dealing with the leaders of a confederal or unified Korea than if it had placed all of its bets on Seoul.

The Case for a Symmetrical Posture

In order to see the options before Japan in their starkest outline, one should also consider, hypothetically, whether it would be wise for Japan to assume the likelihood of eventual unification and give unambiguous support to the most likely winner up to, but not including, the level of direct military intervention. This would presuppose a relatively clear and easy choice between the two rivals. In actuality, however, the situation Japan faces in Korea appears to be quite different. Neither side is sufficiently strong—either militarily or otherwise—to prevail completely over the other in a unification adventure, short of direct foreign intervention on a total scale. The North has a relatively strong basis of nationalist legitimacy as against that of the South on its own home ground but has difficulty in projecting this, as we have observed, given the pre-1945 Korean communist failure to win nationalist preeminence. Pyongyang's current foreign exchange difficulties may betray deeper economic problems, and the growing nepotism in Kim's regime also poses questions about the future political vitality of the North. At the same time, the Seoul regime is far more seriously overextended than Pyongyang in its foreign indebtedness, which adds to its previously suggested inherent political weaknesses. Neither contender has achieved commanding economic and political preeminence, and yet each is just strong enough to feel that the plunge might be worth taking should the other experience a serious economic or political crisis. Seoul's growing military-industrial complex and its intermittent interest in acquiring a nuclear capability serve as a reminder that the possibility of a plunge by the South may well loom larger in future years. It would be an extremely dangerous, long-shot gamble for Japan to become committed to either side; and there are also risks in a halfway policy that allocates increasing resources to the South but stops short of a meaningful commitment to a Seoul-sponsored unification. In the short run, the American presence gives Japan breathing space by reducing the danger of an adventure by either the North or the South. But it also obstructs progress toward a North-South accommodation, as we shall explain later, and it is the indirect economic subsidy provided by the U.S. military shield that enables Seoul to build up its military-industrial complex.

As we have suggested, the Japanese interest in avoiding involvement in the Korean struggle is directly related to the growing Japanese stake in close relations with China. This is not the appropriate place to explore the complex factors affecting Sino-Japanese relations, but it appears likely, as I have argued elsewhere, that Peking will loom larger and larger in Japanese foreign policy calculations.[14] This projection is based not only on changing economic priorities, notably the emergence of China as a major oil producer with massive offshore deposits in the Po Hai area within easy tanker reach of Japan.[15] More important, the new Chinese readiness to export oil and other natural resources to Japan provides a pragmatic rationale for closer ties that many

Japanese would like to have for other reasons. Economics, ethnicity, cultural affinity, and a sense of shared destiny in relation to the West have all combined to give the Sino-Japanese relationship a powerful momentum. In time, this could well lead to a common Sino-Japanese approach to Korea in which Japan backs away from the South in order to avoid a conflict of interests with Peking. Japanese involvement in the South at present would appear to be considerably greater than Peking's aid to the North, though precise figures for the North are difficult to obtain.

Japan, China, and the Soviet Union, as regional neighbors, all have an overriding interest in preempting control of Korea by any of the others. This interest is not served by the polarization now occurring between a Japanese-backed South and a Chinese-backed and Soviet-backed North. On the contrary, the safest eventuality for all concerned would be the emergence of patterns of contact and cooperation that would enable North and South to reduce their external dependence, present a common front toward all outside powers, and move toward eventual confederation or unification.

Japan and Korea: Images and Attitudes

Before proceeding to a consideration of U.S. interests in Korea, it should be pointed out that Japan has been moving fitfully and hesitantly toward a more symmetrical posture but has keyed this movement to its shifting assessments of U.S. plans and desires. Japan's one-sided commitment to the South has been largely predicated on a protective U.S. military presence, and an American decision to maintain a combat presence in Korea for an indefinite further period would strengthen the domestic forces in Japan favoring continued support of the South. By the same token, an American decision to withdraw gradually over, let us say, a five-year or ten-year period would bring the costs and perils of an asymmetrical posture into sharper focus, accelerating the pressures in Japan for a more detached posture balancing Japanese interests in Seoul and Pyongyang.

Adapting to the American Presence

In a perceptive discussion of Japanese policy toward Korea, James W. Morley has observed that

> clearly the word "essential" (*kinyo*) used in the Satō-Nixon communiqué of 1969 and reaffirmed by Miyazawa in 1975 to describe the relationship of the R.O.K.'s security to that of Japan should be given no absolute nor too generalized a meaning. Some "essentials" are more essential than others. Even the conservative governments of Japan most strongly in support of the R.O.K. have never seriously considered making binding military commitments to the Republic itself. There is only one overseas military tie that they have deemed really "essential" to their security. That is the Treaty with the United States. It is primarily to keep that Treaty that the Japanese Government has conceded—to the extent that it has—to U.S. demands on the Korean security issue.[16]

The reference to Korea in the 1969 communiqué was inserted only at the insistence of the United States, it should be remembered, as a quid pro quo for the U.S. agreement to place U.S. bases in Okinawa under the "prior consultation" clause of the security treaty. In American eyes, the reference to Korea in the joint communiqué went hand in hand with the more explicit Satō statement in a National Press Club speech pledging "prompt and positive" Japanese action on any U.S. request for the use of Japanese bases to wage combat operations in the event of "an armed attack against the Republic of Korea." Defending what he had done back in Japan, however, Satō disavowed the English expression *positive*, explaining that the Japanese phrase he had used in his Press Club address, *mao mukini*, could more accurately be translated as "in a forward-looking way." "When we say that we shall determine our attitude 'in a forward-looking way,'" Satō told a Diet questioner, "we mean that we say 'yes' in a forward-looking way or we say 'no' in a forward-looking way. I cannot say under what conditions we will say 'yes' or we will say 'no.'"[17] By April 1974, Foreign Minister Toshio Kimura had further explained that what was "essential" to Japan was not "the security of the republic of Korea" but rather "the peace and security of the Korean peninsula in its entirety." By August, Kimura had taken another step in the direction of greater symmetry with his controversial statements that there is "no threat" from the North and that "the government of the republic of Korea is not the only lawful government in the Korean peninsula."

To a great extent, the partial backtracking on the Korean issue that accompanied the installation of Kiichi Miyazawa as foreign minister in the Miki cabinet mirrored shifting factional alignments within the ruling party rather than a settled national consensus in support of a pro-Seoul policy. This was apparent in a May 1975 *Nihon Keizai* poll of forty-six LDP members of the Lower House of the Diet active in the ruling party's Foreign Policy Council. Asked whether Seoul was a "lifeline" of Japan's security, only nine gave an unqualified yes. Miki's pro-Seoul gestures in early 1975 did not represent a basic policy departure but were part of a tradeoff intended to win conservative support for ratification of the nuclear nonproliferation treaty.[18] When Miki visited Washington in August 1975, he sought to avoid a reaffirmation of the 1969 "ROK clause" in its original form, proposing that his joint communiqué with President Ford state only that "the maintenance of peace on the Korean peninsula is necessary for peace and security in East Asia, including Japan."[19] Even after he had made this concession, as Miki's pro-Seoul critics were quick to point out, it was clear that Satō's "ROK clause" had become a broader "Korea clause."[20] Moreover, Miki had gone still further by carrying an undisclosed message from Kim Il-sung to Ford; and he had done so in a most extraordinary manner, seeking to meet Ford secretly without the presence of Gaimusho advisers. The details of this second Miki-Ford meeting remain unclear, but it would appear that the prime minister urged a more flexible U.S. policy toward Pyongyang that would reduce the risk of a North-South war.

After Miki's return, *Nihon Keizai* pondered the "delicate differences in view" between Tokyo and Washington and likened the shift in Japanese attitudes toward Pyongyang in 1975 to the start of an earlier Japanese thaw in 1966 that prepared the way for the normalization of Japanese ties with Peking.[21] In September 1975, the Japanese government gave new pledges of economic aid to Seoul for the first time since the Kim Dae-jung affair but declined to reaffirm that South Korean security was vital to Japan. Instead, a joint communiqué stressed the need for friendship of the "two peoples." This has since been followed by a succession of contradictory statements regarding the U.S. use of Japanese bases in the event of new hostilities in Korea. Taken collectively, these statements leave considerable doubt about the availability of U.S. bases for combat operations in the event of renewed hostilities in Korea.

Significantly, when Prime Minister Fukuda met with President Carter in 1977, the United States had begun to modify its Korean policy, and Carter agreed to a joint communiqué clause on Korea almost identical to the one that had been propsed earlier by Miki. Omitting a direct reference to Seoul, the operative passage of the communiqué said that "the Prime Minister and the President noted the continuing importance of the maintenance of peace and stability *on the Korean peninsula* for the security of Japan and East Asia as a whole" (italics added).

What Japan Does and Does Not Fear

Japanese attitudes toward the U.S. military role in Korea are clearly much more complicated than is often suggested by advocates of a continued U.S. presence in the South. These attitudes cut across the Japanese political spectrum. To the extent that the U.S. presence keeps the South "safe for Japanese investment" without involving Japan militarily, it is welcome to pro-Seoul conservatives and tolerable to centrist public opinion as one of the necessary costs of the security treaty. To the extent that the danger of fighting in Korea appears real, however, support for the U.S. presence is offset by fears of Japanese involvement. Japanese anxieties focus, in particular, on U.S. tactical nuclear weapons in Korea, and there were anxious Diet exchanges concerning the danger of nuclear retaliation against Japan following former Secretary Schlesinger's 1975 warning that the United

States would not rule out nuclear weapons in Korea.[22] An *Asahi* cartoon hero reminiscent of Sad Sack reflected a characteristic Japanese reaction by carrying baskets of dirt from the west to the east, from the Japan Sea to the Pacific Ocean—doing his bit to move the country eastward out of harm's way.[23]

Still another focus of Japanese anxieties is the instability of the Park regime, for as John W. Lewis and Franklin B. Weinstein have observed,

> even Japanese who view with alarm the prospect of a Communist South Korea are keenly aware of the Seoul Government's narrowing political base and the heightened possibility that an insurgency, perhaps with ambiguous North Korean support, might develop. They can easily imagine circumstances where United States intervention to preserve a non-Communist South Korea might insure a Communist victory and deepen its ultimate impact. Though they prefer a divided Korea, they fear that a clumsy intrusion of American power might increase Chinese or Soviet involvement and make Japan a more inviting target.[24]

As Fuji Kamiya stresses in his chapter, the lack of an effective communist organization in the South makes it unlikely that any insurgency there would command broad-based support comparable to that mobilized by the Viet Cong in pre-1975 South Vietnam, where the communists had won a pre-eminent position of nationalist leadership during the fight against the French. Nevertheless, if mutually reinforcing political and economic difficulties should develop in the South, many Japanese foresee labor and farmer unrest that would invite direct or indirect Northern encouragement.

What most Japanese appear to fear, at bottom, is not a communist triumph in Korea as such, but rather the broader dangers and risks for Japan inherent in the transition from a profitable status quo to an uncertain future. Thus, as the debate preceding the Fukuda-Carter talks showed, even those Japanese who would like U.S. forces to remain in the South are reluctant to say so to Washington. It is one thing to benefit from what the United States does on its own; it would be quite another to ask the United States to bear responsibilities that would, in turn, expose Japan to U.S. pressures for greater defense "burden sharing." On the one hand, many Japanese fear impulsive U.S. intervention in Korea that could embroil Japan militarily; on the other, many fear precipitate U.S. disengagement from Korea that would not allow time for Japan to protect its interests. This latter concern was genuine in the immediate aftermath of the U.S. withdrawal from Indochina and was reflected in a *Sankei* parody, pointedly recalling the "Nixon shocks," in which Henry Kissinger flew secretly to Pyongyang for a settlement with Kim Il-sung, "once again, over the head of Japan."[25]

Kei Wakaizumi, explaining why Japan is fearful of a Korean conflict, put his emphasis not on the danger to Japan from the North but on the "profound apprehension that such a conflict may draw Japan into a conflict with China or the Soviet Union, or that it may damage her relations with the United States."[26] Similarly, when pressed to define the nature of the security threats that would result from a Pyongyang victory, Foreign Minister Miyazawa did not point to the danger of Northern aggression against Japan. Instead, his concern was addressed to the immediate spillover effects of a Korean civil conflict, principally the flood of refugees or "routed troops" who might seek shelter in Japan as a consequence of Japan's current ties to Seoul.[27] To be sure, such spillover effects could pose significant problems, especially in the context of Japan's existing Korean minority, and it is not surprising, therefore, that Japan should want to see peace maintained in Korea. To say this, however, is not to say that fundamental, long-term Japanese interests would be threatened by a Northern victory. Even if the South were to win a new Korean war, as we have observed earlier, Japan would no doubt find it almost as distasteful to live with a unified Korea under Southern leadership as with one dominated by the North. It is the dislocations attendant to a military resolution of the Korean conflict that would be peculiarly costly for Japan, adding to the stresses that are likely to bedevil future Japanese-Korean relations in any case, regardless of how the conflict is resolved. Many pro-

Seoul conservatives who feel that it is up to the United States
to do whatever can be done to perpetuate a noncommunist
South would probably be ready to swallow a communist
victory rather than pay the price of Japanese military
involvement. Edward Seidensticker, analyzing these conservative attitudes, observed that "to such Japanese, it does
not seem fair that Tokyo should be asked now to repair the
damage wrought by Washington thirty years ago" when it
took over Korea, displaced Japanese colonial rule, and
joined with the Soviet Union in dividing the peninsula.
"Such Japanese," Seidensticker recalled,

> remember how America started having second thoughts about
> a disarmed Japan when trouble came up in Korea, and in a
> somewhat hypocritical manner told Japan that although
> naturally the "peace constitution" and the disarmed Japan
> which it called for were here to stay, it would be all right for
> Japan to have a "police reserve." In that police reserve was the
> beginning of Japanese rearmament, and to be told now that
> rearmament should go the whole distance because trouble is
> once again brewing in Korea is too much. It was not for them,
> thank you.[28]

In assessing the probable consequences of a U.S. withdrawal in Japan, one should distinguish between its direct
impact on the Japanese debate over Korean policy and its
larger impact on the balance of strength between right and
left in Japanese politics. As indicated earlier, there is little
doubt that a U.S. withdrawal would strengthen the case for a
symmetrical approach toward Korea made by the Socialists
and the Komeito and would compel a reappraisal of
Japanese options on the part of those forces now favoring
one-sided support for the South. Japan would gradually
adapt to the new situation in Korea, just as it has adapted its
policies to the U.S. presence during the Cold War years. In
the unlikely event of a communist military triumph, rightist
elements would have a new argument to justify the continuing increases in the Japanese military budget that have
already been occurring, in any case, for a variety of other
reasons. But communist control of Korea would not be likely

to bring major increases in the political power of the right or the level of Japanese military expenditures unless it co-incided with drastic changes in Japan's overall economic and political relations with the rest of the world. Given the depth of antinuclear sentiment in Japan, the proposition that a U.S. withdrawal from Korea would in itself trigger a nuclear arms buildup in Japan would appear to be extreme-ly simplistic. Thus Nobuyuki Nakahara, managing director of Toa Nenryo Kogyo, a leading oil firm, has commented that

> the impact of a gradual withdrawal of U.S. forces from Korea would not lead to a violent reaction in Japan. If the U.S. is worried about Japanese rearmament, it should concentrate on those factors which could actually contribute to such a development. For example, the U.S. should assure the flow of agricultural exports to Japan, and it should faithfully carry out its responsibilities to us in the energy field.[29]

During his Washington visit, Prime Minister Miki care-fully sidestepped the persistent efforts of TV questioners who sought to elicit a Japanese request for the indefinite continuance of the U.S. presence in Korea. Three times, Miki responded only that the United States should not make a "very sudden" change in its force deployments. Then he added that "there is only a limited, if any, chance of major hostilities recurring in the Korean peninsula."[30] Similarly, Fukuda was extremely cautious, stressing that the issue of force deployments in Korea was one that should be decided by Washington and Seoul.

The Case for American Disengagement

This analysis has focused on the character of Japanese interests in Korea in order to clear the decks, as it were, for a meaningful consideration of U.S. interests in Korea and a conclusion pointing to American and Japanese policy options. In particular, we have stressed the special sensitivity of the Japanese-Korean relationship in the aftermath of colonialism. For Japan, we have argued, there would be a peculiar danger in a continuing polarization between a

Japanese-backed South and a Chinese-backed and Soviet-
backed North, though Japan, China, and the Soviet Union
have a similar interest in preventing any of the others from
controlling Korea, and all would benefit from a reduction of
tensions that would enable Seoul and Pyongyang to reduce
their external dependence. Japan does not have an exclusive
or inherent interest in the ascendancy of either the South or
the North, in this analysis, but rather a more generalized
interest in a peaceful resolution of the Korean conflict. By
reviewing the internal Japanese debate over Korea policy, we
have demonstrated that Japan has in fact been moving
toward a more symmetrical approach to Korea as a means of
reducing North-South contention but that it has been
constrained by its desire to keep its relations with the United
States on an even keel. At the same time, we have shown that
this emphasis on avoiding a policy conflict with the United
States tends to obfuscate what has become, increasingly, an
ambivalent Japanese assessment with respect to whether an
indefinite U.S. military presence in Korea would necessarily
serve overall Japanese interests.

The Congruence of U.S. and Japanese Interests

Our analysis makes clear that there are no separate and
specifically Japanese interests in Korea differing significantly from fundamental U.S. interests. Both countries have the
same basic interest in a peaceful resolution of the Korean
conflict, a resolution that would minimize the danger of
their direct or indirect involvement. In one sense, Japan has
a more pronounced interest in the avoidance of military
conflict, given its proximity and the possibility of spillover
effects; in another, the United States has far more to lose in
view of its direct combat commitment. Both countries also
have a parallel stake in the insulation of the peninsula from
major power rivalry and in the emergence of a unified Korea
able to act as a buffer state. Like Japan, the United States has
accumulated vested interests in the South, but these do not
outweigh the larger national interests that would be served
by U.S. disengagement from the North-South rivalry. It
should be noted, however, that some of the U.S. vested

interests in the South differ in character from those of Japan, including crude oil sales by American firms, currently exceeding $1 billion per year, and a $2.3 billion military base infrastructure that was being refurbished even in early 1977. If these U.S. vested interests were abandoned, the United States would suffer an even greater economic loss than Japan would suffer if the North took over. Most of the American economic stake in the South, for example, is in the form of equity investment, but the greater portion of Japanese economic involvement is in the form of technical assistance and licensing arrangements. These would be less directly affected than equity holdings, should expropriation occur, since much of the Japanese export trade with the South consists of raw materials and components for Japanese-linked enterprises that would still be needed even if the enterprises concerned were operated by the state.

In considering its future policy options in Korea, including whether and how to disengage all of its military forces, the United States can proceed on the assumption that Japan would not see a threat to its vital interests in an American disengagement, provided that the process is spread out gradually over five to ten years. In addition to the withdrawal of ground combat forces by 1981 or 1982 contemplated by the Carter administration, the United States could also withdraw its air combat units from bases in South Korea at a designated later date without endangering vital Japanese interests, provided Washington keeps its security treaty with Seoul in force and retains a credible capability for intervention in the event of Chinese or Soviet involvement in a new Korean war. One indication of such a capability would be the retention of air wings earmarked for Korea on nearby carriers for an indefinite period. Another would be the continuance of some specialized logistics and technical elements of U.S. forces in South Korea following the withdrawal of U.S. combat forces.[31] This estimate of the Japanese reaction to a U.S. withdrawal is shared by former Ambassador Edwin O. Reischauer,[32] who stresses the distinction between a phased withdrawal conducted in a planned fashion, at a pace set by the United States itself, and a sudden retreat under military pressure comparable to the Vietnam experience.[33] As our analysis has shown, Japan would be most unlikely to intervene in Korea militarily, even in the event of Chinese or Soviet military support of the North; and if it should "go nuclear," this would be for reasons far transcending its concerns in Korea. The greatest risks attaching to a U.S. disengagement do not lie in what Japan would do but rather in what North and South Korea, China, and the Soviet Union might do. Here is where the United States must make difficult judgments, in which a wide spectrum of informed Japanese appraisals should weigh heavily.

Does the U.S. presence promote an atmosphere conducive to a North-South thaw, as administration spokesmen contend?

To what extent is it the U.S. presence that deters a Northern attack?

Is there a significant danger that China or the Soviet Union or both would support a Northern military adventure?

Is the U.S. presence needed to restrain military action by the South?

The Thaw Argument

Since 1958, there have been no foreign forces in the North. Pyongyang has only half the population of the South but has devoted from two to four times as much of its gross national product to military spending as Seoul.[34] By contrast, the combined economic subsidy represented by U.S. forces, U.S. bases, U.S. military aid, and such ancillary economic aid as "Food for Peace" has enabled the South to have a maximum of security with a minimum of sacrifice. The upper- and middle-income minority, in particular, has acquired a vested interest in the status quo. So long as the South has the U.S. presence as an economic cushion, it is under no compulsion to explore the mutual force reductions proposed by the North and has in fact been moving in the opposite direction by expanding its defense-related industries.

Opponents of disengagement argue that the South would react to a U.S. withdrawal by accelerating its defense buildup and that its accompanying anxieties would progressively foreclose any peaceful dialogue with the North. Only the U.S. presence, it is argued, infuses the confidence and sense of security needed to promote a North-South dialogue. This contention does not appear to be borne out, however, by the manner in which the South has approached the North-South dialogue during recent years. On the contrary, it is only in the absence of U.S. forces that Seoul would have to make hard choices, for the first time, between the sacrifices required to match the level of defense strength now provided by the United States and an approach to the North more accurately reflecting the complex mixture of anticommunist and pro-unification emotions in the South. Initially, the South might react to a U.S. withdrawal by expanding its defense buildup, but to do so would impose economic burdens that would soon force a painful reappraisal of long-term options. The objective of U.S. policy should be to promote such a reappraisal, and it would therefore be completely self-defeating to accompany a withdrawal of U.S. forces with the huge amounts of compensatory military aid that were sought by Seoul in mid-1977. At present, the Park regime suppresses public discussion of how far and how fast to go in dealings with the North, and the readiness of the North for compromise has yet to be seriously tested.

For example, the Park regime has made no effort to test the seriousness of the North's repeated proposals for mutual force reductions. At times, Kim Il-sung has talked of reductions that would bring both Northern and Southern forces down to the same level of 100,000 men; on one occasion, in my two-hour interview with him on June 26, 1972, Kim made a more promising proposal for force reductions *of* 150,000 by both sides that would enable the South to retain its superiority in ground forces. Instead of seeking a dialogue to probe Pyongyang's intentions (e.g., with respect to inspection machinery), Seoul has dismissed such proposals out of hand. One of the major sticking points in the abortive discussions of the North-South Coordinating

Committee established in 1972 was a Northern proposal for the establishment of a military committee that would be entrusted with the task of exploring mutual force reductions. Seoul argues that such far-reaching moves should come only after prior agreement on "smaller steps" such as athletic exchanges and postal links. But Pyongyang counters that it wants to gauge Seoul's long-term intentions. Is Park really serious about moving toward confederation and unification, albeit gradually, the North asks, or is he merely seeking token agreements intended to give the appearance of progress toward national unity? Unless Park is willing to discuss meaningful issues at the outset, the North says, the "smaller steps" approach could actually delay unification by enabling Park to appease his domestic critics and prolong a regime that is wedded, in reality, to the goal of indefinite division.

My own conclusion after talking with Kim and lesser North Korean officials was that Pyongyang has a serious interest in force reductions for economic reasons.[35] Similarly, there appears to be more than propaganda alone in Northern proposals for confederation, though I was not able to draw out Northern officials on such key, still-undefined points as how long confederal arrangements would exist prior to full unification. North Korean sources seek to convey the impression that Pyongyang would make no effort to alter the economic system in the South under confederal arrangements, pointing to article five of the revised constitution adopted following the 1972 North-South talks. This article states that Pyongyang "strives to achieve the complete victory of socialism in the northern half" while seeking only to "drive out foreign forces on a nation-wide scale."[36] A more flexible Southern approach to the North-South talks could gradually smoke out what, if anything, specific Pyongyang has in mind when it speaks of confederation. By the same token, the withdrawal of U.S. forces would remove one of the major excuses used by Kim Il-sung to reject de facto coexistence with Seoul and could thus advance, rather than undermine, the prospects for North-South accommodation. Even the limited moves toward force withdrawals made by the United States in 1977 produced a conciliatory initial response on the part of the North addressed to the objective of a diplomatic dialogue between Pyongyang and Washington as signatories to the 1953 armistice agreement (Seoul was not a signatory). Against the background of U.S. force withdrawal plans, Pyongyang might be willing to resume the North-South talks if these were accompanied by a parallel Pyongyang-Washington dialogue, given South Korean readiness to discuss the force reductions issue.

The Deterrence Argument

It would be self-deluding to overlook the deterrent role played by the U.S. presence in past years or to minimize the possibility of a North Korean attack at some time following a U.S. withdrawal. To put this issue in perspective, however, it should be emphasized that the North has been deterred not only by the U.S. presence but also by other important factors, including the disproportionate defense burden already mentioned and serious attendant domestic economic constraints.[37] To the extent that a North Korean attack is a realistic possibility, it could materialize whether or not there is a U.S. presence in Korea and might even be more likely in the context of a continuing American presence. This could apply particularly with respect to low-level pressures deliberately calculated to embarrass the United States and put psychological pressure on Seoul. For example, one Southern military target made more attractive by the U.S. presence is the group of west coast offshore islands located in part just above the thirty-eighth parallel. These were conceded at the last moment by the North during the armistice negotiations and are regarded as militarily vulnerable by the United States today. The South wants to defend these islands in the event of a Northern move there, and Northern pressure could thus lead to intervention by the United States against its own better judgment.

The danger of an escalation of minor military incidents in Korea involving U.S. combat forces is peculiarly explosive as a result of the continued presence of U.S. tactical nuclear forces in the peninsula. This danger is primarily that nuclear storage facilities are exposed to seizure, a danger that will be only marginally reduced by a new $364,000 U.S. program to improve these facilities. However, an added element of danger lies in the fact that U.S. military doctrine does not rule out the use of nuclear weapons in Korea as part of the U.S. deterrent.

The Restraining Hand Argument

On balance, such deterrent value as the U.S. presence has in narrowly military terms would appear to be canceled out, increasingly, by its political impact in freezing the North-South confrontation. Since 1969, the Northern tactical shift to a nonmilitary approach, for reasons largely unrelated to the U.S. deterrent, has created a new opportunity for North-South accommodation, but the U.S. presence impedes the emergence of the indigenous power equation necessary for this process to take place.

Significantly, U.S. government spokesmen have tended to downgrade the danger of a Northern attack in recent years and imply that a more determinative, if unstated, reason for maintaining a U.S. presence in Korea is U.S. fear of Southern adventurism. With its operational control over Southern military forces, it is argued, the United States can keep a restraining hand on the situation and make sure that Seoul does not overreact to Northern provocations or make provocative thrusts of its own that could drag the United States into undesired hostilities.

To some extent, the danger of Southern adventurism would appear to be a valid argument for a cautious approach to a U.S. withdrawal. It is an argument for gradualism, however, rather than for indefinitely postponing a timetable for disengagement. The five-to-ten-year period suggested here would minimize economic dislocations and would permit a stable emotional adjustment on the part of the South. Moreover, Seoul is already acting on the assumption that the United States will withdraw, sooner or later, and is actively moving to expand its defense production base. In effect, the continuation of the U.S. presence without a cutoff point in view serves to underwrite the further militarization of the South, including the steps now being taken to acquire missile manufacturing capabilities.

It is often said that the South could do without U.S. forces in strictly military terms but needs them for psychological reassurance. However, a more critical reason for the Southern desire to prolong U.S. aid and the U.S. force presence is that they release funds for militarily oriented industrial development, funds that would otherwise be extremely difficult to support. At periodic intervals during the past two decades, Seoul has induced each new U.S. administration to supply additional increments of military equipment that would, it was said, enable the South to achieve parity with the North and end its reliance on U.S. aid. Most recently, the 1970 "modernization plan" negotiated by former Defense Secretary Laird, touted as the last such plan that would ever have to be adopted, has been succeeded by new requests for one more "last" five-year plan. On each occasion, it is said that parity would permit the United States to disengage its forces; but it is always possible for Seoul to argue that parity has not been achieved, since each new increment of U.S. aid provokes some degree of countervailing communist aid.

In the short run, the U.S. presence does help to restrain the South. But in the long run, a continuation of the subsidy now provided by the U.S. presence and open-ended U.S. military aid will enable the South to build a much more ambitious military capability than would otherwise be possible and will progressively enhance the danger of a North-South explosion.

The Intervention Argument

The most important deterrent restraining the North may not be the U.S. presence but rather the recognition that it would probably not receive as much Soviet support as it did in the Korean War. The strategic landscape has been radically altered since 1950. Moscow and Peking would now have to judge the impact that any new Korean adventure would have on their improved relations with Washington and Tokyo. Equally important, in the context of the Sino-

Soviet rivalry, Korea now figures in the calculations of the two communist powers not only in relation to the West but also in relation to each other. Each wants to keep the other from establishing a dominant position in Pyongyang, and each would hesitate to risk provoking its rival by intervening unilaterally in a North-South war. At the same time, should the Sino-Soviet rivalry become less intense, the possibility of intervention would be enhanced though large-scale military support for the North would still be unlikely.

Although estimates of communist aid to the North are partly guesswork, there appears to be general agreement in the West and in Japan that Chinese and Soviet military aid to the North has been slowly tapering off and is now less than U.S. aid to the South. According to the U.S. Arms Control and Disarmament Agency, the North received only $922 million in military aid from its allies between 1963 and 1973, as against $2.7 billion received by the South.[38] Some have argued that this has included airpower superior to that provided under U.S. aid to the South; but as General George Brown of the U.S. Air Force told a House Appropriations Subcommittee in 1974, "the North Korean Air Force is essentially defense-oriented and not offensively oriented."[39]

Although the North had more combat aircraft than the South in 1976 (an estimated 573 to 330), only 160 of these were modern, high-performance aircraft, in contrast to 215 in the South. The North's MIGs are interceptors with the limited range and bomb-carrying capacity appropriate for a defensive role. Even the MIG-21 can carry a maximum ordnance load of only 4,000 pounds, less than one-fourth the capacity of the South's seventy-two F-4 Phantom jets. The South argues that the MIGs could play an offensive role, given Seoul's proximity to Northern air bases along the Demilitarized Zone. However, the MIGs' lack of range and payload capacity does not suit them for the close support of sustained ground operations. The South has been seeking upgraded aircraft (e.g. the F-16) as part of compensatory aid provided by the U.S. in conjunction with its force with-drawals. In Washington's eyes, the provision of such aircraft could conceivably be viewed as a prelude to the withdrawal of a direct U.S. Air Force presence in the South. But there is a danger that an F-16 program might stimulate new Soviet or Chinese aircraft assistance to the North and thus perpetuate an open-ended arms race.

In an earlier study, I have argued that the U.S. security treaty with the South should be kept in force indefinitely following a withdrawal of U.S. forces, pending the outcome of diplomatic efforts to coordinate the termination of U.S. treaty ties with the termination of Soviet and Chinese treaty links to the North.[40] I have also suggested earlier here that the continuance of the treaty could be accompanied by the maintenance of air wings on Seventh Fleet carriers near Korea earmarked for possible use there. Should Soviet or Chinese forces intervene in a new Korean conflict, the United States could then respond effectively with its air-power, and the strategic mobility provided by C-5As would even enable the United States to airlift ground forces to the South with the requisite speed if it chose to do so. Ralph Clough ignores the proximity of the Seventh Fleet and the continuing improvement in U.S. mobility in his argument that there is an "underlying asymmetry" in the military security of the North and the South.[41] In military terms, the United States would not be "six thousand miles away" if the North attacked the South and was supported by Soviet or Chinese forces. However, it should be noted that Clough would apparently like to see the United States intervene in any new Korean conflict whether or not the Soviet Union and China do. In this respect, he finds himself an advocate of "asymmetry." By contrast, in my approach, the United States would seek to disassociate itself from the North-South rivalry following the withdrawal of U.S. forces and would not participate directly in a new military phase of the Korean civil war unless Moscow or Peking, or both, should intervene.

The Balance of Power Argument

As Sino-Soviet differences have hardened, the case for a U.S. presence has rested less and less on the danger of Sino-Soviet intervention but rather on the argument that disengagement would threaten the balance of power even in the event of a strictly civil conflict. Given the Sino-Soviet rivalry, it is said, the United States should enforce the peace in Korea unless unification comes with the concerted approval of Moscow, Peking, and Tokyo. Pressed to explain this more precisely, advocates of a continued U.S. presence generally contend that China would like a U.S. presence in Korea to preserve a regional balance with the Soviet Union.

As in the case of Japan, it may well be that Peking does fear the unsettling effects that a precipitate disengagement would entail. If we take a longer view, however, Peking appears to be adapting its overt posture regarding U.S. bases in Korea to the immediate dictates of its relations with the United States. Peking chooses not to make a major issue of the U.S. military presence in Korea for tactical reasons reflecting its overall use of its U.S. ties as leverage against the Soviet Union. Nevertheless, China makes a distinction between U.S. bases on the Asian mainland, which affront its nationalist sensibilities, and its desire for a protective U.S. strategic role underpinned by a U.S.-Soviet missile balance. This has been signalled with growing candor in recent Chinese official statements on Korea.

China appears to be much more sensitive to the explosive potential of Korean nationalism than the other powers directly involved and better prepared than the Soviet Union to contemplate the prospect of a unified Korea under communist rule, even though control of the entire peninsula would make Pyongyang even more difficult to handle than at present. A noncommunist, unified Korea would be another matter, but Peking's attitude would be primarily governed, in any event, by whether the new regime adopted a neutralist posture or became a vehicle of Soviet, Japanese, or American influence. A unified Korea of any complexion would pose much less of a threat to its neighbors than a unified Germany, it should be remembered, and military moves to unify the peninsula would thus be unlikely to invite preemptive intervention. Germany united was expansionist, but Korea before its division was the victim of Japanese colonialism.

The Future of U.S. and Japanese Policy

What should the United States and Japan do in Korea?

The import of this analysis is that concrete initiatives in the diplomatic, economic, and security arenas can profitably take place if and only if both Washington and Tokyo move toward symmetrical policies in dealings with Seoul and Pyongyang. Such movement cannot realistically be conditioned on a close synchronization with Moscow and Peking in which the communist powers are expected to reciprocate U.S. and Japanese moves vis-à-vis the North with directly parallel moves in the South. For nearly seventeen years, there have been no communist forces in the North, and it is for the United States to make a gesture of reciprocity, in the first instance, by initiating a unilateral process of disengagement at a pace and in a manner of its own choosing. In offering the withdrawal of its presence as a bargaining counter, at this late stage, the United States has either been acting on the basis of an extremely distorted view of the actual bargaining situation in Korea or has been attempting to bluff Moscow and Peking in what has so far, at least, proved to be a futile game of diplomatic poker.

The principle of simultaneous reciprocity can be appropriately invoked in Korea only where a basis for reciprocity actually exists, as in the case of the future disposition of the U.S. security treaty with the South and the Chinese and Soviet treaties with the North. As I have emphasized earlier, the U.S. treaty should be kept in force for the indefinite future pending the outcome of long-term diplomatic efforts to phase out the three treaties in a broadly coordinated manner. Such a diplomatic effort would hold promise of success, however, only if the United States were to build upon the plans for the disengagement of ground combat forces initiated by President Carter through his affirmation of the U.S. intention to withdraw air combat units at a designated later stage. Even if some logistical and technical forces remained in Korea, the removal of all combat forces would materially alter the diplomatic climate. This would open the way for meaningful U.S. efforts to obtain Soviet and Chinese agreement on the limitation of arms flows into the peninsula. But an arms limitation agreement would presuppose, in turn, great restraint on the part of the United States in responding to South Korean pressures for military aid as a compensation for force withdrawals. Similarly, arms control measures, notably efforts to establish a nuclear-free zone in Korea or in Northeast Asia as a whole, would hold promise only in the context of the removal of U.S. tactical nuclear weapons as part of the process of U.S. disengagement. Regional arms control proposals should be advanced by the United States in tandem with the announcement of plans for disengagement and should take into account proposals already made by Kim Il-sung for mutual North-South force reductions.[42]

The United States is currently attempting to make any dealings with Pyongyang contingent on a reciprocal readiness by Peking and Moscow to deal with Seoul. Once plans for a U.S. force withdrawal are announced, there would be nothing inherently illogical in attempting to link U.S. recognition of the North with the reciprocal communist "cross-recognition" of the South. As a practical matter, however, such an approach appears unlikely to produce results for several very formidable reasons. One is the Sino-Soviet rivalry and the consequent reluctance of Moscow and Peking to risk alienating Pyongyang. Still another factor complicating this approach is an apparent difference in the Chinese and Soviet approaches to Korea, with China more firmly committed, at this stage, to a pro-Pyongyang posture. Conceivably, the Chinese attitude might be affected by a satisfactory resolution of the Taiwan issue. Together with a unilaterally initiated disengagement of U.S. forces in Korea, the normalization of Sino-U.S. relations might help to bring about a de facto, but not de jure, change in the Chinese approach to Korea. By the same token, a Sino-U.S. impasse on Taiwan could aggravate Sino-U.S. tensions on the peninsula. It should be emphasized, however, that China is not likely to go to the extent of a de jure "two Korea" policy as part of its quid pro quo for a U.S. shift on Taiwan. The most that could be expected would be increased Chinese encouragement of an improved North-South climate and a reinforcement of the other factors militating against Chinese intervention in any new Korean conflict. Regardless of the course of Sino-U.S. relations, therefore, it would appear desirable for the United States and Japan to move toward more symmetrical policies in Korea.

"People to people" exchanges, trade, and measured steps toward the diplomatic recognition of Pyongyang would appear to be essential prerequisites for meaningful diplomatic efforts to promote a North-South accommodation. As suggested earlier, the most promising path to peace in Korea lies in finding a way to link more stable patterns of short-term coexistence with a long-term timetable of projected moves in the direction of confederation or unification. The search for such a formula is not likely to be easy, regardless of what the United States and Japan do, and it is not even likely to begin until Washington disengages its combat forces and joins with Tokyo in adopting more symmetrical policies toward the two Korean regimes.

Notes

1. The concept of the North Korean attack as the first salvo in a worldwide campaign of communist aggression has been effectively challenged by Charles E. Bohlen, *Witness to History* (New York: W. W. Norton, 1973), pp. 288-304; Ernest May, *"Lessons" of the Past* (New York: Oxford University Press, 1973), especially pp. 53-86; and Allen S. Whiting, *China Crosses the Yalu* (New York: Macmillan, 1960), especially pp. 151-172.

2. Robert R. Simmons, *The Strained Alliance: Peking, Pyongyang, Moscow and the Politics of the Korean Civil War* (New York: The Free Press, 1975), especially pp. 107-110.

3. Nikita Khrushchev, *Khrushchev Remembers* (Boston: Little, Brown, 1970), pp. 367-369.

4. Selig S. Harrison, "One Korea?" *Foreign Policy*, no. 17 (Winter 1974-75), pp. 35-62.

5. See article 6 of the Pyongyang-Moscow treaty (July 6, 1961) and article 7 of the Pyongyang-Peking treaty (July 11, 1961).

6. For detailed accounts of my North Korean visit, see the *Washington Post*, May 26, June 6, June 12, June 26, July 2, July 3, and July 4, 1972.

7. An extended analysis of Korean nationalism, including a

discussion of the contrast between the Korean and German cases, is presented in *The Widening Gulf: Asian Nationalism and American Policy* (New York: The Free Press, 1977).

8. Ibid., chapter 7, "After Korea: The Stresses of Division," discusses this significant episode in detail. The hearings of the Special Committee on National Unification were held from September through December 1966, and the 190-page proceedings are reprinted in full in Korean in the committee report. See Taehan Minguk Kuk-hoe [National Assembly], "T'ongil paeksŏ" [White paper on unification], mimeographed (Seoul, 1967). The committee report and numerous other Korean-language materials relating to the unification issue were translated for the author with the support of the Brookings Institution. For example, see a series of thirteen articles by the committee's chairman, Suh In-sok, in *Choson Ilbo*, August 1966; an article by Prof. Kim Hong-ch'ol of the South Korean National Defense College, "Concept of a Friendly Nation," *Chong Maek*, March 1966; and *Han'guk ŭi minjokchuŭi* [Report of a conference on Korean nationalism], Korean Association of International Relations (Seoul, 1967), especially an address by the association's then-president, Yi Yong-hŭi, "Han'guk minjokchuŭi ŭi chemunje" [The problems facing Korean nationalism], p. 13. See also Ch'a Ki-byŏk, "Han'guk minjokchuŭi ŭi tojŏn kwa siryŏn" [Trials and challenges of Korean nationalism], pp. 33-34, and the exchanges on pp. 183-215, especially comments by Ha kyŏng-gŭn, Yi Ki-yŏng, and Ko Yŏng-bok. For a partial English summary of this symposium, see *Korea Journal*, Korean National Commission for UNESCO, December 1966. This was one of the last open discussions of the unification issue among Korean intellectuals permitted by the Park regime before 1969, when the solidification of authoritarian rule began. The unification issue also figures prominently throughout *Han'guk kŭndaehwa e issŏsŏe kaldŭnggwa chohwa* [Conflict and harmony: Report of conference on modernization], April 20, 1968, Publication no. 8, Korean Association of International Relations (Seoul, 1969).

9. "Declaration for Democratic National Salvation," Seoul, March 1, 1976. Signed by Kim Dae-jung, Yun Po-sun, Hahm Sok-hun, Chung Il-hyung, Kim Kwan-suk, Yun Ban-woong, Ahn Byoung-moo, Suh Nam-dong, Lee Oo-jung, Eun Myoung-gi, Lee Moon-young, and Moon Dong-whan.

10. An example of a significant underground document stressing the anti-Japanese theme is Student Government, Korea

University, *Declaration on the Contemporary Situation of Korea,* issued with the approval of the Contemporary Conference on the "New Order of Korea and Asia," Seoul, September 29, 1970. See also the veiled anti-Japanese allusions in "The Five Thieves," by the South Korean poet Kim Chi-ha, a satirical poem confiscated by the Park regime but available in Japanese translation in Sentaro Shibuya, *Nagai Kyrayamai no Kanata ni,* Chuo Koron-sha, December 1971.

Park's official biography (April 1969, p. 5) notes that he graduated at the head of his class in the two-year elementary course in the Manchukuo Military Academy in 1942, winning entry to the advanced course in the Japanese Imperial Military Academy and serving as a first lieutenant until the end of World War II.

11. For example, see the testimony by Ch'oe Mun-hwan, president of Seoul National University, before the National Assembly Special Committee on National Unification, December 6, 1966, followed by the testimony of opposition leader Cho Yun-hyong. See also No Chae-bong, "Han'guk kŭndaehwa e issŏsŏe kaldŭng" [Conflicts in the modernization of Korea], in *Han'guk kŭndaehwa e issŏsŏe kaldŭnggwa chohwa,* pp. 20-30. A more guarded discussion in this vein may be found in *Han kook in kwa sahoe joenui* [Koreans and social justice], Report no. 29 in a series of round table discussions sponsored by the Congress for Cultural Freedom, Metro Hotel, Seoul, April 12, 1967.

12. Yung Tai-pyun, Rhee's prime minister (1953) and foreign minister (1953-55), in an interview with the Dulles Oral History Project, Princeton University, Seoul, September 29, 1964, pp. 8, 20. See also the interview with Admiral Sohn Won-yil, September 29, 1964, p. 11.

13. Pyong Choon Hahm, "Korea's 'Mendicant Mentality'?" *Foreign Affairs* 43, no. 1 (October 1964): 171.

14. "China and Japan: The New Partnership," *Washington Post,* March 4, 1973, p. B5. See also the author's "One Korea?" pp. 55-56; and "The 'State of the Arc': Japan and Korea" (Paper prepared for the Washington Center of Foreign Policy Research Roundtable Series, December 18, 1975), especially pp. 17-21.

15. This is discussed in the author's "China: The Next Oil Giant," *Foreign Policy,* no. 20 (Fall 1975), pp. 3-62; and *China, Oil and Asia: Conflict Ahead?* (New York: Columbia University Prss, 1973).

16. James W. Morley, "How Essential Is the Republic of Korea to Japan?" (Paper prepared for a Conference on Korea and the

Major Powers sponsored by the Institute for Sino-Soviet Studies, George Washington University, Roslyn, Virginia, May 1-3, 1975), pp. 17-18.

17. This is cited in Kwan Ha-yim, "Korea in Japanese Foreign Policy" (Paper prepared for the 1973 Annual Meeting of the American Political Science Association, New Orleans, September 4-8, 1973), p. 12.

18. Morley, "How Essential Is the Republic of Korea to Japan?" pp. 16-17.

19. As examples of Japanese press coverage underlining the divergence in the U.S. and Japanese positions on the communiqué language, see editorials in *Mainichi* ("U.S.-Japan Summit Talks Leave Doubts") and *Tokyo Shimbun* ("Different Evaluation of Japan on Japan-U.S. Summit Talks") on August 8, 1975. Translated in U.S. Embassy Press Translations.

20. "'R.O.K. Clause' Changed to 'Korean Clause,'" *Sankei*, August 7, 1975, p. 2.

21. "Delicate Differences Between U.S. and Japan," *Nihon Keizai*, August 8, 1975, p. 2. See also "We Urge Formulation of Korean Peninsula Policy Which Will Not Leave Behind Roots of Trouble for Future," an editorial on August 2, 1975.

22. "Retaliation Against Japan Will Be Possible in Connection with Deployment of U.S. Forces in Japan to Korean Peninsula: Foreign Minister," *Tokyo Shimbun*, June 14, 1975, p. 1. Translated in U.S. Embassy Press Translations.

23. Cited in Edward Seidensticker, "Japan After Vietnam," *Commentary*, September 1975, p. 56.

24. "Tokyo and Washington," *New York Times*, May 29, 1975, p. 35.

25. "Shaking Asia and Japan's Course: One Day, All of a Sudden, U.S. and Korea," *Sankei*, July 15, 1975, p. 2.

26. Kei Wakaizumi, "Japan's 'Grand Experiment' and the Japanese-American Alliance," Woodrow Wilson International Center for Scholars, October 9, 1975, p. 33.

27. "Foreign Minister Refers to Inflow of Refugees and Routed Troops as Effect of 'War in R.O.K.' upon Japan's Security," *Yomiuri*, August 23, 1975, p. 1.

28. Edward Seidensticker, "Japan after Vietnam," p. 56.

29. Interview, Tokyo, November 14, 1974.

30. "Issues and Answers," American Broadcasting Company, August 10, 1975. Transcript published by Tyler Business Services, Washington. See especially p. 1.

31. For an earlier version of this withdrawal timetable, see Harrison, "One Korea?," pp. 58-62.

32. On "The Robert MacNeil Report," Public Broadcasting System, December 2, 1975, I proposed the withdrawal of combat forces in five years and the remaining forces within ten years. Ambassador Reischauer expressed his agreement with this suggested timetable on this program.

33. "Back to Normalcy," *Foreign Policy*, no. 20 (Fall 1975), p. 207.

34. For example, in 1973, the South reported spending $476 million on defense out of a $9.3 billion gross national product, while the North listed $625 million out of a $3.5 billion G.N.P. In 1976, the South increased its defense spending to 6.2 percent of G.N.P., but this still fell far short of an estimated 15 percent on the part of the North.

35. For a detailed statement of this view by the author, see "North Korea: Fewer Guns, More Butter," *Washington Post*, July 2, 1972, p. C3.

36. "Socialist Constitution of the Democratic People's Republic of Korea," *Korea Today* (Pyongyang), no. 196 (1973), p. 24.

37. I have discussed these constraints at length in "North Korea: Fewer Guns, More Butter."

38. *World Military Expenditures and Arms Trade, 1963-73*, A.C.D.A. Publication 74 (Washington, 1975), Table V, p. 99.

39. This statement was made on April 1, 1974, at hearings on Department of Defense appropriations for 1975. U.S., House of Representatives, *Hearings of the Defense Subcommittee of the Committee on Appropriations*, pt. 2, 1974, p. 379.

40. Harrison, "One Korea?" pp. 58-62.

41. See Clough's "Commentary" in chapter 10 of this volume.

42. Harrison, "One Korea?" p. 61. See also my interview with Kim Il-sung in *Washington Post*, June 26, 1972, p. A18, and an analysis of conversations with North Korean officials, "Kim Seeks Summit, Korean Troop Cuts," p. A1.

10

Commentary: Two Views on Peace and Dialogue in Korea

Ralph N. Clough and Toru Yano

Ralph Clough

I agree generally with Professor Kamiya's main theme—that there will be no large-scale military conflict on the Korean peninsula in the near future. I believe that Kim Il-sung will continue to be deterred from starting such a conflict by the strength of South Korean forces, the presence of U.S. forces, the warnings issued by the highest U.S. authorities, and the disinclination of either China or the Soviet Union to back him in an attempt to unify Korea by force of arms. The differences between Korea and Vietnam pointed out by Professor Kamiya are great and pose a radically different problem for Pyongyang from that formerly faced by Hanoi. Consequently, the exaggerated fears of war in Korea such as those expressed in the immediate aftermath of the collapse of South Vietnam and Kim Il-sung's trip to Peking can be discounted.

I agree with Professor Kamiya that South Korea today is far more resistant to infiltration and subversion than was South Vietnam, but I have certain misgivings as to its future three or four years from now. First, South Korea skates on thin ice in its drive for economic development by relying so heavily on foreign long-term and short-term loans. It came close to going through the ice in April 1975, but recovered rather well in the latter part of the year. So long as economic recovery advances in the United States and Japan, the

South Korean economy will probably continue to grow fairly rapidly, but if a renewed world recession checks this growth, there would be serious political repercussions.

Given South Korea's past record, there is probably less call for misgivings about its economic future than about its political performance. Can President Park's repressive measures continue to be effective over the next three to four years? Or will periodic further tightening of the screws be necessary, which would intensify anti-Park feelings and make South Korea more vulnerable to North Korean subversion? The form and extent of government controls most conducive to public order and the modernization of society in a besieged state such as South Korea is extraordinarily difficult for an outsider to judge, yet any prediction of the future must be based on a judgment concerning this basic point.

Although I concur in Professor Kamiya's view that large-scale war is unlikely in Korea in the near future, it seems to me that his analysis could give more attention to the danger of incidents that might escalate the fighting to a level that neither side anticipated. It is clear that North Korea has entered a period of renewed radicalism, as Professor Kamiya asserts, although Kim Il-sung has not as yet resorted to extensive infiltration efforts such as those attempted in the late 1960s. Nevertheless, the tunnel digging and the positioning of forces in more forward positions are worrisome. North Korean rhetoric, particularly the detailed accusations that the United States and South Korea are preparing to attack the North, has grown more intense. The western islands held by South Korea off North Korea are dangerously exposed. Tension is such that incidents and escalation may easily occur.

Finally, although neither the Soviet Union nor China seems likely to support North Korean military action against South Korea, neither seems willing to consider international actions that would reduce tension between the two Koreas. They may find the status quo in Korea in their interests, but they have been unwilling to take steps to consolidate it. Far from moving in the direction of reciprocal recognition of North and South by the big powers, China has moved in the opposite direction: in the communiqué with Kim Il-sung in April 1975, it announced its acceptance of the Democratic People's Republic of Korea as "the sole legal sovereign state of the Korean nation." Although I strongly favor the concept of reciprocal recognition by the big powers and membership of both Koreas in the United Nations as a means of making the Korean confrontation less dangerous, the Sino-Soviet rivalry and the consequent ability of Pyongyang to play off its supporters against each other make this a remote possibility for the near future.

Mr. Harrison presents an eloquent case for the gradual withdrawal of all U.S. forces from South Korea over a period of five to ten years and deliberate steps by Japan and the United States toward diplomatic recognition of North Korea even though neither the Soviet Union nor China makes comparable moves toward the diplomatic recognition of South Korea. He argues that such policies by the United States and Japan would help to stabilize the security of the Korean people, reduce the danger of military conflict in Korea, and improve the prospects for Korean unification. I find Mr. Harrison's argument unconvincing, partly because I disagree with some of the judgments on which he bases his argument (points to which I will return later), but mainly because in urging on the United States and Japan "more symmetrical policies" toward North and South Korea, he totally ignores the underlying asymmetry in the situations of the two Koreas, an asymmetry that current U.S. and Japanese policies help to redress but that his recommended policies would accentuate.

I refer to the fact that Kim Il-sung is backed by China and the Soviet Union, which demonstrated in 1950 that they could not tolerate the destruction by military force of a friendly, communist state on their borders. There is every reason to believe that they would take the same view in the future. Park Chung-hee's ally, on the other hand, is six thousand miles away. Although the United States rescued the South Korean state from destruction in 1950, the geographical disadvantage of Park's position compared to that of his rival makes it impossible for him (or any other South Korean leader) to have the same confidence in his ally that the North Koreans have in theirs. Because of the asymmetry in self-confidence growing out of this situation, Kim can demand unification on his terms, and Park is placed on the defensive. Both he and Kim know that Peking and Moscow would never permit a South Korean attempt to unify Korea by military force to succeed, although it is by no means unthinkable for the United States and Japan to disengage from South Korea and thus make possible a successful invasion by North Korea.

Given the asymmetry in the situations of the two Koreas, the policies Mr. Harrison recommends for the United States and Japan seem likely to increase rather than decrease the danger of military conflict in Korea and diminish rather than improve the prospects for fruitful negotiations between the two Koreas. The South Koreans would feel more isolated, less confident of the support of their ally, and the North Koreans would be inclined to discount the risk of U.S. intervention once all U.S. forces had been withdrawn from South Korea and once the United States and Japan had begun the process (as North Korea would probably interpret their actions) of shifting their diplomatic relations from Seoul to Pyongyang.

If one assumes (as Mr. Harrison may, although this is not entirely clear from his chapter) that the result of this weakening of Seoul's position and the strengthening of Pyongyang's would be a series of negotiating concessions by the government of South Korea until it had, in effect, peacefully accepted North Korea's terms for confederation or unification, then the risk of armed conflict would indeed be reduced. But it seems to me more realistic to assume that the government of South Korea would work even more vigorously to strengthen its own defenses, even to the extreme of producing nuclear weapons, rather than capitulate without a fight. And I do not see how Mr. Harrison's proposed policies would increase the pressure on Pyongyang to make compromises in its negotiating position—quite the contrary. Mr. Harrison points out that "the readiness of the North for compromise has yet to be seriously tested." I would point out that it is likewise true that the readiness of the South for compromise has yet to be seriously tested. In my view the kinds of step-by-step proposals put forward by South Korea offer a far more promising ground for testing willingness to compromise than the sweeping proposals advanced by the North.

One might infer from portions of Mr. Harrison's argument that he thinks present trends in U.S. and Japanese policies involve such great risks that it would be preferable to adopt the policies he recommends *even though the result would be increased danger of war on the Korean peninsula.* He would thus be prepared to accept the military conquest of South Korea: it would not be sufficiently damaging to U.S. interests (once gradual disengagement had been accomplished) to justify continued involvement. He does not, however, quite take this position. He insists that the Japanese "have an overriding interest in a peaceful resolution of the North-South rivalry"—a view with which I thoroughly agree—and holds out hope that the assertion of nationalism will lead eventually to patterns of contact, collaboration, and confederation. Mr. Harrison does not adequately face up to the possibility that the policies he recommends might increase the risk of conflict rather than improve the chances for a peaceful reunification. I find it hard to believe that the U.S. force in the South has no deterrent effect on North Korea—as Mr. Harrison implies in his statement that a North Korean attack "might even be more likely than would otherwise be the case in the context of a continuing American presence."

I do not want to leave the impression that I favor no change at all in current U.S. policies toward Korea. I do favor a gradual reduction of U.S. forces in South Korea, although I question the advisability of total withdrawal—particularly of U.S. air units—in the absence of any international understandings or a decline in tension between the two Koreas that would reduce the risk of conflict. I do not think we should assume that the present hard line being taken by

Kim Il-sung and Peking, and, to a lesser extent, Moscow, will necessarily continue indefinitely. Patience and a refusal to weaken unduly our military and diplomatic positions regarding Korea are more likely to encourage favorable change than premature unilateral concessions.

Toru Yano

When we discuss the subject of Korea, we must consider carefully the public mood in each of the countries concerned with the problems of the peninsula. In this connection, I would like to call attention to the general mood in Japan since the end of the Vietnam war. There is the keenest interest among the Japanese in the future of Korea. For one thing, North Korea is the last country with which we have to establish diplomatic relations. Certain pressure groups in Japan represent those who sympathize with North Korea, and others represent those who support the South, which means that discussions of the Korean situation are bound to be filled with tension and even a certain "immobilism." Because the subject of Korea is so sensitive in Japan, it is difficult to discuss it freely and openly. Japanese policies toward Korea have also reflected these tensions, contradictory tendencies, and immobilism.

Let me relate something that happened in 1975. The *Chose Maru*, a Japanese fishing boat, was attacked by North Koreans, and two Japanese lives were lost. When this occurred, Japanese policy-makers were very concerned, and they held intense discussions to determine the appropriate course of action. The policy that emerged from these deliberations was an interesting mixture of both "hawkish" and "dovish" elements. The Foreign Ministry decided to issue a very sharp protest to North Korea, a move intended to placate hawkish elements of the Japanese population. But the act of delivering the note to the North Korean representative in Stockholm represented, at least implicitly, a conciliatory gesture. Indeed, new guidelines were established in 1975 for contacting North Korean diplomatic representatives all over the world. In considering how to approach North Korea, Japanese thinking has been very heavily influenced by Professor Kamiya's well-known proposal of "cross-recognition."

To sum up, following the end of the Vietnam war, there was a new mood concerning Korea among the Japanese. There was heightened concern about North Korea's intentions, but there was also an intensified interest in developing contacts with the North Koreans.

Let me review some of the central elements in current Japanese thinking on Korea. First, when the Japanese people think about Korea, they do not see the problem as one of preparing for the possibility of a new war on the peninsula. Rather, the key problem is defined as the creation of a mechanism that would guarantee a dialogue between the two sides in order to preserve peace and stability. This is a very important element in the way Japanese think about the Korean problem.

Second, it is generally thought that Japan has a stake in the maintenance of two Koreas, rather than in unification. Although some Japanese pay lip service to the goal of Korean reunification, there seems to be a consensus that in reality it is preferable to keep the two Korean states in existence. Third, we think of South Korea as a long-term ally; we attach a high priority to our friendship with the South Koreans. On the other hand, it is not desirable to isolate North Korea internationally as Japan's adversary. This, too, is a consensus.

Fourth, the balance of power on the Korean peninsula is in reality a product of two different sets of power balances in the region. At one level, there is a balance of power between the two Koreas. That balance is supported and, indeed, guaranteed, by the existing balance among three or four external powers—notably, Japan, the United States, China, and the Soviet Union. Japan and the Soviet Union should be counted as countries with an equally great interest in what happens in Korea. This also is the Japanese consensus.

Finally, Japan and the United States should cooperate with each other in their efforts to maintain peace and stability in Korea, but it should be appreciated that the two countries cannot play symmetrical roles. This is because of the basic differences, arising out of historical experience, in the way Japanese and Americans relate to Korea. Japan's concern about the future of the Korean peninsula is more intense than that of the United States, but it is also characterized by certain peculiarities—ambivalences—such as I depicted earlier. When Americans think about the problems of the Korean peninsula and the role Japan might play in helping to maintain peace and stability there, they should therefore take into consideration two basic elements: (1) the conflicting strains of thought among the Japanese people, which tend to immobilize both the discussion of Korea and the formation of government policies concerning the peninsula, and (2) Japan's strong interest in fostering a dialogue with North Korea while maintaining both Korean states in existence backed by a balance of power at two levels.

I liked Mr. Harrison's paper very much. It is penetrating and demonstrates a true sense of idealism, as well as realism. I would prefer, however, to see a more complete scenario explaining how the reduction of U.S. military forces in South Korea is to be carried out. There is need for a discussion in more concrete, technical terms: which military elements are to be withdrawn, to what place, and when? It is also necessary to consider the crucial bearing that the United States–Japan Security Treaty may have on this question. The treaty may serve as an obstacle to what seems a rational scenario for the Korean peninsula. The treaty is sometimes a matter of irrationality for us because, as you know, it has been interpreted in ways that may hinder the free movement of U.S. military personnel and weapons through Japan.

We should recognize the difficulties that exist in accommodating the different approaches of our two countries to the Korean problem. Americans often say that since the Korean matter is so vital to Japan, let the Japanese play a role in South Korea's defense, but this is totally contrary to our expectations. On the other hand, Japanese usually evaluate very highly America's historical commitment to Korea, and we tend to view the U.S. military presence as multi-functional. A U.S. military presence represents not only a legal commitment and a military guarantee. It may also discourage irrational acts on the part of the country in which the forces are stationed. U.S. military forces also give the Americans a degree of diplomatic leverage vis-à-vis potentially hostile countries in the region. So we view the U.S. military presence in terms of its several functions, and we assess very highly the contributions of the United States to the achievement of peace and stability on the Korean peninsula.

In closing, let me call attention to a pitfall into which both Japanese and Americans may fall. In considering the timing of possible approaches to the normalization of relations with North Korea, we should be careful to avoid what I call the *"après vous* pitfall." The Americans may say, *"après vous, messieurs les Japonais,* you go first" in normalization efforts with North Korea, and the Japanese may say, *"après vous, messieurs les Americains,* please go first." So we should be very concerned about this *"après vous* pitfall."

11

Japan and the Future Balance in Asia

Henry S. Rowen

President Carter's decision to withdraw all U.S. ground forces from Korea by 1981 or 1982 has evoked expressions of concern not only from many Koreans but from many Japanese as well. The Japanese concern is not so much that the removal of the U.S. Second Division could trigger a North Korean invasion, but rather that this move, together with others, may signal a U.S. retreat from East Asia and even from the western Pacific. They see the possible end position as the virtual disappearance of the U.S. military presence in Asia.

Much evidence is offered in support: the U.S. withdrawal of forces from South Vietnam and its subsequent collapse; withdrawal from Thailand; the reduction of U.S. manpower in East Asia and the western Pacific to one-half the pre-Vietnam intervention level; and American statements that U.S. forces will be oriented toward the defense of Europe.

Latent Instabilities in Asia

The American perception of dangers in Asia has changed remarkably in the past decade. Most important has been our recognition that war with China is extremely unlikely; planning for a possible major conflict with that country has come to a halt. Today, China is seen as strongly inward-looking; the Sino-Soviet relationship seems to have achieved quasi-stability; the Soviet Union poses no major threat elsewhere in the region; and Southeast Asia is now low on our scale of interests. Improvements to the forces of South Korea, the suitability of its terrain for defense, and the more modest levels of economic and military support that the North has been receiving support the proposition that military stability is attainable there without U.S. ground forces.

In contrast, our perception of dangers in other regions has not receded proportionately. The Soviet buildup in Europe, the continuing possibility of another Middle East war, Soviet and Cuban activities in Africa, and across-the-board increases in Soviet nuclear and general-purpose forces have been eroding the American belief that disengagement from Vietnam and détente with the Soviet Union would produce an era of relative international calm and permit wider American disengagement.

Today's sense of stability in East Asia owes a great deal to the nature of Japanese-American ties. The postwar transformation of Japanese political institutions, the enormous growth of the Japanese economy, and the predominantly constructive character of Japanese relations with the rest of the world have contributed substantially to the well-being and security—in a broad sense—of others, including Americans. The United States has provided the secure environment in which Japan flourishes. There is little inclination in Japan today to modify successful behavior. The current generation of leaders, who have experienced both war and intimate collaboration with the United States, is resisting basic changes; their successors might do the same. The December 1976 and July 1977 elections in Japan signal little change in this regard.

Nor is there much inclination in the United States to make changes. Incremental costs for the defense of Japan are small; so are the risks. Neither the Japanese nor the Americans have perceived the need for more than a modest Japanese defense effort. But today, many Japanese view the future with uneasiness, not so much with regard to threats to Japan's territory—for the defense of the Japanese islands against (non-nuclear) sea and air attack appears manageable—but rather with regard to latent instabilities in the region and the possibility of significant shifts in the military balance within the region and outside it. Three potential sources of instability are particularly important:

1. In *Korea,* a quick thrust by the North might capture Seoul, which now has a population of more than six million. Our knowledge of the workings of the Pyongyang regime is scant. We cannot predict what Kim Il-sung will do; but his major preoccupation is to end partition, and he has not ruled out force. Alternatively, North Korea, which has been balancing between the two communist giants, might move closer to the Soviet Union or to China; the former move would appear especially threatening to others in the region. Stability in the South is not entirely assured, and disturbances would offer an occasion for intervention by the North.

2. The *Sino-Soviet relationship* could shift sharply toward rapprochement or toward war. Although neither now seems likely, the consequences would be far-reaching. Rapprochement would free Soviet forces for reallocation against the West and, more important, would reduce Soviet worries about a two-front war. A Sino-Soviet war, on the other hand, could spill over, involve others in a major, perhaps nuclear, conflict, and even upset drastically the global balance of power.

3. The *Soviet-American military balance* has undergone important military changes. Soviet activities in the Indian Ocean and East Africa, with further development of naval and air bases, could threaten sea routes from the Persian Gulf. Moreover, U.S. forces might be drawn farther back to cope with crises or conflict in Europe, the Atlantic, or the Mediterranean. Across-the-board growth of Soviet military power and an increasing Soviet ability to project that power to remote areas suggests that our more limited forces will be thinly spread out. These trends have not been lost on the Japanese—or on the Chinese, who repeatedly express concern about the growth of Soviet naval forces in the Pacific. And these regional changes are taking place against a background of large increases in the strength of the Soviet

Union's long-range nuclear forces.

The United States' forces in East Asia and the western Pacific have a strategic significance much broader than that of dealing with a direct attack on South Korea; they also symbolize political support for Japan, Korea, and other U.S. allies.[1] Moreover, they seem to signal to the Chinese that we are positioned to help deter Soviet moves and perhaps, under circumstances unspecified, to render some direct help. They also confront the Soviets with an American capacity to conduct military operations against the Soviet Far East in the event of a Soviet move against Europe.

For some years now, U.S. spokesmen have emphasized psychological, political, and global strategic objectives for our military forces in Asia.[2] This is in sharp contrast to the emphasis in the 1960s, when force requirements for specific conflicts dominated. Some critics who favor additional U.S. force cuts in the area accept the importance of the political criterion but conclude, nevertheless, that sizable reductions can be made with only slight risk.[3] President Carter evidently agrees, at least in regard to Korea. This conclusion is a natural consequence of overconcentration on scenarios— i.e., on specific force-planning.

Even if we conclude that these latent instabilities are powerful reasons not to make further cuts, Soviet pressures elsewhere may yet cause us to create a partial vacuum, one that we would prefer to see filled by friends and with our cooperation and participation. Among our Asian allies, only Japan can play a significantly greater security role.[4]

Remote as a larger Japanese security role might appear, given Japanese politics, it is marginally less remote than it was before the president's announcement that U.S. ground forces would be withdrawn from Korea. In order to understand how the Japanese defense role might evolve over the next decade, it is important to be clear on the potential threats Japan may face.

Direct Military Threats to Japan

Despite Japanese reluctance to name adversaries, insofar as any is perceived it is the Soviet Union. Soviet forces in the Far East include forty-three divisions in eastern Siberia, fifty-five amphibious ships (plus escorts), around 300 medium bombers, and growing numbers of new tactical fighters (SU-17s, SU-19s, MIG-23s). Other forces that might be used to reinforce those in the Far East include some seventy amphibious ships, seven airborne divisions, and 1,000 heavy and medium bombers. To counter this threat, Japan has the 144 ships of the Maritime Self-Defense Force (MSDF), the thirteen divisions of the Ground Self-Defense Force (GSDF), four of which are in Hokkaido, the Japanese island most exposed to attack, and the 350 interceptor aircraft of the Air Self-Defense Force (ASDF). U.S. air units in Japan and the U.S. Seventh Fleet also have to be considered, together with reinforcements that could be sent from the United States.

This Soviet threat has not alarmed Japanese or American planners. Almost all the Soviet divisions are on the Chinese border, and the Soviets' simultaneous amphibious capacity in the region is only about 4,000 men. Soviet tactical-air offensive strength has been sharply limited by short-range aircraft and poor air-to-ground weapons. To invade successfully, the Soviets would have to establish a strong beachhead, gain air superiority, hinder the movement of Japanese troops, damage U.S. forces in the area, and block U.S. reinforcements. The prospects must look unpromising. The odds are high that the Soviets would find themselves in a prolonged and highly dangerous conflict with both Japan and the United States, and Moscow's worries over its differences with Peking make such an attack even more remote.

How might the Soviet threat look by the late 1980s? After all, Soviet amphibious strength is growing, and new technologies, including air-cushion vehicles, might be available for such an attack. If differences with China have lessened, more forces could threaten Japan. Even so, improved surveillance and precision weapons such as Harpoon and the tactical cruise missile will be especially dangerous to concentrated hostile forces that must make close approaches to the defending shores. In short, it does seem within Japan's capacity to throw back an invasion attempt a decade from now.

The vulnerability of Japan's sea lines of communication is potentially more serious. More than 80 percent of Japan's fuel and most of its annual $56 billion of exports are carried by ship, about 2,000 vessels arriving in Japan's ports each month. Stocks of many raw materials, including oil, appear to be sufficient for 45 to 90 days of consumption, and efforts are being made to increase oil stocks to 180 days. With reductions in nonessential production, the Japanese economy might be able to continue functioning reasonably well for four to six months, even with a sharp reduction in imports; thereafter, output would decline sharply.[5]

The seventy-five attack and cruise-missile submarines in the Soviet Union's Pacific Fleet, thirty of which are nuclear-powered, together with the Soviets' medium-range and long-range aircraft, pose a real threat to Japan's sea-lanes. Increases in the number of Soviet nuclear attack submarines and long-range aircraft over the next decade will intensify this threat. (China's submarines, all conventional, present a much smaller danger.) The outcome of a sea interdiction campaign is sensitive to a number of uncertain parameters, and it is not clear how such a campaign would develop. However, the outcome is likely to be favorable to the Japanese if their stocks were built up, if Soviet ports and narrow exits from the Sea of Japan to the Pacific were mined, if ships were rerouted to southern routes in order to maximize the distance and transit time for attacking submarines, and if U.S. as well as Japanese ASW forces were used. Much of Japan's trade, moreover, is carried in foreign bottoms; the Soviets would have to challenge many countries. Nonetheless, although the probability that the Soviet Union would undertake such a campaign is low, it is not independent of the probability of success. More important, Japan's sense of vulnerability could influence its behavior in undesirable ways. It is worth making sure that the Soviets cannot succeed.

Soviet naval and air activities around Japan, which have been given uncharacteristic prominence in the latest Japanese Defense White Paper, present something of a puzzle. From the Soviet perspective, Japan must seem an unthreatening country with the capacity of becoming a big problem. The Japanese economy is now perhaps two-thirds the size of the Soviet Union's, and it is likely to overtake the latter economy before the year 2000. Why should the Soviet Union want to make the Japanese nervous, increase their dependence on the United States, and perhaps cause them to rearm on a substantial scale? Moscow may be trying to impress the Japanese with its power and to persuade them to shift their more-or-less equidistant stance between China and the Soviet Union. Another explanation is that this behavior is business as usual for the powerful Soviet military bureaucracies. Whatever the reason, behavior that heightens the possibility of increased Japanese armament seems imprudent.

Japan, like the United States, has no defense against ballistic missiles; and, at best, only a small portion of attacking aircraft or cruise missiles could be intercepted. Moreover, many of Japan's key air-defense facilities are vulnerable even to non-nuclear attack. (True, there are feasible improvements that would make non-nuclear attacks costly, and Japan has an important defense advantage in that it cannot be reached overland.) Nuclear attack is guarded against by the prospect of retaliation by the United States, but as Soviet long-range nuclear forces have grown, questions have arisen in Japan, as elsewhere, about the efficacy of the U.S. nuclear guarantee. This is not yet a serious issue in Japan; however, in time, concern about America's nuclear strength will affect Japanese views about that guarantee. If accompanied by perceptions of other dangers, Japanese concern will be heightened.

Japanese Regional and Extraregional Concerns

President Carter's move toward Korean withdrawal has evoked strong opposition from Japanese legislators.[6] The seriousness with which potential shifts on the Korean peninsula or in the Sino-Soviet relationship are regarded depends critically on assumptions about America's role. At the least, we are seen as essential to preserving stability in Korea, countering Soviet naval and air power in the Pacific and Indian oceans, and deterring direct threats to Japan, including the nuclear threat.

Among the developments outside the region that are of concern to Japan is the possibility of another 1973 oil crisis. Despite political and financial concessions to the Arabs, the Japanese ended up paying as much for their oil as did other importers, and their supplies seem no more assured. Japan has slowly been reducing its dependence on Persian Gulf oil—by obtaining some oil from China and shifting to nuclear power to generate electricity. It now appears that in 1985, Japan's nuclear power plants will be producing around 25,000 MW—or about half the target adopted by Tokyo after the 1973 crisis. The Japanese also worry that future Chinese activities might affect their large and growing economic stake in Southeast Asia.

In this set of potential troubles, the nature and scale of future Soviet activities are dominant and not easily predicted. On the one hand, Soviet ground and air forces deployed along the Chinese border were greatly expanded in the late 1960s. The Soviet Pacific Fleet, which constitutes about 30 percent of the navy, has participated (with a lag) in the Soviets' overall naval modernization effort and has progressively engaged in more distant exercises and deployments, especially in the Indian Ocean. On the other hand, the Soviet Union has had little success in developing ties in Asia, Vietnam and North Korea aside. From a strategic standpoint, it suffers from a severe shortage of bases for its naval and air forces. Even a larger and more modern fleet could be bottled up in the Sea of Japan. Therefore, the acquisition of bases in the Pacific and the Indian oceans, especially bases that could support combat operations, would greatly increase Soviet naval effectiveness.[7] The growth in the number of independent states in the Pacific will increase Soviet negotiating opportunities in this regard.

Consider, for example, the implications of a major Soviet naval and air base in Southeast Asia (e.g., at Cam Ranh Bay, unlikely as it now seems, given Vietnam's independent stance and Chinese opposition). The strategic position of the USSR in this region would be greatly changed: the security of the Japanese sea lines of communication—and those of China—would be put in question; so would the naval balance in the Indian Ocean. Consider the further impact if the United States were to lose its air and naval bases in the Philippines, a possibility that cannot now be excluded.[8] Moreover, tankers supplying Japan and Soviet naval vessels ply the same routes, a coincidence of paths not comforting to the Japanese. In short, it is dangerous to assume that Soviet power in the Pacific and Indian oceans is modest and that the Soviet presence there will not grow.

Possible Japanese Defense Postures

According to its 1976 Defense White Paper, Japan stands tenth in the world in defense spending (expenditures in 1975 were roughly $4.5 billion), despite the fact that the share of GNP devoted to defense in that year (0.84 percent) put Japan near the bottom among all nations. The apparently rapid growth in defense expenditures under the Fourth Defense Buildup Plan—from $2.7 billion in FY 1972 to $5 billion in FY 1976—is almost entirely a reflection of inflation. The current national defense plan, which is to be funded year by year, shows no significant change in pattern. The FY 1977 budget of $5.6 billion, which allows for real growth less than the expected GNP growth of 6 percent, means a small decrease in the share of GNP allocated to defense.

The Fourth Defense Buildup Plan was designed to maintain the existing size of ground forces and to increase Japanese firepower and mobility; Japanese-made tanks, armored personnel carriers, and helicopters were to replace older American equipment. The MSDF was to grow from 140,000 tons to 240,000 tons by adding fifteen destroyers and destroyer escorts and five submarines; improvements were to be made in antisubmarine forces and in fleet air defense. The ASDF was to concentrate on quality by replacing obsolete F-86s with F-4s. However, the unexpected inflation of the past three years has caused this program to fall short. Out of the FY 1976 budget, only around $900 million was spent on procurement, an amount much less in real terms than originally planned.

Weapons modernization has also been impeded by the government's policy of producing about 80 percent of all military hardware domestically. Often the cost is much higher than that of imported weapons because of the small volume of production. Some aircraft cost two or three times more to produce than they would in the United States, and Japanese-made improved Hawk missiles may cost eight times as much. But this policy does give Japan greater capacity to expand its production in the event of a crisis.

An important constraint on an independent Japanese defense posture is the low level of research and development funded in the defense budget—a remarkably small $50 million a year, or about 1 percent of the defense budget. In contrast, the United States devotes about 10 percent of its (much larger) defense budget to R&D. (The Japanese have, however, been able to carry out a surprising number of projects with these modest resources, including a tank, a transport vehicle, a trainer/support-fighter aircraft, artillery pieces, and air-defense missiles.) A low level of R&D is consistent with the Japanese industrial practice of buying technology and adapting it to Japanese needs. This practice has been criticized on the grounds that Japan has special defense needs, that some equipment (e.g., electronic-countermeasures devices) is secret and difficult to import, that it is difficult to adapt and improve equipment acquired under license, that foreign countries have become reluctant to transfer technology to Japan, and that Japan needs to acquire technical power on an equal level with other countries. Increases in R&D to 2 percent or more of the defense budget have been advocated by the Japan Defense Agency.

As they view the international environment, many Japanese perceive two principal rivalries: the Sino-Soviet and the U.S.-Soviet. In regard to the former, they have been trying to maintain a posture of "equidistance" (recently with a tilt toward Peking). They have not seen themselves centrally involved in the latter rivalry.

Perhaps the fact that Japan is more immediately under pressure in its relations with China vis-à-vis the Soviet

Union makes that contest especially prominent. U.S.-Soviet competition is seen as more remote. Moreover, to many on the Left, the American ties and troop presence suggest that Japan could be drawn unwittingly into a conflict. On the other hand, the United States' role in offsetting Soviet strength is important to most Japanese' sense of security.

The Japanese have, understandably, a strong preference for the status quo, which enables them to concentrate on economic growth. Their low-profile foreign policy minimizes the likelihood of being pulled into a conflict, and Japan's alliance with the United States, its strong economy, and its capacity to mobilize give the Japanese hedges against uncertainty. However, the trends described above raise the possibility that the status quo may not survive. We must examine, therefore, the several broad directions that Japan might choose in the next decade:

1. *No Major Change.* This course implies continuing with a narrow self-defense orientation, continuing to depend on the United States for essential protection, retaining a low political profile, and continuing to focus on economic growth.

2. *Strengthened Self-Defense.* This course could lead in time to Japan's playing a wider, tacit regional role; later, Japan might take on an explicit regional role.[9]

3. *A Heavily Armed, Neutral Japan.* At some point in the future, perhaps in response to a major international shock, Japan might strike out on an independent path, build a large defense establishment, develop nuclear weapons, and loosen or even end its mutual defense relationship with the United States.

These three positions do not exhaust the possibilities. For instance, a Japan that no longer had a treaty relationship with the United States could, as Japanese on the Left have argued, seek to be both neutral and disarmed. This prospect seems remote.

Course 1: No Major Change

The "no major change" course provides for incremental improvements in the Japanese defense posture as the economy grows. It finds powerful support in the long-standing view that there are no serious threats to Japan. This alternative would produce a level of defense spending in 1986 of about $10 billion (in 1976 dollars), assuming an annual 5 percent real growth rate for the economy and defense spending at 1 percent of GNP. Spending in this amount would permit maintenance of present force levels and limited missions, and substantial improvement of antisubmarine, air-defense, and ground-force equipment. The resulting posture would not be insignificant, but Japan, by itself, would not have the capacity to defend its sea lines of communication at a distance or to influence regional developments strongly. Within this framework, however, useful cooperation between Japan and South Korea could take place—improvements in their political relationship permitting.

Whether future Japanese governments will judge that "no major change" will be adequate, we can only guess; at present, the odds substantially favor this course.

Course 2: Strengthened Self-Defense

A policy of "strengthened self-defense" would mean increases in defense spending. Over a decade, the share of GNP devoted to defense might approach that of the NATO countries, 3 or 4 percent. At 3 percent of GNP by 1986, the defense budget would be about $30 billion (1976 dollars), and over the ten-year period the aggregate would be around $150 billion. Allowing for increasing real costs, maintenance of the existing force would cost perhaps $60 billion, leaving a substantial $90 billion for force modernization and expansion.

With resources of this magnitude, Japan could create a strong and technologically advanced military force. In addition to being far better able to counter Soviet naval and air strength in the Pacific, Japan would have the capacity to alter the military balance in Korea and to influence the Sino-Soviet balance.

An almost certain issue would be Japan's possession of capabilities that would appear to be offensive in nature—

longer-range ships and aircraft, tactical cruise missiles, and so on. The ASDF might also acquire a ground-attack mission. An even greater departure from Japan's post-1945 posture would be the acquisition at some point of sea-based air power (e.g., V/STOL aircraft on sea-control ships).

This course, while offering important advantages in an uncertain environment, would have palpable risks. The most critical would be the heightened possibility of involvement in a U.S.-Soviet conflict not centering on Japan or perhaps not even originating in the region. Plausible Japanese objectives in such a contingency would be (1) to avoid direct involvement, (2) to prevent domination of Japan by any hostile power, and (3) to avoid isolation from the United States as a consequence of Japan's failure to help us in a serious struggle with the Soviet Union.

These objectives, however, could be in sharp conflict. The Japanese would have strong reasons to avoid direct involvement while at the same time wanting us to succeed.[10] Many possible options exist in the case of a conflict originating elsewhere: (1) stay out altogether and deny Americans the use of bases in Japan; (2) provide only tacit support (e.g., substitution of Japanese for U.S. forces in Japan or at sea, thus freeing our forces for use elsewhere); (3) provide some symbolic and material support (e.g., giving only logistic support to U.S. forces and allies); (4) allow U.S. use of bases in Japan except for direct combat operations, or allow the United States to use them even for combat operations; (5) use Japanese forces in "defensive" missions only (e.g., escorting convoys and providing other ASW surveillance around Japan); or (6) use Japanese forces "offensively." How far the Japanese would be willing to go down this list would depend not only on the perceived threat to Japan and the strength of Japanese forces but also on the balance between their desire for noninvolvement and their fear of the possible consequences of noninvolvement. It is important to note that the Japanese might be able to provide considerable help without actively involving themselves in combat (viz., through option 4), and even a modest probability of Japanese participation would go a long way toward deterring some conflicts.

The "strengthened self-defense" course might also pose problems for the United States, despite assumed close ties between Japan and the United States. Certainly, Japan's capacity to make trouble would be greatly increased, and an armed Japan would have a political character somewhat different from the character it has today.

What would be the likely effect on other nations? Which nations might feel threatened? It has been widely held in Japan and elsewhere that a rearmed Japan would be an alarming force in the world. This was understandable in the 1950s and 1960s, but would it be in the 1980s? After more than thirty years, it is difficult to see what the Japanese could do that they have not already done to make it clear that they do not have political and military designs against others. Those who express concern about Japanese militarism have memories, understandably bitter, about a now remote past, or they hold unpersuasive theories about innate characteristics of the Japanese people. Nonetheless, many Koreans might be alarmed and many Chinese as well. For instance, how might China view a Japanese navy regularly patrolling the sea-lanes off the coast of China? Such worries would be greatly eased if the U.S. commitment and a tangible U.S. military presence continued. This also would be true for more distant countries in Southeast Asia, as well as for Australia and New Zealand. In time, some of these countries might even favor alliance ties to Japan through a collective security system including the United States as well.

This course is also consistent with Japanese development of closer ties to China. Indeed, a Chinese-Japanese-United States alignment is not excluded, although it is likely to come about only in response to clearly threatening Soviet moves.

On balance, some approximation to this course seems most likely to meet American needs for the 1980s, and may meet Japanese needs. But change from a narrow self-defense concept, if it comes, will be slow. We should not press the Japanese on this doctrinal issue; instead, there are many specific tasks, described below, to be carried out.

Course 3: A Heavily Armed, Neutral Japan

The third course, that of a "heavily armed, neutral Japan," is consistent with the view that the period since 1945 has been unnatural for the Japanese, since they have been so dependent on a foreign power. Indeed, this is an unprecedented relationship for Japan, inconsistent with its geographic, cultural, and linguistic insularity. Although practiced in assimilating ideas and techniques from others, the Japanese have done so selectively and have adapted these borrowings to the Japanese culture.

This tendency toward political and cultural isolationism conflicts with the powerful outward pull of Japanese global economic interaction. But the Japanese have shown great skill at separating economic relationships from political and military ones. In time, Japan might sharply reduce its dependence on the United States and acquire much greater military capacity—possibly including nuclear arms—while vigorously pursuing its worldwide economic interests.

What processes or events might bring about such a change? One possibility is a grave crisis in which it suddenly becomes evident that the United States cannot or will not protect Japan. Another is a political victory by a faction committed to a policy of nondependence on the United States. Whatever the cause, it is clear that Japan could over time acquire very substantial military strength.

This "heavily armed, neutral Japan" course includes, more than the others, the possibility of Japanese nuclear weapons, which might be proposed in accordance with the theory of "proportional deterrence," wherein a medium-sized nation can deter a larger one by its ability to inflict civil damage on the latter, even though the medium-sized state might suffer far more damage. There is something to this theory, but the asymmetry in capacity suggests that there would be an important difference in bargaining strength. And, too, some kinds of risks would be heightened. Moreover, a Japanese nuclear force designed to kill large numbers of Russians or Chinese is not likely to appear to meet realistic national defense needs.

Yet Japan's economy is nearly at the great-power level,

and it seems entirely in the Japanese national character that
if Japan were to acquire nuclear weapons at all, it would do
so on a substantial scale. The British and French model of
small, largely symbolic forces does not fit the Japanese style;
the Japanese do not do things by halves. Japan could
allocate $10 billion a year to a nuclear force, an amount quite
sufficient to support a substantial nuclear program. Even so,
Japan would face serious difficulties. The essential requirement of having a *secure* force is not met simply by
assumption. Fixed bases (e.g., missile silos) are already
vulnerable, and mobile nuclear forces would be difficult to
operate on Japan's terrain.

In the field of nuclear submarines, Japan would be
starting from scratch, and it would have to contend with
Soviet undersea surveillance and attack techniques of the
late 1980s. If the Japanese submarine fleet were to be small in
order to limit costs (say, on the scale of Britain's force, which
at times has no more than one of its four submarines on
station), then Soviet antisubmarine forces might have a good
chance of locating most or all of that fleet. Moreover, if the
Japanese were to seek the ability to strike most of the Soviet
Union, they would have either to face long transits or to
build missiles and submarines with ranges comparable to
that of the U.S. Trident 1.[11]

Another possibility is the use of cruise missiles in diesel-
electric submarines such as Japan already has. The high
accuracy attainable with these missiles means that small
warheads producing low collateral damage would be feasible. Also, very high accuracy means that, for some missions, they could be effective with non-nuclear warheads, a
capability that might be of particular interest to the Japanese.

Japan has a broad industrial base that could be put to
work on nuclear weapons and delivery vehicles. Further,
neither the international system of IAEA safeguards nor U.S.
agreements in regard to cooperation on nuclear technology
precludes Japan from having—without violation—direct
and ready access to nuclear-explosive materials. Indeed,
these agreements (not only in the case of Japan but,

unhappily, much more widely) do not prevent non-weapon states from being within days of the ability to explode a nuclear device—again, without violation. In the Ford and Carter administrations, we have begun to understand the incoherence of existing rules on nuclear energy as they relate to our nonproliferation objectives, and the United States has begun to try changing them. Whatever rules emerge from the current rethinking, Japan will nevertheless have a formidable capacity to develop nuclear weapons if it so chooses.[12]

It seems most unlikely, however, that Japan will do so in the foreseeable future. The domestic political obstacles are formidable, and non-nuclear weapons seem adequate for almost any military mission Japanese forces might have to undertake. The strongest case for Japanese nuclear weapons is that they could deter a nuclear attack; thus, so long as the U.S. guarantee has essential credibility, Japan is not likely to want nuclear weapons. This judgment, however, also assumes that South Korea, Taiwan, or some other country in the region will not acquire nuclear weapons. It should be an important objective of U.S. and Japanese policy to encourage these regional states to maintain their non-nuclear status.

Japanese nuclear weapons aside, a more independent, armed Japan that has preserved its democratic institutions and has no ambition to greatly extend its influence over the smaller states of Asia could contribute importantly to regional stability. Japan might, in effect, assume the role of "protector" of the small states against the power of the Soviet Union or China. In this role, Japan might partially or even wholly replace the United States. But this course of action poses dangers much more serious than those of the two alternatives. For one thing, great and dangerous changes in Japanese domestic politics might occur. For another, a more heavily armed Japan without ties to the United States would be viewed with alarm. Remote as this prospect seems, major and sometimes abrupt shifts in Japan's external relations have occurred before, and they cannot be excluded for the future.

Two conflicting political trends will affect Japan's

defense policies: (1) the progressive weakening of the Liberal-Democratic party (LDP) and (2) the gradual lessening of political opposition to the self-defense forces and to the U.S.-Japanese security treaty. The first trend makes it more difficult for the government to muster a majority on defense issues and on defense spending. The Socialist and Communist parties still formally oppose the security treaty, although JSP (Japanese Socialist party) opposition has been weakened by Chinese support of the treaty. Only the JSP proposes unarmed neutrality. Even the Communists support a people's armed force. Clearly, then, defense is acquiring greater legitimacy. This suggests that if Japan's external environment worsens, a political basis for a substantially larger defense program will exist.

The results of the 1976 elections, in which the conservative LDP lost heavily, do not imply a popular shift against defense. The votes lost went predominantly to the New Liberal Club and other middle-of-the-road parties. That opponents of the self-defense forces and the security treaty are now generally less militant means that contention on these issues is now within the range of normal politics.

The public opinion polls show increasing support in Japan for stronger defense. In a poll taken in 1976 on attitudes toward security issues, 76 percent of the respondents supported the self-defense forces, and 59 percent supported both the self-defense forces and the security treaty with the United States. Support for the treaty varied predictably by party, but members of the Japanese Communist party (JCP) were evenly divided on this issue—31.5 percent in favor, 32.6 percent opposed.[13] Furthermore, JCP supporters favored the self-defense forces by 51.1 percent to 28.9 percent.[14]

This support, to be sure, is for defense spending beneath the threshold of 1 percent of GNP. Assuming little change in Japan's external environment and given the loss in LDP strength, the 1 percent barrier, or something close to it, will probably remain effective. The environment is changing, however, and if it is seen to become more dangerous, that barrier is likely to be breached.

Possible Areas for Increased U.S.-Japanese Cooperation

At the very least, this analysis suggests the importance of strengthening ties between the United States and Japan. Despite notable obstacles of culture and language, there is much that supports the relationship, and the Japanese see it as worth the cost. Increased cooperation implies reducing the asymmetry of the present relationship—although that asymmetry will not be eliminated soon. The United States should accept some changes in its independent stance and operating procedures with regard to Japan. For its part, Japan should gradually broaden its concept of self-defense.

Complementarity

Both partners should take the idea of "complementarity" more seriously and exploit comparative advantages in their mutual defense effort. The United States has not done so, the nature of the security treaty has not required it, and the sense of threat has not motivated it. To date, unilateral U.S. and Japanese decisions have given the United States flexibility and have suited Japan's desire to avoid involvement in dangerous situations. Looking ahead, the case for complementarity is stronger.

Japan has advantages in surveillance around Japan ground facilities, availability of skilled people, close-in naval operations, merchant-ship operation, deployment of surface-to-air defensive missiles, and its large and accessible industrial base. America's advantages include its advanced and rapidly deployable air and naval forces, its worldwide intelligence and surveillance network, its airlift capability, its sophisticated munitions—non-nuclear as well as nuclear—and its ability to operate in areas remote from Japan. The tailoring of our forces to exploit these respective advantages would build a strong sense of commitment and improve efficiency; it would somewhat reduce both parties' capacity for independent action, a price that the United States, at least, should be willing to pay. Taking Japanese defense more seriously also implies that Americans should not hesitate to make recommendations to the Japanese on the basis of our technical and combat experience, and also that the United States should be more consistent in its support of Japanese efforts.

Specific Contingencies

Much is to be gained by jointly focusing on specific contingencies. The absence of specific goals makes it difficult to establish performance standards for our forces or even to present a plausible justification for their existence. Contingency planning has been much easier for West European and Korean defense: the clear and present danger of attack helps focus attention.[15] But there are meaningful and concrete tasks to be carried out—especially in air defense and the protection of Japan's sea-lanes. Possible goals are to assure that a certain minimum number of ships could get in and out of Japan each month (subgoals might include criteria for undersea surveillance and target acquisition, provision of escorts, and armament of merchant ships) or to assure that the Soviet naval route from the Sea of Japan to the Pacific could be effectively and rapidly blocked. Another possibility is to cooperate in protecting the sea lines of communication to Alaska. A related possibility—to think what was once completely unthinkable—might be to arrange for MSDF use of bases in the Philippines under certain circumstances (if we retain those bases).

Contingencies in Korea should be reexamined. For example, the ability to send air-defense tracking information directly between Japan and South Korea would be of mutual benefit, and the creation of such a link would be a useful signal to the Soviet Union. Also, the gains from Japanese-Korean cooperation in the production of some types of weapons and in the operation of repair facilities could be large.

Specific performance goals would also have the useful effect of shifting from a nearly exclusive focus on resource input (i.e., the share of GNP allocated to defense) to output (i.e., the tasks ahead). In the end, if neither we nor the Japanese can identify important, specific goals for our forces, we should not be surprised to find that they have low combat effectiveness or that they are subject to budget cuts.

Intelligence and Surveillance

Intelligence and surveillance activities are consistent with Japan's restrictive definition of defense. Yet, one of Japan's weaknesses is its poor ability to collect information on the strength, technical characteristics, and movements of other countries' forces. The United States shares some of its intelligence information, but this is largely general in character. There are problems in regard to sharing information with Japan (which has an even more porous security system than we do), but there is reason to ask whether we are doing enough. Part of the problem may be that the relevant U.S. bureaucracies want a quid pro quo; it might help if the Japanese had more trading material. Geography puts the Japanese in a good position to supply information on critical undersea movements, on the airspace around Japan, and on adjoining land areas, especially the Soviet maritime provinces. Japan may have other areas of information advantage, in North Korea, for example.

Mobilization Preparations

Japanese preparations for possible crises could be made more effective if coordinated with U.S. provisions for reinforcements, logistic support, and increasing weapons production. The time required in a crisis for a large increase in strength could probably be greatly shortened.

Cooperative Research and Development

Many Japanese and Americans hold that Japanese-style R&D is adaptive and incremental rather than original. This view seems somewhat overstated. Japanese products in many lines (e.g., ship designs) are superior to those offered by others, and Japanese auto producers have recently been more innovative than have those in Detroit. But very large investments in defense technology, over a long period of time, will be needed if Japan is to build up a competency comparable to that of the Soviet Union or the United States. This suggests that military R&D ventures with U.S. firms might be attractive. The United States is weak in some fields of technology, most obviously in ground-force equipment.

Perhaps the Japanese could be of help here, as well as in other fields in which they excel or have promise. U.S. firms, too, should be interested: the Japanese military-procurement market is growing rapidly, despite Japan's preference for producing most of its hardware domestically. Today, there is a billion-dollar market annually, and this could well become much larger in the 1980s.

Conclusion: Now Is the Time To Act

It will be objected that the present state of Japanese party politics and the American preference for autonomy preclude moving very far along these lines. However, those enmeshed in American domestic politics may well find the reality of growing Soviet strength, combined with a continued low-profile military policy on the part of Japan, increasingly hard to accept; the inherent tension of such a situation would undermine political support for a continued U.S. presence in Asia. There is no doubt that action along the five lines described above would have to be taken step by step and implemented over a long period. Improved consultative machinery, however, does exist in the U.S.-Japanese Subcommittee on Defense Cooperation, one of whose functions is to discuss joint countermeasures for emergencies. Now is the time to press more vigorously on substance.

With any luck at all, the more troublesome possibilities will not emerge. We should certainly hope so, for the present balance in Asia, with all its latent problems, will be difficult to improve on. But if unfavorable trends continue to develop in East Asia, both Japan and the United States will face some hard choices. Japan's political culture and the leaders it produces have been conservative in both familiar senses. This implies little change, but it also suggests latent support for defense efforts that, sooner or later, may be seen as important to undertake. It is very much in the U.S. interest to see that these efforts develop within a framework of close cooperation—which implies a continued, visible, and strong U.S. presence in the region.

Notes

1. On withdrawal of the Second Division from Korea, U.S. forces in East Asia will consist of two-thirds of a marine division (on Okinawa), nine tactical fighter squadrons, and amphibious "lift" sufficient for two battalions. We will then have around 115,000 men in the region.

2. For recent examples, see the FY 1978 Posture Statement by Secretary of Defense Rumsfeld. Secretary Schlesinger's FY 1976 Posture Statement included the objective of preventing Soviet forces in Asia from being deployed west of the Urals and discouraging the Soviets from opening another front in Northeast Asia.

3. See Henry Owen and Charles Schultze, *Setting National Priorities: The Next Ten Years* (Washington: Brookings, 1976); and Charles A. Sorrels, *U.S. General Purpose Forces Related to Asia* (Washington: Congressional Budget Office, 1977).

4. To be sure, as A. Doak Barnett observes, we have a tacit security relationship with the PRC based on a mutuality of interest. But, though we should try to strengthen this relationship, it must still be regarded as fragile. *China Policy* (Washington: Brookings, 1977).

5. For an analysis of how Japan, in cooperation with the United States, might counter a Soviet or Chinese campaign directed against Japanese sea lines of communication, see David Schilling, "A Reassessment of Japan's Naval Defense Needs," *Asian Survey* 16, no. 3 (March 1976).

6. The tension within Japanese politics on security issues is illustrated by Japanese statements since January 1977. These have included expressions of deep concern over U.S. withdrawal, opposition to withdrawal, repetition of the position adopted in 1969 that the security of Korea is essential to the security of Japan—but also the assertion that the withdrawal issue is primarily a matter between the United States and South Korea.

7. The term *base* may refer to a great variety of logistic and combat functions. At one extreme, there may be limited port-visit privileges and minor supply-and-repair facilities; at the other, there may be major resupply, training, and even combat capabilities, including airfields from which patrol and bomber aircraft can operate.

8. At this writing, President Marcos has rejected the U.S. position on continued base rights, although negotiations continue. It certainly cannot be taken for granted that the United

States will have access to these bases over the next decade.

9. This option does not exclude the possibility of eventual Japanese possession of nuclear weapons. A Japan so armed might maintain, as do Britain and France, an alliance with the United States. However, the internal political changes associated with Japanese acquisition of such weapons might open a good deal of political distance between the United States and Japan.

10. The Japanese are not likely to forget that it does not pay to be allied to a loser. Recall that the Soviets, after the defeat of Germany in 1945, quickly transferred forces to the east in order to defeat the Kwantung Army in Manchuria.

11. For further analysis of the problems a Japanese nuclear submarine program would face, see A. Wohlstetter et al., *Moving Toward Life in a Nuclear Armed Crowd?*, a report to the U.S. Arms Control and Disarmament Agency, 1976.

12. Japan is in a key position to help bring about changes in the international rules that might reduce the dangers of nuclear energy while still enabling nations to enjoy its benefits. The proposed changes, which would limit wide access to plutonium and highly enriched uranium, would restrict technically unnecessary, economically dubious, and exceptionally dangerous activities. The problem is not that Japan is likely to make a sudden move to acquire nuclear explosives—domestic opposition is powerful. But if there is to be wider international appreciation of the proliferation dangers inherent in certain types of nuclear power, then Japan, and other major industrial states, will have to be in the vanguard. So far, it is not clear that a consensus on the changes needed will emerge among the industrial powers.

13. *Sankei Shimbun*, January 1, 1976. See also the poll results published in the November 3, 1976, issue.

14. Masamichi Inoki, "Japan's National Security," *Japan Echo* 3, no. 3 (1976) (trans. from *Shokun*, May 1976).

15. To argue that *some* Japanese-American planning should focus on specific contingencies is not inconsistent with my earlier observation that decisions on America's Asian force posture should not be *dominated* by a focus on a few specific scenarios.

12
Conclusions and Policy Recommendations

Franklin B. Weinstein

The questions considered in the preceding chapters have, as noted in the Introduction, been the subject of an ongoing dialogue between Japanese and American specialists on security affairs and arms control. These discussions have not aimed at producing a set of conclusions and policy recommendations that all could agree on. There is enough diversity of opinion—not only between Americans and Japanese but also within each national group—to preclude such a product. Nevertheless, some conclusions may be drawn from the discussions we have had. The following proposals, which I put forth as the project director, represent my personal views. They reflect my own assessment of the degree of consensus on basic goals and assumptions as well as my estimate as to the kinds of policies that might serve those goals. In preparing these conclusions and recommendations, I have drawn not only on the chapters included in this book and the conference discussions that accompanied their presentation but also on subsequent conversations and correspondence with many of the participants and with other knowledgeable specialists. Several participants expressed disagreement with certain of my proposals. Thus, it should be clearly understood that although these proposals have emerged out of a process of formal and informal discussion involving a sizable group of Japanese and American experts, they do not represent the view of all who have taken part in the dialogue.

The Defense of Japan

The Significance of Changing Japanese Attitudes

The end of the Vietnam war brought into sharp relief certain changes in Japanese attitudes toward their own defense. The discussion of defense issues at our 1976 meetings and in informal talks during 1977 differed markedly from our previous discussions. In conference sessions and informal conversations during 1974 and early 1975, attention was drawn to the lack of broad support among the Japanese people for the security policies pursued by their government. We were reminded of the unpopularity of the SDF, the sharp criticism aimed at U.S. bases in Japan, and the wide currency enjoyed by proposals for the abrogation or revision of the mutual security treaty. The central question was how to reduce the U.S. presence in Japan to the "bare essentials" without jeopardizing Japanese and U.S. security needs.

Since 1975 public attitudes toward the security treaty, U.S. bases, and the SDF have grown considerably more tolerant. The 1976 and 1977 discussions focused on the significance of these changed attitudes and, in particular, on the feasibility of proposals for intensified U.S.-Japanese cooperation in the security field. Now the key question is whether the diminished hostility toward the SDF and the security relationship with the United States in fact signifies a willingness on the part of the Japanese to play a more substantial defense role.

The implications of the changes in Japanese thinking on defense issues are in dispute. Certain American scholars and officials believe that from the standpoint of Japanese public opinion, the present period may be an opportune time to press Japan finally to shoulder its full share of the defense burden. These analysts are inclined to interpret the new Japanese attitudes as proof that the U.S. defeat in Vietnam, together with such other developments as the buildup of the Soviet Pacific Fleet, shocked the Japanese into an awareness of the need for them to undertake greater defense responsibilities in cooperation with the United States.

The thrust of our discussions, however, suggests that it would be a serious mistake to interpret the change in

Japanese attitudes as an opportunity for the United States to put pressure on Japan to expand its role as a "military partner." Although no one questioned the desirability of closer and more continuous consultation, the participants seemed generally to move toward the view that any significant increase in the level of Japanese-American military collaboration involving an expanded role for the SDF would not be politically feasible in Japan.

To begin with, even Japanese who personally favor more rapid expansion of the SDF observe that increasing public tolerance of the defense establishment does not necessarily indicate a readiness to assume a military role. Japanese defense specialists are quick to note that the new attitudes are not merely a response to the Vietnam war's end and the Soviet naval buildup; they can also be traced to the Okinawa reversion, to the rise of multipolarity and the easing of Cold War tensions in Asia, and, in particular, to Chinese acceptance of the mutual security treaty, which means that the U.S.-Japanese security relationship is no longer an impediment to the improvement of Sino-Japanese relations. It may well be that the Japanese military forces have become more easily tolerable, mainly because they now seem less likely to be employed in a conflict. America's defeat in Vietnam need not be viewed as increasing the danger to Japan. On the contrary, with the United States finally at peace in Asia and likely to remain so, there is less reason to fear that the security treaty will be used to involve Japan in direct or indirect support of U.S. military operations. Furthermore, when a majority of the Japanese people say that they now look upon the SDF with favor, are they expressing support for the accelerated expansion of those forces or merely for continuing to develop them at a pace that will keep them in a relatively weak state? Public opinion polls and the fiscal 1977 budget, which allocates a lower percentage to defense than any previous budget since the birth of the SDF in 1950, indicate the latter.[1] All of this suggests that the key to the new public acceptance of the SDF and the security treaty is not a heightened sense of danger, requiring a military response by Japan, but a diminished likelihood that Japan will be drawn into war with the communist powers.

Japanese specialists emphasize, moreover, that the decline of animosity toward the SDF and the security relationship with the United States does not mean that domestic criticism has grown insignificant. Although some opposition leaders have indicated that the security treaty should be maintained in the "first stage," these leaders and others continue to call for further reduction of the U.S. military presence in Japan. If 79 percent of the population now say they support the existence of the SDF, there is still very strong opposition to larger defense outlays. Finally, although the critics may be relatively quiescent at present, any move toward a significant increase in Japan's military role could easily revive militant opposition.

Japan's Strategic Requirements

The persistent pacifism of the Japanese people is reinforced by a widespread belief that there is no convincing strategic justification for an accelerated military buildup by Japan. Indeed, Japanese and American strategists agree that Japan faces no imminent security threats.

In time, of course, this perception concerning the absence of threat may change. The major question marks on the horizon are the situation in Korea and the Soviet naval buildup. The Japanese certainly fear that if armed conflict erupts in Korea, they may find it hard to escape involvement, but few conceive of a military threat to Japan emanating from the Korean peninsula. If either Korean government were to acquire an independent nuclear weapons capability, however, Japanese perceptions of the Korean threat could change dramatically.

Some U.S officials and defense specialists view with alarm the Soviet naval buildup in the Pacific; the Japanese tend to be uneasy about the possible implications of the buildup, but they do not necessarily assume that it is directed against Japan or that it significantly weakens the credibility of the U.S. commitment. In August 1976 Director-General of Defense Michita Sakata noted that the Soviet navy, like the armed forces of China and North Korea, had reached an impressive state of development, but, he added, "they are not pointing their guns against us." Indeed, Sakata observed that except for two unsuccessful Mongol attempts in the thirteenth century, "no one has ever come to conquer us."[2] Only if Sino-Soviet relations were to improve dramatically or if the Soviet navy appeared capable of dominating the Pacific would Japanese concern about Soviet intentions escalate to alarm.

This is not to suggest that the Japanese feel they now live in a world without potential danger. Japanese defense planners assume that three kinds of threats are at least conceivable: direct nuclear attack, conventional attack by the Soviet Union along Japan's northern frontier, and harassment of Japanese ships at sea. All of these are viewed as very unlikely, though the third is not quite so remote as the others. Japanese strategists assume that U.S. assistance would be needed not only to deter nuclear threats but to deal with conventional challenges as well, especially to help maintain Japan's access to sea-lanes and provide some capability for counterattack beyond the Japanese homeland.

That the United States must continue to play an important role in Japan's defense was not disputed by any of the conference participants. Indeed, all agreed that the U.S.-Japan alliance remains an indispensable ingredient in Japan's defense strategy. If it is necessary to effect changes in the mutual security treaty, this should be done by re-interpreting the document rather than by formally amending or abrogating it.

The crucial U.S contribution to Japan's defense is, of course, the nuclear umbrella. The credibility of the U.S. nuclear umbrella was judged to be adequate by those who took part in our discussions. No one argued that credibility requires the certainty of a U.S. nuclear response; whatever doubts allies may have about the willingness of the United States to risk its own destruction by entering a nuclear war on behalf of another country, the umbrella will serve to deter so long as potential adversaries believe there is even a small chance of U.S. nuclear retaliation. It also makes it unnecessary for the Japanese to consider seeking their own nuclear weapons. There was agreement that an independent Japanese nuclear force could prove provocative and, therefore, dangerous from the standpoint of Japan's own security.

Although the Japanese and American specialists involved in our discussions could agree on the credibility of the nuclear umbrella and the importance of maintaining it, they could not agree on the question of whether U.S. nuclear weapons are intended to deter conventional, as well as nuclear, attacks on Japan. Nor could they agree on the relative importance attached to tactical nuclear weapons, which would presumably be used to counter a conventional threat. Some Japanese expressed the view that the possibility of using nuclear weapons, strategic or tactical, to repel a conventional attack should be kept open, but the Americans seemed to assume that such use of nuclear weapons was not contemplated. There was apparent agreement, however, that the use of nuclear weapons against a conventional attack might safely be ruled out if a no-first-use agreement for nuclear weapons were concluded. But such an agreement, though acceptable to most participants on both sides, was considered unlikely in light of the U.S. government's known opposition to the concept. Another uncertain aspect of the nuclear umbrella is whether it would be more credible if Japan's non-nuclear principles were modified to permit the entry of nuclear weapons under certain circumstances—e.g., in an emergency, such as an attack on Japan, or routinely if such weapons are deployed aboard U.S. naval vessels docked in Japanese harbors. As several specialists observed, even if nuclear weapons had to be used for the defense of Japan, there would be no need to base them on Japanese territory; they could be just as effectively deployed offshore.

Concerning the possible entry of nuclear weapons aboard ships in transit, as in the case of the potential use of the nuclear umbrella to counter conventional threats, the Japanese argued that it is better to leave these questions ambiguous. As one of the Japanese participants put it, "You will be happier if you believe that your wife is beautiful." Ambiguity certainly has its advantages. It may help defuse sensitive domestic political issues, as in the matter of nuclear transit. Even the remote possibility of a nuclear response to a conventional challenge may have some deterrent value. But there is need for caution. Ambiguity may promote a false sense of confidence. And it may impede the building of the domestic political consensus needed to make commitments viable in times of crisis. With vital Japanese and U.S. interests at stake, it would seem prudent to seek the clearest possible understanding of what the two countries may expect of each other in a given contingency.

The Burden-Sharing Issue: Three Fallacies

The lack of political support in Japan for an accelerated buildup of the SDF and the absence of any real strategic justification for such a move are, of course, closely related. Because the Japanese see the threats to their security as remote and the U.S. commitment, especially the nuclear umbrella, as credible, they feel no sense of urgency to develop a stronger military establishment. Yet it may be anticipated that the United States, or at least certain American leaders and particular government agencies, will press Japan even harder than before to expand its military capabilities at a rate faster than most Japanese would prefer. The long-standing American belief that Japan, like other U.S. allies, should do more to lighten the defense burden borne by the United States is likely to grow stronger in the future. Indeed, Mr. Carter's inauguration as president evoked expressions of Japanese concern that his plans to reduce U.S. forces abroad might lead to a U.S. request that Tokyo assume a greater share of the defense burden. In light of President Carter's earlier statement that "interdependence means mutual sacrifice," even his generally welcomed call for increased consultations between Washington and Tokyo raised fears that the discussions might focus on the augmentation of Japan's defense role. And outgoing U.S. Ambassador James Hodgson was said (on reviewing his tenure in office) to have indirectly urged that Japan be ready to assume responsibilties for maintaining security in East Asia.[3]

In fact, the burden-sharing issue had already begun to complicate the Carter administration's relations with Japan within a few months of the inauguration. There was a good deal of displeasure among the Japanese because the administration's decision to withdraw U.S. ground forces from Korea in four to five years was taken without consulting its allies in advance. At the time of Vice-President Mondale's early 1977 visit to Tokyo, however, it was reported in the press that ranking Japanese officials had indicated the government's desire not to be consulted on the timing of any withdrawal. This reticence on Tokyo's part reflected not only a concern that Seoul might object to Tokyo's involvement in these decisions but also a fear that U.S. officials might exploit consultations on withdrawals from Korea as an opportunity to press Japan to make a greater contribution to regional security.

American pressure on Japan to undertake a larger share of the defense burden may well become an important source of conflict between the United States and Japan during the next decade, especially if the political position of the long-dominant LDP continues to erode. To be sure, Mr. Carter has exhibited sensitivity to the importance of avoiding further "shocks" in U.S.-Japan relations. Where the Japanese indicate a desire to be consulted, he will presumably ensure that Tokyo is fully briefed on any planned U.S. moves that may affect Japan's vital interests. But the achievement of more harmonious relations depends not merely on consultations intended to convey to the Japanese a clearer understanding of American purposes and expectations; it is also essential that Americans make a serious effort to acquire a deeper comprehension of the way Japanese view their own security and that of the rest of Asia. Moreover, the logic of American thinking about burden sharing needs some hard scrutiny. Why is it so important that Japan make a larger defense contribution?

As traditionally conceptualized by U.S. spokesmen, burden sharing has two principal dimensions—political and economic. Allied nations that are willing to develop their own military capabilities thereby demonstrate the strength of their anticommunist commitment and of their determination to defend themselves. Why, many Americans ask, should the United States pay the costs of defending nations that are unwilling to make the maximum sacrifice for their own security? The viability of the U.S. commitment to Japan, it is argued, depends on the determination of the Japanese to defend themselves. The United States may not be prepared to bring on the holocaust of nuclear war in order to protect people who are unwilling to fight in their own defense. Similarly, it is said, the duration and strength of the U.S. response to a conventional attack on Japan will depend ultimately on Japan's own will and capacity to resist aggression.[4]

An equally important part of the case for greater burden sharing resides in the presumed economic benefits for the United States. It is assumed that if allies expand their military forces or undertake broader responsibilities with existing forces, it will be possible for the United States to make a corresponding reduction of expenditures, thereby easing the load on the American taxpayer. The political appeal of this argument, always considerable, becomes almost irresistible when the ally, like Japan, is an economic power whose products often compete directly with American goods.

A Mistaken Linkage. There are three major fallacies in the way in which the burden-sharing concept has been applied to Japan. First, it is a mistake to link the viability of the U.S. commitment to the determination of the Japanese to defend themselves, as manifested by increasing burden sharing. This mistaken linkage reflects in part a misinterpretation of the meaning of Japan's reluctance to play a more substantial military role. Japan's extraordinary pacifism is rooted in the country's peculiar historical circumstances and is reinforced by a belief that there are no imminent threats to Japan's security. Of course, no one would deny that the Japanese are moved by economic motives as well; like many Americans, they would like to keep their defense budget low in order to have more money to spend on other needs. But it would be inaccurate to dismiss Japanese pacifism as a mere pretext for shirking an unwanted economic burden. The significance of the factors that differentiate Japan from other U.S. allies should not be underestimated.

For example, the U.S. experience in Vietnam is often cited as evidence of the difficulty of securing the support of the American people for the sustained defense of a country that does not wish to defend itself. But the relevance of the Vietnam case is dubious. The will to resist was a critical factor in the case of Vietnam because the viability of South Vietnam as a nation was very much in question. Moreover, there was serious doubt about the intrinsic importance of Vietnam to the United States.

The case of Japan is exactly the opposite. The pacifism of the Japanese people does not reflect any lack of support for the Japanese nation. There is no question whatever about the viability of Japan as a nation or about the intrinsic importance of Japan to the United States. A Japanese military buildup is not needed to prove that Japan is worth defending.

Nor is it easy to see why the willingness of the United States to risk nuclear holocaust should increase as a result of a marginal further development of the SDF. Questions about the Japanese determination to fight might be more relevant in a protracted conventional war, but it is very difficult, given the basic geographical facts, to envisage the Japanese having to fight such a war for the defense of the home islands. One can conceive of Japan's being involved in a lengthy conventional conflict beyond the home islands, but it strains credulity to imagine an invader fighting mile by mile for Japanese soil.

In this connection, it is important to recognize clearly the difference between Japan and those European NATO members that see their principal external threat coming from the numerically superior conventional forces of the Warsaw Pact countries. NATO countries that perceive such a threat could reasonably be expected to make a substantial contribution to their own defense. In Europe, U.S. nuclear weapons are intended to help deter a conventional attack. In Japan, the chief purpose of the U.S. nuclear umbrella is to prevent nuclear blackmail. Because Japan faces a threat different in nature and magnitude from that facing some European

NATO members, there is no reason to apply to the Japanese burden-sharing arguments that may be appropriate in Europe.

Increased burden sharing by Japan thus ought to be irrelevant to the viability of the U.S. commitment. The central reason for defending Japan is the country's unquestioned importance to the United States in strategic and economic terms. So long as they wish U.S. protection, the Japanese should be able to count on the United States to defend Japan whether or not they are prepared to mount a major defense buildup in their own behalf.

Moreover, it is necessary to distinguish between criticism of Japan for not carrying its share of the load and real doubts among Americans as to whether Japan is worth defending. Although Americans may voice resentment at seeing Japan prosper without having to carry a heavier military burden, this does not mean that they would urge abandonment of the commitment simply because Japan is not spending more on defense. The danger, however, is that criticism may be stated so strongly as to raise doubt about the viability of the commitment, even where the critics may not intend to create such doubts.

Ultimately, those who speak of Japan's determination to resist are really speaking more of capabilities than of will. What does it mean to say that the Japanese are determined to defend themselves in the absence of any real capability to do so? Is a determination to fight in the absence of adequate military capabilities anything more than a willingness to commit suicide? The real question, therefore, is not one of a will to resist but of a capacity to do so and the costs of acquiring this capacity.

An Illusory Contribution. This brings us to the second fallacy of burden sharing, which lies in the assumption that a modest expansion of Japanese military capabilities would necessarily increase Japan's security and reduce dependence on the United States. A minor increment to Japan's defense forces may be taken as an earnest of Japan's willingness to pay for its own defense, but what precisely would it contribute to Japan's security?

To answer this question, it would be useful to spell out precisely what it is that advocates of greater burden sharing are asking the Japanese to do. This is not easy, however, because those who urge that the Japanese shoulder a larger share of the defense burden often fail to specify what military capabilities the Japanese should develop. Many, perhaps most, of those who speak of the need for the Japanese to assume a larger role in their own defense define Japan's defense broadly—that is, they assume that the security of neighboring Asian territories will contribute to that of Japan. Spurred on by the growth of Soviet naval forces in the Pacific, they focus their efforts on prodding the Japanese to assume regional security responsibilities, from the Sea of Japan to Southeast Asia. President Ford, John Connally, and several senators have been among the outspoken pro-ponents of the view that Japan should assume greater responsibility not only for its own defense but for that of the rest of Asia as well.[5] When specific weaponry is mentioned, highest priority is attached to Japan's naval development, especially to the improvement of its antisubmarine warfare (ASW) capability in the Sea of Japan. Occasional reference is made to the desirability of Japan's providing military aid to South Korea and to certain Southeast Asian countries.

A modest expansion of Japanese Maritime Self Defense Force (MSDF) capabilities might enable Japan to make some added contribution, but in comparison to the U.S. naval forces deployed in the area, that contribution would be marginal. If Japan were to play more than a minor role, the MSDF would have to be expanded far beyond the level presently contemplated. The question, therefore, is whether the marginal contribution that Japanese forces or Japanese aid might make—in both military and psychological terms—would be commensurate with the costs likely to be incurred.

What are those costs? To begin with, we have alrady noted the existence of an important difference between American and Japanese perceptions of Soviet naval development in the Pacific. Because the Japanese do not assume that the Soviet naval buildup threatens them, they find it hard to see how their development of naval forces in response to the Soviet buildup would add to their security. On the contrary, it would send hostile signals to the Soviets and perhaps to other adversaries as well, thereby complicating Japan's relations with them; who can calculate the opportunity costs in lost chances for economic or political relationships that might have helped ensure stability? Moreover, a Japanese buildup aimed at countering the Soviet navy might well provoke a Soviet response, which could increase the chances of conflict.

Nor should one underestimate the potential costs to Japan's relations with other Asian countries. Many Asian nations would probably react against any Japanese move toward a regional military role, and this could easily create tensions capable of undermining economic relationships that the Japanese do recognize as important to their security. Regardless of how sincerely advocates of such a buildup assure their critics that only a limited expansion is envisaged, many will conclude that once the process of military development picks up momentum, it will not be easy to slow it down.

Moreover, given the low perception of threat, a reallocation of resources toward greater defense expenditures would probably antagonize important interest groups and segments of the public. The acquisition of any Japanese role in the defense of areas beyond the Japanese islands would raise the greatest political controversy in Japan, given the constitutional stipulation that Japan's military role be limited to "self-defense." In fact, by attempting to do too much, advocates of a faster military buildup may so mobilize opposition to defense outlays as to jeopardize even those expenditures that are clearly needed. If burden sharing is pushed too hard, it could inspire a wave of anti-Americanism that could jeopardize the foundations of the U.S.-Japanese alliance. Even America's friends in the LDP may feel compelled to take steps to prove that they are not merely doing Washington's bidding. In sum, there may be high costs in developing unneeded military forces merely to demonstrate Japan's willingness to share the burden.

Japan's acquisition of a minor regional role in the name of burden sharing could well result in a net diminution of security for Japan and for the United States.

Furthermore, there is no reason to assume that a modest Japanese buildup would in fact make possible a corresponding reduction in the U.S. presence. It is not at all clear whether these Japanese forces would substitute for U.S. ones or merely supplement them, in which case there would be no saving for the American taxpayer.

The SDF are, of course, continuing to develop, if not as rapidly as the advocates of burden sharing may wish. There are political, economic, and bureaucratic elements in Japan that favor this military development for their own reasons, quite apart from the imperatives of burden sharing; certainly, the Defense Agency has an interest in expansion of Japan's military establishment. The lines along which the Japanese have chosen to build their forces, as laid out in the 1976 Defense White Paper, aim not at the assumption of a regional role but at filling a presumed "gap" in the country's defense by establishing a "basic standing force" to provide a "denial and resistance" capability—that is, to deal with small-scale aggression in the early stages. The emphasis is on a variety of qualitative improvements in existing weapons and equipment, as well as on the addition of one mixed brigade to the Ground Self Defense Forces (GSDF), which would then consist of thirteen divisions and two mixed brigades; one escort flotilla to the MSDF, which would then have five escort flotillas; and the introduction of an Airborne Early Warning (AEW) capability into the Air Self Defense Forces (ASDF). This force would be expected to hold the line until U.S. power can be brought to bear, which the Japanese estimate would take about three days.[6]

Such an approach clearly poses far fewer problems than one designed to give the Japanese a regional defense role. But it is not at all apparent just how this would reduce the burden presently assumed by the United States, since the new Japanese forces are intended to fill a presumed gap, not to supplant an existing U.S. capability. There are, moreover, questions that need to be raised about the probable benefits for Japanese security of putting further resources into the development of a small "denial and resistance" force. Such a force is likely to prove either too much or too little for the situation. One cannot easily devise credible scenarios to which such a force would be a relevant response. It has been suggested that an attack might begin with the interdiction of air- and sea-lanes, followed by bombing raids, and finally by invading ground assault forces. Another scenario has a potential aggressor creating internal disturbances in Japan and then, in response to "an invitation" from some element in Japan, launching a limited armed attack in the hope of establishing a limited military fait accompli before the United States has time to take action.

But how realistic are these scenarios? And against whom would these small-scale wars be fought? Does anyone really think that the Soviet Union or China would initiate a war with Japan by launching a small-scale conventional assault? So long as U.S. naval and air forces remain committed to the defense of Japan, such an invasion seems almost inconceivable. The U.S. forces designed to deter a massive invasion would also deter a small-scale attack; the "gap" that the basic standing force is designed to fill may be imaginary. Japanese forces created to deter a small-scale attack are likely to be redundant. Only if the U.S. commitment were to be drastically reduced would there be a strong case for building up a Japanese force, and in that event, a much larger force than the one presently contemplated would be needed. In short, if the U.S. commitment continues, an expanded, but still modest Japanese defensive force is unnecessary; if the U.S. commitment is curtailed, such a force is inadequate.

It is hard, therefore, to see how the Japanese can lift a significant share of the defense burden from the shoulders of the United States unless they are prepared to undertake a major buildup, which would either assume, or lead to, a basic change in the nature of the U.S. commitment. As already indicated, a modest expansion might actually diminish Japanese security without facilitating any reduction in the U.S. presence. Moreover, U.S. forces serve primarily as a deterrent, backed by the full weight of U.S. military might; they cannot be substantially replaced by Japanese forces without diminishing their deterrent value. This is not to say that U.S. forces cannot be reduced; they probably can, and the United States can also save several hundred million dollars in its balance of payments by further rationalizing and consolidating its base system in Japan.[7] But this can be done without any corresponding Japanese buildup. A modest Japanese buildup of the sort being urged in the name of burden sharing thus makes little sense—unless it is viewed as merely a first step toward a substantially larger buildup aimed at giving Japan a major military role. The relevant question then becomes: are the seriousness of the threat and the likelihood of its becoming a reality sufficient to justify the great costs that this major military expansion would involve? The answer would almost certainly be in the negative.

A Misunderstood Burden. The third fallacy of burden sharing resides in the assumption that the burden can accurately be measured by the size of a country's armed forces and defense expenditures. The burden of defense and security should not be defined so narrowly. To begin with, the Japanese feel that the substantial economic aid they provide to other Asian countries, though it serves a variety of purposes, does contribute to regional security. The Japanese have often noted that the military bases they make available to the United States represent an extremely important contribution to U.S. defense needs. Although the Japanese derive some economic benefit from the U.S. presence, they incur considerable financial costs by making available the land for bases and contributing to their maintenance. More difficult to gauge, but no less important, are the substantial political costs, specifically the infringement on sovereignty inherent in the bases and the tensions that sometimes arise between the bases and the surrounding community. The bases are criticized for their impact on the environment, especially "noise pollution," and for their interference with urban development.

Rarely is it noted that a country can contribute to security by not doing certain things. Japan helps to promote stability in East Asia by not rearming more rapidly. If Japan were to acquire a military role in the region, this would not only enflame anti-Japanese feelings; the resulting turmoil would jeopardize U.S. interests as well. It is important to recognize that by limiting their own rearmament and relying on the United States to deter potential aggression against Japan, the Japanese are paying a certain cost in the form of the risk they take. This cost is perceived as modest, because the risk is low, given the remoteness of the threats to Japan and the reliability of the U.S. commitment. But there is still some risk, which ought to be calculated as part of the burden borne by the Japanese.

It is not without irony that the strongest argument against burden sharing may lie in the possible long-term consequences of success in persuading the Japanese to expand their defense role. By prodding Tokyo to undertake moderately increased military development, Washington may help set in motion within Japan a process that will generate irresistible pressures to make the country a major military force in the world, perhaps a nuclear power. Once military development picks up momentum, it may create its own dynamic to push the process further; certainly, it is risky to assume that this process can be controlled.

Japan presently offers the world a model of a nation that possesses major power status without the military attributes usually associated with such status. This enables Japan to make a virtually unique contribution to the creation of a peaceful world order. In itself, Japan's example will not drastically change the attitudes of other nations, but it is a step in the right direction. Rather than undertaking military development that would make at best a marginal contribution to security, Japan can do more to foster stability in Asia by developing its political and economic relations with potential adversary nations, without, of course, abandoning the security treaty with the United States. Because their military capabilities are so limited, the Japanese believe that they must make greater use than other nations of economic and diplomatic levers for maintaining their security.

Reliance on such nonmilitary instruments ought to be encouraged; hopefully, other nations may come to place greater faith in them as well. Thus, rather than pressing the Japanese for military contributions that are likely to prove only marginally useful, if not redundant or actually counter-productive, it would seem wiser to encourage Japan to make the kind of contribution to peace and security that it alone among the major powers can make.

Future Development of the SDF

The foregoing critique of burden sharing should not be taken to suggest that there is no possible justification for the expansion of the SDF. At the very least, the SDF's important nonmilitary functions—such as its role in rescue and disaster relief—should be developed further.[8] Japan might also contribute more to the maintenance of U.S. bases, especially when doing so creates jobs for Japanese. Changes in the international environment may at some point dictate ac-celerated development of Japan's military capabilities. Even now qualitative improvement in particular areas may be appropriate. The central point is that the SDF ought to be developed within the country's constitutional limitations at a pace reflecting Japan's own defense needs as perceived by the Japanese people, not as a meaningless gesture of burden sharing in response to pressure from the United States.

Some Possible Guidelines. The discussions of Japan's defense strategy that took place in our conferences point toward some possible guidelines for the future development of the SDF. Most countries prefer to settle their conflicts without having to go to war, but the Japanese aversion to war is truly extraordinary. The Japanese are very aware of their country's vulnerability should a serious threat emerge. Indeed, Japan may be unique, especially among major powers, in its emphasis on avoidance of armed conflict as a component of its strategic doctrine. If faced with the threat of war, it is up to Tokyo either to find a peaceful settlement or to activate the U.S. forces committed to Japan's defense. Japan needs an independent capacity to assess potential threats and the longest possible warning time so that Tokyo can bring to bear all the nonmilitary means at its disposal to avoid the actual outbreak of hostilities. In the event of failure, Japan must then have time to decide whether to take whatever steps are necessary to ensure the realization of the U.S. commitment. It would thus seem sensible to give highest priority to the development of the military capabilities that directly contribute to successful avoidance by giving Japan the earliest possible warning of any potential hostile move.

This suggests the desirability of focusing the SDF's development on the improvement of Japan's capabilities for gathering and processing intelligence. Some Japanese members of our group have emphasized the importance of Japan's acquiring its own satellite reconnaissance system. Better antisubmarine warfare capabilities, especially tracking and surveillance, and airborne early warning, which is one of the focal points of the defense plans outlined in the recent white paper, are examples of goals that would seem consonant with the emphasis on avoidance. To be sure, these ASW and AEW capabilities would provide primarily tactical intelligence, which might lengthen the warning time only marginally. But might not even a marginal increment to warning time be of potentially critical importance in framing a Japanese response to a threat?

One must, of course, recognize the problems involved even in a buildup focused mainly on capabilities related to avoidance. The kinds of intelligence capabilities mentioned above, especially a satellite reconnaissance system, are extremely expensive to acquire. There is also a problem of redundance, since these costly capabilities would duplicate those already possessed by the United States. Could the territory subject to satellite coverage be subdivided in order to reduce the burden on the existing U.S. satellite system, or would both systems have to be comprehensive in order to be effective? If such complementarity could be achieved, would the United States be willing to rely on Japan for a portion of its strategic intelligence, thereby eliminating duplication? If such an arrangement proves infeasible, would duplication be justified by the possibility that Japan and the United States may reach different conclusions as to the correct interpretation of intelligence data?

An obvious alternative is the establishment of better consultation between Japan and the United States, beginning with improved arrangements for the sharing of U.S. intelligence, including selected raw data. The inadequacy of existing arrangements for intelligence sharing was a theme emphasized by the Japanese participants in our discussions. The security considerations that previously inhibited such sharing are less relevant now, in view of the reliance on satellite photographs. Improved contingency planning might also be helpful. This apparently is being undertaken by the new Subcommittee for Defense Cooperation (SDC), set up in the summer of 1976 to consider, among other things, precisely what would be expected of each party in an emergency. Similarly, it is important that decisions about the level of U.S. forces and facilities in Japan be made through a process of genuine consultation and collaborative study, rather than a one-sided process in which the Americans make the determinations and the Japanese merely respond.

Improved consultation of the sort described above becomes all the more important in view of the likelihood that there will in fact be little expansion of the SDF. The 1976 Defense White Paper reports that because of financial constraints a "considerable portion" of the major equipment additions scheduled in the Fourth Defense Plan, which expired at the end of fiscal 1976, will not be implemented.[9] As already noted, the fiscal 1977 budget allocates a lower percentage to defense than any previous budget since the birth of the SDF. It is doubtful, therefore, that Japan will wish to pay for greatly augmented intelligence capabilities.

Conclusion. Whatever the Japanese may decide, the United States should refrain from pressing Japan into an unwanted military role in the name of a misguided conception of burden sharing. Basic to Japan's security, and to the preservation of U.S. security interests in East Asia, is a high degree of mutual understanding, embracing political and economic concerns, that will make manifest to both countries the importance of the interests they share. Such an understanding can be sustained far more easily if each country's security policies have broad national support. The United States should help the Japanese government build public support for the U.S.-Japan security relationship by removing irritants wherever possible. This not only means making it unmistakably clear that the U.S. commitment is not contingent on any increased burden sharing by Japan; it also means attaching a high priority to further consolidation of U.S. facilities in Japan and to the reduction of the U.S. presence to a level the two sides determine to be the minimum necessary for effective deterrence. And the Japanese, for their part, should understand that pressures exerted by the American people to reduce the U.S. presence in East Asia do not mean that the United States would diminish the strength of its commitment to Japan.

Asian Security and the Problem of Korea

It is easy to oversimplify the relationship between Japan's security and that of the rest of East Asia. The Pentagon Papers reveal a tendency on the part of U.S. policy-makers, dating back to the early 1950s, to look upon Japan as the "ultimate domino" in Asia. Many commentators have emphasized Japanese concern about the steadfastness of U.S. commitments; they have portrayed the Japanese as fearful that Washington's failure to fulfill its other Asian commitments would portend the abandonment of Japan. Most recently it has become a commonplace that the United States must hold to its commitment to South Korea because the Japanese consider this essential for their own security. Any substantial reduction of the U.S. military presence in Korea, it is argued, could undermine Japanese confidence in the U.S. commitment to Tokyo and propel the Japanese toward a major rearmament program, which might include nuclear weapons. Thus, the Japanese interest has generally been interpreted as a plea for the perpetuation of existing policies, as a vote against change.

U.S. Commitments and Asian Security

Our conference discussions suggest that there is reason to question the validity of the widely accepted view that the Japanese stand unalterably against any change in U.S. commitments. To be sure, the Japanese do worry about the reliability of U.S. commitments, and government spokesmen do say that the United States should maintain its current posture in Korea lest the precarious balance there be upset. But there is much more to Japanese thinking than that.

To begin with, the Japanese do not necessarily see any clear-cut relationship between the U.S. commitment to Japan and Washington's other Asian commitments. They recognize the limitations of America's capacity to ensure the survival of allied regimes through a projection of U.S. military power. Japanese and American participants seemed generally to agree that Washington should continue to move toward a more selective approach to its Asian security commitments, assuming, of course, that Japan remains among "the selected." No one argued that a more discriminating approach to the implementation of U.S. commitments would endanger the credibility of truly vital commitments such as the one to Japan. We found no disagreement with the proposition that the need for and feasibility of implementing each commitment should be reassessed on a case-by-case basis in close consultation with the allied government.

Of course, it is not an easy task to make the necessary judgments concerning each commitment. Nor is it easy to overcome the strong temptation to resist making hard decisions until they are forced upon us by events. But there would seem to be considerable advantage in reviewing the need for and feasibility of commitments in a calm, noncrisis atmosphere, rather than waiting until the government finds itself pressed to make a rapid response and, having done so, to justify that response to the public.

A reassessment of commitments might focus on the following questions: (1) What potential threats does each ally face at present, and what is the extent of its capability to defend itself without assistance? (2) To what extent is it in the interests of the United States to assist its ally in meeting each of those threats and under what circumstances, if any, would the direct involvement of U.S. forces be required? (3) Given conditions in the allied country and in the United States, what is the likelihood that U.S. military intervention would prove feasible and effective? (4) What is the minimum U.S. military presence required to make the commitment credible? (5) What particular circumstances might cause the commitment to be considered wholly or partially invalid?

There were some differences of opinion among the conference participants on both sides concerning the desirability of publicly specifying the conditions under which each commitment might be implemented. Some felt that "going public" in the redefinition of commitments would excessively politicize them and weaken their deterrent value. Congress, it was feared, might attach "irrelevant conditions," presumably stipulations concerning matters unrelated to the strategic calculus, such as the allied government's policies with respect to human rights. Besides, publicly ruling out intervention might invite aggression, but even the remote possibility that a questionable commitment will be fulfilled might help to deter adventurous gambles by a potential aggressor.

The counterargument to the fear of politicization was that without the early involvement of Congress and the public in the process of reassessing and redefining U.S. commitments, it would be hard to build the broad base of popular support needed to ensure the successful implementation of any commitment. And what is an "irrelevant" condition? If something bears upon the prospects for developing a domestic political consensus behind a commitment, is it not therefore relevant to the feasibility of carrying out the commitment? It will be necessary to "go public" at some point if the commitment ever needs to be implemented, and all the "irrelevant" considerations are likely to be raised then. In that case, the United States may have to respond before a popular consensus can be developed in support of the commitment, only to discover later that those "irrelevant" factors thwart the building of the needed consensus.

Nor can it safely be assumed that publicly narrowing the scope of a commitment to a particular country, or even terminating a security arrangement, would invite aggression. It would depend on how vulnerable the ally is to the kind of threat being excluded from the commitment. The presence or absence of a U.S. commitment is only one of the factors that a potential aggressor must calculate. It is possible that the curtailing of a U.S. commitment might lead either to a stiffening of the ally's will to resist based on more effective mobilization of its own resources or to an accommodation of interests between the potential disputants, thus averting hostilities. In any case, even if publicly circumscribing a U.S. commitment does lead to aggression, the countries concerned are, by definition, of peripheral importance to the United States, and, therefore, their "loss" would not seriously jeopardize U.S. security interests. Indeed, it is probably only because Washington says it is committed to such countries that this "loss" involves a cost to the United States. On the other hand, those important commitments that are publicly reaffirmed would find their credibility enhanced.

There was an apparent consensus among the participants that commitments requiring counterinsurgency activities by the United States are not viable and should be curtailed. Indeed, few expect the United States to become involved in such activities. This has clear implications in Southeast Asia, where the principal threat faced by America's remaining allies is that of insurgency. Even relatively conservative Japanese specialists on Asian security affairs could agree in early 1977 that the United States should resist any possible overtures from the Thai government for the reintroduction of U.S. forces or increased military aid to deal with the growing insurgent challenge. There is very little evidence of any concern on the part of the Japanese at the prospect of a further diminution of U.S. commitments in Southeast Asia. A second guideline suggested was that the United States should demonstrate the high priority it attaches to nuclear nonproliferation by making its commitments contingent on the willingness of allies to refrain from seeking an independent nuclear weapons capability. This would be especially relevant to South Korea and Taiwan.[10]

The participants in our discussions agreed not only on the need for a more discriminating approach to U.S. commitments but also on the desirability of placing greater emphasis on nonmilitary instruments for the achievement of security. They could not agree, however, on the extent to which economic and diplomatic relationships with communist nations could reduce the degree of reliance on military commitments.[11] There is need for systematic study aimed at clarifying how particular kinds of economic activities might help deter aggression. A number of specific questions were suggested by our discussions. What kinds of economic relationships with the communist countries would give them the greatest stake in the preservation of peace? How far should the United States go to encourage a multiplicity of relationships? Should it facilitate the transfer of military-related technology to the People's Republic of China? Is the French sale of tanks, fighter planes, and other such equipment to China a good precedent? Should the United States and Japan encourage other noncommunist Asian nations to normalize and develop their relations with communist states, or should they merely allow events to follow their own course? And how important is ideology as a limiting factor in these relationships?

The discussion of commitments ultimately came to focus on the Korean case, for this is clearly of greatest concern to Japan. Although nothing approaching a consensus emerged from this lively discussion, some important aspects of Japanese thinking were clarified. Because the subject of Korea occupied so much of our attention, I have presented here a rather lengthy analysis of the problem, drawing on those discussions. The reader should be aware that several participants have expressed their disagreement with my proposals concerning force withdrawals and diplomatic relations with Pyongyang.

Japanese Flexibility on Korea

Although the official Japanese position, which urged no change in the existing U.S. presence in Korea, was expressed, the Japanese participants displayed considerable flexibility concerning the possibility of major U.S. withdrawals. There was little alarm among the Japanese at the prospect of such withdrawals if accomplished over time and after careful consultation. Indeed, the Japanese generally gave the impression that they expected the United States to withdraw its forces from Korea before long and that the relevant question was not whether that should be done but how to do it in a way that will minimize destabilizing effects.

This flexibility is but one of the nuances and countercurrents in Japanese thinking on Korea often ignored by Americans. Several Japanese participants emphasized their belief that Washington has never really understood Japanese thinking on the Korean question. In particular, Americans do not sufficiently appreciate the importance of *process* to the Japanese. It is hard to overemphasize the significance that the Japanese attach not merely to the substance of policies but to the process by which they are developed and implemented. Since President Nixon "shocked" the Japanese by failing to inform them in advance of his plan to visit Peking, Americans have tended to understand the importance of consultation, but merely as a means of ensuring that the Japanese are briefed before a decision is announced publicly. Indeed, some Americans, knowing that U.S. decision-makers are unlikely to be swayed by the Japanese, seem inclined to regard consultations in advance of a decision as something of a charade. This ignores an important cultural difference. As noted by two students of Japanese corporate decision making, Japanese who are consulted about an impending decision will normally indicate their consent, but this does not imply approval, as it might in an American context. The fact that he has been consulted, and given an opportunity to express his reservations, may lead a Japanese to acquiesce in a decision he might otherwise have resisted.[12]

As for force withdrawals from Korea, some Japanese who reflect government thinking argued that these should be accomplished through a "definite, carefully laid out plan" formulated in consultation with Japan and South Korea and made public. The allies may not agree on all points, but they must be consulted. A number of Japanese participants made clear their belief that a withdrawal of U.S. forces from Korea undertaken in such a manner would not lead to any major military buildup or a move toward nuclear weapons in Japan; nor was there any indication that this would lead Japan to question the viability of its security relationship with the United States. Although there has in fact been considerable dissatisfaction among the Japanese with the character of the Carter administration's consultations in connection with the decision to withdraw ground combat forces from Korea, the Japanese have apparently not found it too difficult to adjust to the decision. They probably recognize that in this particular case the inadequacy of consultations cannot be blamed entirely on Washington, since the Japanese sent conflicting signals concerning their desire to be consulted.

There are, of course, certain developments that clearly would upset the Japanese. They fear that a precipitate U.S. withdrawal from South Korea based, for example, on disapproval of Seoul's policies on human rights would be viewed as a complete repudiation of the ROK by the United States and could invite hostile action by North Korea. Withdrawals should be undertaken in a way that would "build confidence" among the South Koreans and would not send misleading signals to Pyongyang. Ideally, asserted one of the senior Japanese participants, there should be "some arrangement" to maintain peace after the departure of U.S. forces.

In any case, it was made clear that the overriding Japanese interest in Korea is the avoidance of hostilities that would polarize the Japanese people and could lead to Japanese involvement in the conflict. Avoiding an "explosion" on the peninsula is deemed even more important than preservation of a noncommunist South Korea. To be sure, a unified Korea, especially under Pyongyang's aegis, would be undesirable from the Japanese standpoint. The concern is less with the military threat that a unified communist Korea might pose to Japan than with the psychological shock of a communist victory. The Japanese fear that the process of determining how they should deal with the new situation would produce a bitter debate during which extremist groups of both the Left and Right might gain strength. A rush of Korean refugees into an already highly polarized Korean minority in Japan would add to the turmoil. And, of course, Japan's substantial economic stake in South Korea would be in grave jeopardy.

But Japan's reaction would depend on a number of factors, not the least of which would be the attitude of the unified Korean state toward Japan. The Japanese participants seemed confident that their country could live with a unified Korea; they predicted that if it were attained peacefully, the reunification of Korea, even under communist auspices, would produce no fundamental changes in Japan's defense policies. Tokyo would not abandon the security relationship with the United States, nor would it undertake any sharply increased military development. The problem is that few people, on either the Japanese or the American side, can envisage the reunification of Korea without violence.

Our discussions suggest that the Korean development most likely to lead to a military buildup in Japan, including pressure for the acquisition of nuclear weapons, would not be a withdrawal of U.S. forces but a move by either Korean government to obtain an independent nuclear weapons capability. There seems little likelihood of Pyongyang's acquiring such a capability, but the same cannot be said of Seoul. Although it would take the South Koreans a long time to develop nuclear weapons, the repercussions of a move in that direction (acquisition of some necessary components, such as reprocessing facilities) would begin to be felt immediately. One cannot predict with certainty, however, that South Korea's acquisition of nuclear weapons would lead Japan to follow Seoul's example. Some senior Japanese specialists on security affairs, noting that a nuclear-armed South Korea would be internationally isolated and that a few low-yield bombs would not make the Koreans a serious threat to their neighbors, believe that Japan would continue to rely exclusively on the U.S. nuclear umbrella. But even if the Japanese did so, there is no denying that emotionally based pressures to develop a nuclear weapons capability would be intense.

In sum, Japanese attitudes toward Korea manifest a greater degree of flexibility than is generally acknowledged. Though they may prefer the status quo, the Japanese can accept U.S. force withdrawals, so long as they are undertaken in a way that will minimize any potentially destabilizing effects. The United States need not feel constrained in its consideration of Korean options by the assumption that Japan stands resolutely opposed to any change in the U.S. role.

Can Washington withdraw its military forces from South Korea without jeopardizing the peace and stability of the peninsula? There is, of course, no agreement among either Americans or Japanese concerning the pace or extent of any force withdrawals. In my view, Mr. Carter's announced plan to withdraw U.S. ground combat forces within four to five years is a reasonable and safe policy. I believe there is also a need to take a longer-term perspective and consider not only the rationale for withdrawing ground forces but also the other steps to which this process may lead and the implications of those steps. It is time to begin thinking seriously about the logic of a complete withdrawal, carefully planned and staged over a period of time sufficient to minimize destabilizing effects. There is no need for haste in setting timetables, but it would be appropriate before too long to begin discussing with Seoul and Tokyo a comprehensive withdrawal plan. This would involve the early removal of the U.S. tactical nuclear weapons presently stationed in Korea, followed by the withdrawal of ground forces on the schedule set by President Carter, and finally, over a period of perhaps several additional years, the evacuation of the remaining air and naval forces. Air forces earmarked for Korea should be retained in Japan, at Pacific island bases, and at sea, as a manifestation of the readiness of the United

States to intervene in Korea in the unlikely event that it becomes necessary to do so. If this plan is properly constructed and explained, I do not believe that the Japanese will oppose it. But the reasons for these withdrawals must be made clear.

Removal of Nuclear Weapons

The least controversial element of a U.S. withdrawal plan, judging from our discussions, would be the removal of the tactical nuclear weapons presently stationed in Korea. Some of these weapons are already being withdrawn as the U.S. ground forces that control them come out. There are several reasons for removing the rest of these weapons. To begin with, the Japanese and American participants agreed that the weapons are not needed for the defense of South Korea. U.S. government officials with Northeast Asian responsibilities indicate that it is virtually impossible to imagine how they could be used effectively. Whatever deterrent effect they may have can be brought to bear from weapons deployed offshore. But if they remain on the peninsula, there is always a danger that somehow they may be used if a conflict breaks out. Even in the absence of hostilities, one cannot rule out the possibility of theft or capture.

Two related arguments have been brought forth in support of keeping these weapons in Korea. First is the fear that their removal might diminish the South Koreans' confidence in the U.S. commitment. This has led some to propose removal of the weapons if it could be kept secret. One must question, however, whether such a move could in fact be kept from the public. Surely the South Koreans will know and, assuming they disapprove, they may well leak the information to their American friends to use as evidence of U.S. "softness" in fulfilling its commitments.

The other argument concerns the possibility that withdrawal of U.S. nuclear weapons from South Korea would provide an important added incentive for Seoul to seek its own nuclear weapons capability. Yet, prior to U.S. intervention quashing the French sale to South Korea of reprocessing facilities, the South Koreans were moving toward the components of a nuclear weapons capability—even though American tactical nuclear weapons were deployed in their country. Keeping these weapons in Korea is no guarantee that Seoul will not seek to go nuclear. We must acknowledge that on this or any other issue, the Koreans may prove to be beyond U.S. influence. But assuming that the U.S. presence gives Washington some continuing (though limited) influence over Seoul, one cannot deny that any diminution of that presence would probably reduce U.S. leverage. The critical question, however, is: would the United States, with its nuclear weapons withdrawn from Korea, retain enough influence to keep Seoul from seeking its own nuclear weapons?

While deferring a fuller answer to the discussion of the potential impact of troop withdrawals on U.S. influence over Seoul, it may be said here that the added leverage provided by U.S. tactical nuclear weapons is very likely to prove marginal. It is a case of overkill. If it were made clear to Seoul that (1) in the unlikely event it is needed, the U.S. nuclear deterrent remains available from offshore and (2) a Korean decision to opt for an independent nuclear weapons capability would almost certainly lead to the abrogation of the U.S. commitment, the South Koreans would find it hard to escape the conclusion that they, unlike the Indians, could go nuclear only at the sacrifice of a much more credible U.S. deterrent. Assuming that the Koreans believe what they say about the importance of the U.S. commitment, it would seem very unlikely that they would be willing to pay the heavy price of developing their own nuclear weapons.

Finally, contrary to the assumption that a withdrawal of U.S. nuclear weapons would encourage Seoul to seek its own, it may well be that the United States, by keeping such weapons in Korea, suggests that they are essential for Korea's defense and, therefore, actually stimulates Korean desires to have their own nuclear weapons.

The Military Rationale for Withdrawal of U.S. Forces

Over the years the military requirement for U.S. forces in Korea has diminished as South Korean capabilities have grown. Most analysts agree that the armed forces of South and North Korea are now, overall, in balance. Despite North Korean advantages in certain areas, U.S. military analysts have concluded that neither side could win a decisive victory in a full-scale war conducted without the participation of any foreign forces.[13] In ground forces the South Koreans have a significant numerical advantage, in addition to superior combat experience and excellent defensive terrain. It is widely agreed that they can repel any ground attack from the North without the assistance of U.S. ground forces; President Park himself confirmed this publicly in August 1975. Although, as reported in the press in May 1977, North Korean firepower had previously been underestimated, it is questionable whether the new figures represent any significant change in the overall balance. It is also important to note that the increased inventories, mainly of tanks, now attributed to the North Koreans reflect improved intelligence collection capabilities on the U.S. side, not a sudden buildup by the North Koreans.

There is no reason to believe that U.S. ground combat forces will be needed in 1982, the outer limit set by the president for completing the withdrawal of those forces. Indeed, a strong case can be made that they are superfluous even now, but a gradual withdrawal is desirable in order to give all parties time to adjust. Even if one takes a pessimistic view of the implications of the revised estimates of North Korean firepower, it is hard to imagine that the South Korean army has any deficiencies in equipment that could not be remedied within the four- to five-year period designated for the withdrawal of U.S. ground forces. The issue raised by the Carter withdrawal plan, it should be remembered, is whether the South Koreans will be able to defend themselves without U.S. ground combat forces four or five years hence, not whether they can do so today.

The military justification for the continued presence of U.S. air forces is also disappearing. There is no doubt that U.S. air forces play a more important military role in the defense of South Korea than do U.S. ground forces. It is generally acknowledged that without U.S. support to Seoul,

North Korea has a substantial quantitative advantage in air capabilities. But the margin of North Korea's superiority in the air shrinks considerably when qualitative factors are taken into consideration, and the gap is being narrowed further as South Korea procures additional F-4s and F-5Es, both of which are superior to any aircraft possessed by the North Koreans.

The speed at which U.S. forces may be withdrawn without threatening the stability of the peninsula would depend in part on the answers to certain questions: How long will it take at current rates of procurement for the South Koreans to attain a level of parity with North Korea in air-defense capabilities? Can Washington help, through commercial credit sales of military equipment, to accelerate the augmentation of South Korean capabilities as part of an overall understanding about the withdrawal of U.S. forces from Korea? Can the United States help provide the needed increments to South Korea's air power without provoking a counter-buildup on the other side, thus stimulating an escalation of the Korean arms race? If such a development of South Korean capabilities proves infeasible within a reasonable period of time, can the gap in air capabilities presently filled by U.S. forces in Korea be adequately filled by U.S. air forces stationed offshore?

It is impossible to give definitive answers at this point, but some observations may be offered. Augmentation of South Korea's air-defense capabilities to a level of parity with the North is presumably possible at some level of expenditure. Of course, care would have to be taken to assure that South Korea does not acquire offensive capabilities that would threaten North Korea and thereby jeopardize the stability of the peninsula. This may not be so simple, for the distinction between offensive and defensive weapons is usually ambiguous. For example, some commentators have noted that F-4s, which the South Koreans are now acquiring and which represent the mainstay of the U.S. air presence on the peninsula, may be dangerously close to having offensive capabilities. The F-4, given its range and payload, can be used for long-range penetration missions.[14] South Korea's acquisition of additional long-range aircraft or even of ships that might be used to harass Japanese fishing boats clearly is worrisome to the Japanese.

The principal constraint on an American-assisted augmentation of South Korean military capabilities is likely to be the unwillingness of the Congress and public opinion in the United States to support any additional aid to Seoul in light of that government's domestic repression and its lobbying practices. But a coupling of increased commercially based military sales guaranteed by the U.S. government with a plan for the complete withdrawal of U.S. forces from Korea might well make such expanded aid politically feasible.

Distance, as a Japanese defense planner has noted, is not likely to be a crucial matter if U.S. forces stationed outside the country have to fill any remaining gap in the ROK's capabilities. If a sufficiently high degree of alertness is maintained by U.S. forces stationed offshore, they can very quickly be deployed from aircraft carriers, bases in Japan, and even from as far away as Guam. This means that bases in Korea and in Japan would have to be kept in a state of readiness that would enable them to receive and service a large number of aircraft. Whether bases in Japan would be available for this purpose is not certain. The Japanese are reluctant to make a public commitment. But there is every indication, based on our discussions with the Japanese, that in an emergency the bases could be used.

In any case, given the vitality of South Korea's economy, it is hard to imagine that Seoul will not be able to attain parity with the North Korean air forces within, say, five to eight years. The willingness of the United States to facilitate this process through military aid should become less important as Seoul increasingly finds itself in a position to buy what it needs from a variety of sources. When South Korean air forces are the equal of North Korea's, there will be no military justification for the continued presence of U.S. forces.

The Political Rationale for Withdrawal

Many of those who acknowledge that the military justification for the continued presence of U.S. forces in Korea is diminishing argue that the real importance of those forces is political. By serving as a trip-wire to ensure immediate U.S. involvement, these troops are said to deter a North Korean invasion. Withdrawing them, even if they are superfluous from a military standpoint, allegedly would have a dangerous psychological impact on the South Koreans and could invite North Korean aggression. A U.S. withdrawal, if interpreted by Seoul as a critical weakening of the U.S. commitment, could lead South Korea to undertake some drastic action, such as seeking its own nuclear weapons capability.

The political justification for a U.S. presence is stronger than the military rationale, but I believe there is need for substantial rethinking of the reasoning behind that political justification. It is easy to argue that the U.S. military presence in Korea has achieved its purposes in the past and that it is therefore foolhardy to tamper with a successful policy. But, that success has had its costs, and these costs have received insufficient attention. It is time for leaders in Washington, Seoul, and Tokyo to consider whether there may not be other ways, less costly for all of them, to deter conflict in Korea and prevent the proliferation of nuclear weapons in Northeast Asia.

The Question of Deterrence. The first question to be asked is whether an indefinite U.S. military presence on the peninsula is in fact indispensable to deter a North Korean attack. The presence of U.S. forces as a symbol of a security commitment has one overriding political purpose: it makes U.S. intervention in the event of hostilities virtually automatic. That U.S. ground forces stationed just below the DMZ serve this role is clear beyond doubt; the desire to avoid such automatic involvement is reportedly one reason for the Carter administration's decision to withdraw those forces. But it is not clear that removing ground combat forces eliminates the trip-wire effect. Although air forces positioned farther south could theoretically be held in reserve during the early stages of hostilities, in reality it would be extremely hard to keep them out. Even if U.S. air forces were not assaulted by enemy airplanes, troops, or saboteurs, there would be enormous pressure on them to intervene immediately in order to convince the aggressors of the hopelessness of their cause and to avoid giving the appearance of retreating under fire.

Automatic U.S. intervention in a foreign conflict is clearly desirable when two conditions are met: (1) the defense of the country concerned is of indisputable strategic importance to the United States; and (2) the country clearly needs and wants direct U.S. military intervention to help defend it in case of attack.

In 1950, South Korea was believed to be important to the United States not primarily because of its intrinsic worth but because the North Korean attack was seen as a projection of Soviet influence in a bipolar Cold War world. That U.S. intervention was required to repel the North Korean invasion was beyond doubt, given the assumptions of the policymakers. Today, the original rationale for defending South Korea has lost much of its force. In this multipolar world, it can no longer be assumed that North Korean expansion would increase Soviet power and influence vis-à-vis the United States. Neither the Soviets nor the Chinese seem to have any clear interest in a reunified Korea; on the contrary, the Soviets may actually prefer a divided Korea in the belief that this would help assure access to the Straits of Tsushima. The dissipation of the original rationale for U.S. intervention in Korea does not necessarily mean that the United States should refrain from coming to the defense of South Korea. But it is difficult to make a strong case that the U.S. interest in defending South Korea is now so overriding as to justify the automatic intervention that the presence of U.S. forces practically assures.

An even more striking change since 1950 is the ability of South Korea to defend itself without direct assistance from U.S. forces. South Korea is on the verge of being able to assume full responsibility for its own defense against a North Korean attack unaided by the Soviets or Chinese. There is every reason for the South Koreans to feel confident about their prospects and for the North Koreans to think twice before contemplating any invasion. This goes beyond the strictly military calculations outlined in the preceding section. Whatever dismay Americans may justly feel at the undemocratic and corrupt nature of the South Korean regime Washington has supported, it is a mistake to ignore the impressive strength of South Korea in several areas.

South Korea is often compared to the American-supported regime in South Vietnam; though there are some valid parallels to be drawn, Seoul is in a vastly stronger position to defend itself than Saigon ever was. Unlike South Vietnam, South Korea not only has a military machine that can, in most respects, match its adversary's; it also has more than double the population of its rival, a physical environment relatively hostile to large-scale guerrilla insurgency, reasonably strong support in the rural areas reflecting both an intense anticommunism and a reasonable degree of economic improvement in recent years, and a dynamic industrial sector. To be sure, South Korea has serious problems—ranging from the ruling elite's narrowing base among the political intelligentsia to economic policies that have produced deepening inequities in income levels, sharply rising foreign debts, and a dependence on foreign capital that threatens to undermine national autonomy. There is, nevertheless, good reason for the South Koreans to assume that they will have the military, economic, and political resources to withstand any threat the North may mount.

What worries the South Koreans most is the possibility that North Korea may launch a blitzkrieg attack against Seoul, which stands merely thirty miles below the DMZ. There is no denying Seoul's vulnerability to this kind of attack. It is a painful fact of life for the South Koreans. But given the residual strength of South Korea, such an attack would almost certainly prove suicidal for the aggressor. This is not 1950. Even with the advantage of a surprise attack on the capital, a North Korean invasion undertaken without Soviet or Chinese support (as seems likely) would still confront the substantial retaliatory capacity of the South Korean armed forces and the hostility of the general populace, along with such additional backing from the United

States as may be needed.

Of course, Pyongyang could launch an attack that it knew to be doomed to ultimate failure merely to divert the attention of the North Korean people from their own problems; for that matter, so could Seoul. This, however, would provide at best only a temporary diversion. Moreover, either a North or a South Korean regime pressed to attack its rival in order to obscure its own failures might find it hard to mobilize people for a difficult struggle. To be sure, either leadership could defy rationality and try to drag its adversary down in an act of national suicide. But there is no reason to think that Seoul, with all the material progress it has made in recent years, would contemplate such madness. Nor do South Korean officials, including some members of the Korean CIA interviewed in 1976, regard Kim Il-sung as a man crazy enough to commit national suicide. In any case, if he were inclined to pursue such a course, there is no reason to assume that even a U.S. military presence would deter him.

It is often observed that the South Koreans find the prospect of a gradual withdrawal of U.S. forces unsettling, even though they may be able to accept the logic of analyses showing that their security would not be jeopardized. American and Japanese specialists have noted that the South Koreans in only one way seem inferior to their northern rivals—that is, in their perception of themselves; the presence of U.S. forces in Korea, it is said, will always be needed to bolster the South Koreans' self-confidence. The South Koreans sometimes seem consciously to foster this impression. A former commander of the Korean armed forces told me in 1976 that U.S. military forces should stay in Korea "for 200 years." But are these Koreans really so lacking in self-confidence? Or are they merely trying to persuade Washington to keep its forces in Korea so that, as a high-ranking U.S. official put it, "Kim Il-sung will have to think not merely twice before invading the South but three or four times." A continued U.S. military presence makes that much more unlikely an invasion that Pyongyang must already calculate to be unpromising. From the Korean standpoint, it is said, there is no such thing as too much security. One can easily understand why the South Koreans feel as they do, but it is necessary for us to weigh the marginal increment to security against the costs of maintaining forces far beyond those needed for deterrence.

As the South Koreans' capability to inflict unacceptable costs on any invading North Korean force grows, so should Seoul's capacity, on its own, to deter a North Korean attack. A gradual U.S. withdrawal over, say, five to eight years, might well be made contingent on the maintenance of a rough balance between North and South Korea. If the announcement of plans for such a withdrawal leads to a major North Korean buildup, the timetable can always be revised. There is no more reason to view planned withdrawals as irrevocable than to regard past commitments of forces as fixed in concrete.

Even after the completion of a U.S. withdrawal, the United States would have to be considered as an element in the calculus of deterrence. After all, nothing in the security treaty requires the presence of U.S. troops as a manifestation of the commitment. A U.S. response would no longer be automatic, but it could hardly be discounted by the North Koreans. As in the case of the nuclear umbrella, the United States can play a role in deterrence even when there is no certainty that Washington will in fact intervene. A U.S. presence close to, but not in, Korea would serve not only to reinforce the deterrent capabilities of the South Koreans but also to demonstrate that Washington remains committed to intervene in the unlikely event that Moscow or Peking should decide to do so on North Korea's behalf. Since there are no Soviet or Chinese military forces in North Korea, one can hardly argue that U.S. forces must be kept in South Korea merely to deter the Soviets and Chinese. The proximity of North Korea's allies as opposed to South Korea's distance from the United States may argue for keeping some U.S. forces close to Korea, but there is no need to station U.S. forces *in* South Korea itself to redress that asymmetry.

If an attack can almost certainly be deterred without maintaining U.S. forces in Korea, is there any reason to ensure the automatic involvement of the United States by keeping a trip-wire force in South Korea? In the very unlikely event that the North Koreans were to defy logic and invade, why not see first whether the South Koreåns can handle the situation without U.S. intervention? Cold War logic led many Americans to conclude that the United States should commit itself to the defense of as many allies as possible because only U.S. military power could deter attacks by communist nations against their neighbors. It is time to shed such outmoded assumptions and adjust to the new strategic context. Allies such as South Korea that no longer need the automatic U.S. intervention implied by a U.S. military presence should be permitted, indeed encouraged, to stand on their own to the maximum extent possible. It is in the interests of the United States to keep its options open and to hold military intervention as a last resort, limited to those situations in which it is manifestly required.

Enhanced Credibility of a Redefined Commitment. The announcement of a plan to withdraw all U.S. forces from Korea over a certain period of time, and subsequent implementation of that plan, might well facilitate the building of a consensus in this country behind a redefined commitment to Seoul. The open commitment to automatic intervention, implied by the retention of U.S. forces in Korea, is becoming increasingly difficult to sustain from a domestic political standpoint. Growing numbers of Americans balk at committing U.S. forces and funds to automatic involvement on behalf of a regime that denies its citizens the human rights cherished by Americans and bribes U.S. officials in order to win their political support.

If it were understood that U.S. intervention is not automatic, except in the unlikely event of Soviet or Chinese intervention, it would probably be easier for the American people to support this narrowed commitment. Though more limited in scope, such a commitment would be more credible because it is backed by a political consensus. Besides, a decline in the level of U.S. support for South Korea is likely to bring a corresponding reduction of criticism of Seoul by Americans. South Korean officials resent what they regard as U.S. interference in their country's domestic affairs, but they understand that it is the presence of U.S. forces and U.S. aid that gives many Americans the feeling that they have a right, even an obligation, to protest against Seoul's domestic policies. Though Seoul may object initially to any plan leading toward a complete withdrawal, in the long run a more self-reliant South Korea, less open to American criticism of its domestic policies, might actually find its relations with the United States smoother.

The Costs of Unneeded Dependency. In fact, maintaining U.S. forces in South Korea beyond the time when they are really needed may be damaging to the South Koreans. Some people, as noted above, argue for continuation of the U.S. military presence in Korea to bolster the South Koreans psychologically. But both Japanese and American members of our group commented on the cyclical nature of the problem: whatever "psychological inferiority" the South Koreans may feel vis-à-vis the North will only be perpetuated by a continued U.S. presence. Such feelings of inferiority can be overcome only by showing that they can in fact stand without U.S. support. U.S. forces symbolize a dependency relationship, and providing this "crutch" only deepens the psychological inferiority it is allegedly intended to alleviate. If it is made clear that the withdrawal of U.S. forces is undertaken neither as an abandonment of the Koreans nor as a punitive measure but as a vote of confidence in Seoul's ability to defend itself, this may help to break the psychological dependence of the South Koreans on the United States. From the standpoint of the United States, a withdrawal from South Korea may be viewed not as a sign of our weakness but as evidence of a successful policy. One of the main goals of U.S. commitments, presumably, has been to help strengthen our allies so that they might be able to defend themselves. The United States should be bold enough to recognize a success as such.

The costs of perpetuating a dependence that need not exist are even clearer if one considers that doing so plays into the hands of Pyongyang. The U.S. military presence in Korea is easily exploited by the North Koreans as a psychological weapon; it causes considerable embarrassment and frustration for South Korean youth, as both Japanese and American participants noted. It serves to buttress the North Koreans' claim to the mantle of Korean nationalism and their characterization of the South Korean government as a mere puppet of the United States. Pyongyang can argue to its own populace and to receptive audiences in the Third World that the Seoul regime would collapse if U.S. military support were withdrawn.

Why not deprive Pyongyang of this argument? Once U.S. forces have withdrawn and South Korea continues to thrive, Seoul's standing among Third World nations is likely to rise. More important, the continued viability of South Korea after the departure of the Americans, together with Pyongyang's perception that Seoul's military power makes the costs of invasion unacceptably high, may even lead the North Koreans to accept the existence of the South Korean state and to begin moving toward some sort of modus vivendi with it. So long as the South Koreans remain clearly dependent for their security on the United States, as manifested by the U.S. military presence, it will always be easier for Pyongyang to dismiss Seoul as an American puppet than to come to terms with the reality of the southern state.

Relations with Pyongyang. Perhaps the ultimate reason for withdrawing unneeded U.S. forces from Korea is that the redundancy these forces represent is almost certainly purchased at the sacrifice of opportunities to develop relationships with Pyongyang that might ease tensions and reduce whatever incentive there may be for the North Koreans to attack the South. These opportunity costs are impossible to calculate, for no one can be sure what possibilities might be opened by a termination of the U.S. military presence. Nor can we be certain that the retention of U.S. forces rules out any chance of progress. But it is reasonable to assume that these forces pose an obstacle to any significant relationship between Washington and Pyongyang and impede normalization of relations between the two Koreas as well. Even the mere announcement of a plan for a complete withdrawal of U.S. military forces might help open the way for negotiations. Although no one can guarantee a positive response from Pyongyang, the announcement of such a plan would at least make it harder for the North Koreans to refuse to enter discussions with the South.

The Japanese have generally put more emphasis than the Americans on the need to develop relationships with North Korea as a first step toward a long-term solution of the Korean problem. Even if the prospects of success are uncertain, these relationships represent the best hope for such a solution. The assumption is that if Pyongyang has economic and diplomatic ties with countries such as the United States and Japan, it will acquire a greater stake in maintaining peace. When going to war means jeopardizing a host of beneficial economic relationships, Pyongyang is more likely to calculate that the costs of war are too high.

Some may think it unrealistic to view such relationships as a basis for security. The real danger, however, is not that people will expect too much of these relationships but too little; an overemphasis on military commitments as the basis of security may prevent any real effort to test the deterrent potential of other means.

The Japanese participants in our discussions seemed especially sensitive to the dangers of isolating North Korea. Indeed, some Japanese claim that the most important aspect of the Korean problem is to arrange some contact between the United States and North Korea, perhaps in a third country. There is every indication of Tokyo's continued readiness to serve as an intermediary between Washington and Pyongyang should the Americans indicate that this is what they wish. Even if they do not help to arrange the meeting, the Japanese would at least want to be informed about it in advance. A number of Japanese have reported North Korea's eagerness to talk with the U.S. government. The major economic difficulties that North Korea has recently encountered are said to have given Pyongyang important new incentives to develop cooperative relations with noncommunist states and, in pursuit of that end, to ease tensions with the South.

Japan has already begun the process of building relationships with North Korea by developing modest economic ties

with Pyongyang. For its part, the United States might begin
by relaxing its trade embargo on North Korea and by
encouraging exploratory economic contacts. Some move
toward diplomatic relations also seems in order. A number
of Japanese leaders, including one with close ties to Seoul,
have urged unilateral recognition of Pyongyang by Tokyo
and Washington. This ought to be considered. Diplomatic
ties would not only draw Pyongyang out of its isolation, but
would also enable us to improve our intelligence on North
Korea and develop better means of communicating with
Pyongyang in a crisis. They might also enhance the development of economic relations that could help to stabilize North
Korea's economy and make the country less dependent on
Moscow and Peking.

Obviously, cross-recognition—in which the communist
powers establish relations with Seoul as we do with Pyongyang—would be the preferred course. Some Americans, and
some Japanese as well, feel strongly that no move should be
made toward establishing "official" relations with Pyongyang until the Soviets and Chinese are prepared to reciprocate with Seoul. For that matter, many would have preferred
to make the withdrawal of U.S. ground forces contingent on
some move by Pyongyang to ease tensions between the two
Koreas. The problem is that insistence on such precondi-
tions is likely to mean perpetuation of the status quo.
Moscow and Peking may well recognize Seoul after Tokyo
and Washington have taken the lead by establishing ties
with Pyongyang. The Soviets already have fragmentary
unofficial relations with South Korea.

The central point, however, is that even in the absence of
reciprocity, neither the withdrawal of ground forces nor
steps toward the establishment of relations with North Korea
need be narrowly viewed as a concession to the communists
that must be balanced by some concession on their part. In
the case of force withdrawals, insistence on a quid pro quo
tends to undermine the rationale that the forces are being
withdrawn mainly because they have become superfluous.
As indicated above, economic and diplomatic ties with
Pyongyang are useful in themselves for both sides. The

promised benefits are not significantly diminished by the absence of reciprocal relationships between the communist powers and Seoul.

Consideration must, of course, be given to the impact on Seoul of any unilateral move toward relations with Pyongyang. U.S. policy has been to rule out any talks with the North Koreans unless Seoul's representatives are in attendance. One may assume that the South Koreans' initial reaction to any departure from this policy would be one of alarm, but there is little justification for such concern. There is no reason to think that U.S. or Japanese relations with Pyongyang would lead to any diminution in the relations they or other countries maintain with South Korea; Seoul's position is in no way analogous to that of Taipei. The South Koreans should be further reassured by the knowledge that improved U.S.–North Korean relations are likely to prove a restraining force on Pyongyang. This could well be formalized at the outset by coupling the establishment of diplomatic relations with a North Korean pledge that, although both Koreas may feel they have a "right" to use any means at hand to unify the country, the use of force in resolving the conflict is not contemplated. If the North Koreans are unwilling to make such a pledge directly to the United States, it could be made indirectly through a forum of Pyongyang's choosing.

There are obviously limits to what the United States and Japan can do to help bring about the normalization of relations between the two Koreas. A total withdrawal of U.S. forces would at least remove one source of tension. It could well stimulate both sides to constructive action, for each could in some sense claim the U.S. withdrawal as a "victory." Seoul could point to the departure of the Americans as evidence of South Korea's strength and independence; Pyongyang could celebrate fulfillment of one of its stated long-term ambitions. The establishment of economic and diplomatic relations between Washington and Pyongyang would help to create a conciliatory climate conducive to negotiations between the two Koreas.

In particular, Washington might consider encouraging

South Korea to reopen discussions of force reductions. One can hardly be optimistic, but there is some reason to be hopeful. There is some sentiment in Seoul, especially among younger scholars and government officials, favoring a more active posture concerning negotiations with the North. These people feel that the South Korean government should accept Pyongyang's long-standing proposal for a reduction of armed forces to 100,000 on each side if the North Koreans agree to constraints on the availability of weapons and surprise attack capabilities, including air power. It has been reported by a Japanese Diet member from the LDP that Kim is almost "desperate" for force reductions because of pressures stemming from North Korea's current economic crisis. Kim is said to have complained in an interview with the Diet member that South Korea gets grant aid from the United States but that he has to pay for all the equipment he receives from his Chinese and Soviet allies. This may, then, be a particularly opportune time to launch conciliatory moves toward North Korea.

Seoul's Nuclear Option

Ultimately, the strongest argument against a withdrawal of U.S. forces and the establishment of economic and diplomatic relations with North Korea seems to lie in the potential impact of these moves on nuclear proliferation. Even a phased withdrawal, it is argued, would be so unsettling to the South Koreans that they would be willing to defy the United States and move toward a nuclear weapons capability. Would Seoul feel that a complete U.S. withdrawal had so weakened the value of the commitment that there was no longer need to be concerned about American attitudes? Would the United States retain enough leverage to dissuade Seoul from going nuclear?

The South Koreans may feel that if they are able to acquire an independent nuclear capability, they will strengthen their bargaining position with the United States, but they must also realize that exercising that option could well mean the sacrifice of any remaining U.S. commitment. This commitment might be worth less to Seoul than before, but it would still serve to deter Soviet or Chinese involvement and to hold open the possibility, if no longer the certainty, of U.S. intervention even against the North Koreans alone. Indeed, if Pyongyang knew that South Korea were moving toward a nuclear weapons capability in defiance of the United States and at the cost of any U.S. commitment, this could conceivably provoke a preemptive attack by an alarmed North Korea. A South Korean decision to seek nuclear weapons under such circumstances would thus be an exceedingly dangerous course.

Even if Seoul were to dismiss as valueless the U.S. security commitment, a decision to go nuclear would incur another major cost: the United States could deal a crippling blow to South Korea's nuclear power program by cutting off the supply of enriched uranium. Given the magnitude of investment required to put a nuclear power plant into operation, this would not be an insignificant consideration. Moreover, the Japanese might bring economic levers to bear.

Assuming the worst—that is, a decision to embark on a nuclear weapons program at any cost—the South Koreans would still face some major technical obstacles. Lacking the facilities to produce the highly enriched uranium required for nuclear weapons, they would have but one route to a bomb: separation of plutonium from spent fuel rods. If the present agreement among the nuclear supplier nations to refrain from selling reprocessing technology is maintained, the Koreans would not be able to import the required facilities. The only alternative would be to develop their own capability to separate the very modest amount of plutonium that would be required to build three or four bombs. It is hard to predict with confidence how long this would take. Some experts contend that the Koreans could not acquire such a capacity before 1990; others feel that they could conceivably do it by 1985. If, as some have proposed, there is an international agreement that spent fuel be shipped abroad for storage in multinational facilities, rather than retained in each country, it would be much more difficult for the Koreans to gain access to the necessary plutonium. In any case, there would be some doubt about whether the weapons produced in this manner would work. And, it is not clear just what military value a nuclear arsenal of several bombs would have. Thus, although one cannot discount the danger that the South Koreans might defy rationality and pursue a nuclear weapons program, it would be a mistake to minimize either the costs involved or the technical difficulties they would have to overcome in order to produce an effective weapon.

In addition to the high price the South Koreans would pay for nuclear weapons, there is a more positive reason why they are unlikely to move in that direction. If a withdrawal of U.S. forces leads gradually to the establishment of constructive U.S. and Japanese relationships with Pyongyang and to progress in normalization of relations between the two Koreas, Seoul will have little incentive to build nuclear weapons. They are very expensive, after all, and South Korea's resources can certainly be more usefully deployed. Thus, it may well be that a withdrawal of U.S. forces would discourage, not promote, nuclear proliferation by helping to set in motion a process leading to relaxation of tensions and reducing whatever need the South Koreans may feel to possess nuclear weapons. In the long run, that would be the most effective means of stemming nuclear proliferation.

Toward a More Meaningful Stability in Korea

To sum up, it is a mistake to interpret Japanese statements on Korea as a vote against any change in existing policies. There is need for greater appreciation of the crosscurrents, ambivalence, and flexibility in Japanese thinking. Japan and the United States share an interest in the stability of the Korean peninsula, but it is important to develop a more sophisticated understanding of the meaning of stability.

It can always be argued that initiatives undertaken without reciprocity pose a threat to stability. This, I believe, represents a shortsighted view of stability. Unilateral initiatives may be required in order to create a foundation for a less precarious stability. The only viable long-term solution to the Korean problem lies in the gradual establishment of a security structure less dependent on U.S. military power on the peninsula. For two reasons, U.S. forces, though they may help to maintain a somewhat artificial stability in the short run, frustrate the creation of a basis for a more secure and lasting stability. First, U.S. forces represent an alien force; they cannot stay forever, and there will always be uncertainty about how the situation will change after they leave. Second, they tend to foster tension and obstruct détente between the two Koreas. A stability that is self-perpetuating, rather than artificial, must come from within—through the establishment of a modus vivendi between the two Koreas. Progress toward that end is unlikely, however, unless one side takes the initiative. The proposed withdrawal of U.S. forces from Korea should be viewed as a first step toward the creation of conditions for a more genuine and lasting stability.

Prospects for Arms Control

The problem of nuclear proliferation and, more generally, the prospects for arms control in the Pacific comprise the final set of issues raised in our meetings with the Japanese. To what extent, we asked, might the security of Asia be advanced by formal arms control agreements? Can Japan, a nation itself only lightly armed, take a leading role in the process of developing such arrangements?

It proved extraordinarily difficult to obtain clear answers to these questions. Though arms control issues were considered indirectly in a variety of contexts, when we focused on them directly we discovered that communication was difficult because U.S. and Japanese conceptions of arms control differ significantly. Arms control questions as they are typically posed in this country elicit little interest among "establishment" Japanese specialists. At our 1975 meeting, the Japanese showed little inclination to discuss such broad questions as the future role of Japan in arms control, how to get China involved in arms control negotiations, how to deal with nuclear proliferation as a global problem, potential arms control measures in the Asian region, and the relevance of SALT to Japan. They tended to view nuclear-free zones, no-first-use agreements, and other formal arms control measures as unrealistic in the present context and, in any

case, of secondary importance. Most of the Japanese, and
some of the Americans, maintained that such arms control
measures could only be discussed fruitfully as the culmina-
tion of a consideration of broader security issues.

The 1976 and 1977 discussions, both inside and outside the
formal conference sessions, made two things clear: (1) there
is, among a minority of Japanese specialists, a rising interest
in arms control; and (2) what appears to be a lack of interest
on the Japanese side may simply be a reflection of constraints on discussion imposed by the terms in which arms
control issues have usually been raised by Americans. There
is also evidence of some frustration among the Japanese with
respect to American posturing on the question of nuclear
proliferation. Some of the Japanese suggested that the
United States seems preoccupied with the proliferation issue
and inclined to preach on the subject without making any
sacrifices itself. To be sure, the Japanese do not seem to view
the problem with quite the same urgency as the Americans,
except as it applies to specific areas, such as Korea. The
Japanese have been especially troubled by Washington's
apparent unwillingness to make the hard choices necessary
for a consistent nonproliferation policy. The readiness of the
United States to supply nuclear materials to India following
the latter's detonation of a nuclear device, the promises to
supply reactors to Egypt and Israel, and the uncertainty
concerning the reliability of the United States as a supplier
of enriched uranium to nations that forego developing their
own capabilities—all were cited as evidence that the United
States is not prepared to follow a consistent nonproliferation
policy. If the United States cannot develop and sustain a
policy that makes the export of nuclear technology and
materials consistently subject to the test of its implications
for proliferation, rather than commercial or political criteria, then, it was argued, Washington should stop talking
about the proliferation problem.

Of course, one cannot assume that a more consistent U.S.
nonproliferation policy would lead to a convergence of U.S.
and Japanese perceptions of the issue. As indicated by the
hostile Japanese reaction to the Carter administration's

policy opposing the commercialization of reprocessing facilities, Japanese and American interests are not identical. Tokyo may share Washington's dismay at the access that nations with reprocessing facilities will have to plutonium that can be used to build nuclear weapons, but the Japanese also view reprocessing, and the plutonium-burning fast breeder, as a means of reducing their dependence on imported raw materials. There is nothing more vital to Japan's security than an assured supply of energy. Given their ratification of the NPT and the strength of their commitment to remain militarily non-nuclear, the Japanese find it hard to understand why the U.S. nonproliferation policy should require that they make such a heavy sacrifice.

For the Japanese, arms control has three relevant dimensions: (1) encouraging mutually satisfactory economic and diplomatic relationships so as to reduce the likelihood that Asian disputes will be resolved by warfare; (2) insulating Japan from the effects of such wars if they do break out; and (3) reducing pressures on Japan, both internal and external, to accelerate the development of Japanese military capabilities and the militarization of its foreign policies.

From the Japanese standpoint, then, arms control is important—less as an end in itself than as a means to reduce the danger of a war that might involve Japan (either directly or through the U.S. bases in Japan). This means, in the first instance, paying less attention to the formalities and mechanics of potential arms control arrangements and paying more attention to the political interests and motivations of the nations concerned. It also suggests that ways should be sought to foster de facto arms control in Asia and that less attention should be given to devising formal arms control agreements.

Throughout the discussions, both Japanese and American participants agreed on the need to conceive of arms control and security in broader than military terms. The Japanese appear to believe that the critical question is how to create, through economic and diplomatic steps, conditions in which viable arms control arrangements become feasible because there is a sufficiently high degree of confidence that nations can maintain their vital interests and ensure their security without resort to war.

The Japanese thus state that efforts at limiting arms ought not to focus merely on the negotiation of agreements but also on the creation of conditions that discourage aggression. From the Japanese standpoint, drawing China into arms control discussions is not important in itself; affecting Chinese military capabilities and reducing China's motivations for exercising its military power are of the utmost importance. Discussing what Japan would like the United States and the Soviet Union to do in SALT strikes the Japanese as unrealistic, for they perceive their influence over the course of U.S.-Soviet negotiations as extremely limited. Yet the Japanese have a strong interest in learning more about the strategic perceptions of Soviet and U.S. policymakers and how they relate to their arms control policies. Nor is it inconceivable that Japan may influence the process to the extent that the United States justifies certain strategic policies with reference to Japanese interests. A clarification of how the Japanese perceive these interests might exercise an influence on U.S. policy making.

Similarly, a general discussion of arms control measures in the Asian region has an air of unreality to the Japanese, but the possibility of denuclearizing the Korean peninsula or limiting naval force levels and deployment is of great interest to them. The question of nuclear proliferation as a global problem evoked little response from the Japanese; all participants, however, were interested in discussing ways to discourage South Korea from seeking its own nuclear weapons. Finally, the subject of conventional arms transfer, from which American arms control specialists have tended to shy away as being beyond effective arms control, was of real concern to the Japanese participants, because the Japanese themselves are faced with a decision on whether to relax restrictions on the export of conventional weapons. How, they ask, should Japan respond to the growing pressures, both internal and external, to export military-related technology?

There are several areas in which efforts might be made to

deal with the problems illuminated by our discussions concerning arms control. The United States should take seriously Japanese criticism about the inconsistency in U.S. policies on nuclear proliferation. A move toward a stronger U.S. commitment to halt nuclear proliferation did emerge from the Ford administration during the final days of the 1976 presidential campaign, and the Carter administration has continued this trend. One way to give greater force to Washington's assertions on the subject would be to declare that a clear decision by an Asian ally of the United States to acquire a nuclear weapons capability would almost certainly void the U.S. commitment. At the same time, positive inducements devised to assist allies in meeting their legitimate energy needs might help dissuade them from seeking facilities that could be used to support a weapons program.

In pursuing its nonproliferation policies, Washington should also show greater sensitivity to Japan's special energy needs and strong commitment to a non-nuclear weapons future. Japan's readiness to refrain from seeking nuclear weapons depends, at least in part, on the degree of confidence the Japanese have in the U.S. nuclear umbrella and in the trustworthiness of the United States. U.S. policies that tend to undermine Japanese trust in the United States, even if undertaken in the name of a consistent global policy on nonproliferation, may only serve to stimulate the Japanese to consider more seriously the expansion of their defense capabilities and, ultimately, the nuclear option.

It would also be desirable to have greater clarity as to Japanese views on arms control questions, whether arms control is defined in Japanese terms or American terms. Not only is it important to keep Japan informed about the progress of SALT; greater efforts should also be made to elicit Japanese views about the impact of potential strategic arms limitation agreements on the security of Japan. What do the Japanese think about cruise missiles, for example, and how would their inclusion in a SALT agreement affect Japan's interests? In particular, Japanese views concerning possibilities for controlling the naval arms race in the Pacific should be sought. As already indicated, Japan may be able to have some impact on U.S. policies when Washington rationalizes those policies in terms of Japanese security interests—as in the case of Korea and U.S. naval force deployments. Finally, there is evidence of growing concern in the United States about the problem of conventional arms sales. Americans should pay greater attention to the arms control implications of Japan's self-denying policies restricting the transfer of conventional weapons and military-related technology.

Summary

The conclusions and recommendations advanced in the preceding pages deal with diverse issues. The key proposals may be recapitulated as follows:

1. The United States should refrain from pressing Japan into an unwanted military role in the name of a misguided conception of burden sharing. The SDF should put greatest emphasis on improvement of intelligence capabilities and the development of better intelligence-sharing arrangements with the United States. The United States should help the Japanese government build public support for the security relationship by removing irritants wherever possible, which means reducing the U.S. presence to the minimum level the two sides consider necessary for effective deterrence of conflict in Japan and Korea.

2. The United States should take a more selective approach to its security commitments in Asia. Commitments involving counterinsurgency operations should be curtailed. Washington should resist any possible overtures from the Thai government for the reintroduction of U.S. forces and should look very critically at any new aid requests from Bangkok.

3. The United States should soon begin discussing with Seoul and Tokyo a comprehensive plan for the gradual, phased withdrawal of all U.S. forces from South Korea. This would involve the early removal of the U.S. tactical nuclear weapons presently stationed in Korea, followed by the withdrawal of ground combat forces on the schedule set by President Carter, and finally, over a period of perhaps several additional years, the evacuation of the remaining air and

other forces. Air forces earmarked for Korea should be retained in Japan, at Pacific island bases, and at sea, as a manifestation of the readiness of the United States to intervene in Korea if it should become necessary to do so. The United States and Japan should seek economic relations with North Korea and encourage both Koreas to work toward force reductions. Washington and Tokyo should explore the possibility of establishing diplomatic relations with North Korea, coupled, if possible, with a North Korean pledge not to use force in the resolution of its conflict with South Korea.

4. The United States should continue efforts to develop more consistent policies to stem nuclear proliferation, but should do so with greater sensitivity to Japan's special energy needs and strong commitment to a non-nuclear-weapons future. Washington should make it clear that a decision by South Korea or any other Asian ally of the United States to acquire a nuclear weapons capability would almost certainly make it impossible to sustain the U.S. commitment to them. The Japanese should be encouraged to express with greater clarity their views on a variety of arms control issues.

Taken together, these recommendations provide for preservation of the U.S.-Japanese security relationship, while seeking to foster the evolution of policies, in both Washington and Tokyo, that will encourage a greater reliance on nonmilitary means of ensuring security. Many serious security problems remain in the post-Vietnam era, but there are also important new opportunities. As the confrontative relationships of the past gradually soften, the prospects for establishing a security structure less dependent on U.S. military power grow. There is much that the United States and Japan, acting alone and jointly, can do to advance this process.

Notes

1. See the English-language version of *Defense of Japan* (Tokyo: Defense Agency, 1976), pp. 55-56; and *Mainichi Daily News*, January 21, 1977.

2. *Far Eastern Economic Review*, August 20, 1976.

3. *Asahi Evening News*, January 19, 1977; *Japan Times*, January 20, 1977; *Mainichi Daily News*, January 21, 1977.

4. For elaboration of this view, see James William Morley, "A Time for Realism in the Military Defense of Japan," chapter 3 of this volume.

5. *Wall Street Journal*, August 24, 1976.

6. *Yomiuri*, July 9, 1976.

7. See Fred Greene, *Stresses in U.S.-Japanese Security Relations* (Washington: Brookings, 1975), p. 106.

8. According to a public opinion poll reported in the 1976 Defense White Paper, rescue-relief operations were named more often than any other activity as the SDF function most requiring expansion.

9. *Defense of Japan*, p. 91.

10. There was some feeling expressed on the American side, however, that it might be too "abrasive" to attach such a condition to U.S. commitments, especially given the leverage afforded by the U.S. position as a nuclear supplier.

11. For an elaboration of the view that such relationships are important, see chapter 7.

12. Richard Tanner and William G. Ōuchi, "Made in America (Under Japanese Management)," *Harvard Business Review*, September-October 1974, pp. 61-69, quoted in *Managing an Alliance: The Politics of U.S.-Japanese Relations*, I. M. Destler et al. (Washington: Brookings, 1976), p. 102.

13. See Ralph N. Clough, *Deterrence and Defense in Korea* (Washington: Brookings, 1976), pp. 14-15; and Donald H. Ranard, "The Korean Peninsula and U.S. Policy," reprinted in *Congressional Record*, March 24, 1976, p. E1522.

14. See "Korea and U.S. Policy in Asia," *The Defense Monitor 5*, no. 1 (January 1976): 6.